HENRY COOPER'S
100
GREATEST
BOXERS

HENRY COOPER'S
100
GREATEST
BOXERS

Macdonald
Queen Anne Press

A QUEEN ANNE PRESS BOOK

First published in Great Britain in 1990 by
Queen Anne Press, a division of
Macdonald & Co (Publishers) Ltd
Orbit House
1 New Fetter Lane
London EC4A 1AR

A member of Maxwell Macmillan Pergamon Publishing Corporation

British Library Cataloguing in Publication Data
Cooper, Henry *1934–*
    Henry Cooper's 100 greatest boxers. – (100 greatest).
    1. Boxing – Biographies – Collections
    I. Title   II. Series
    796.830922
    ISBN 0–356–18837–X

PICTURE CREDITS

Allsport: 51, 78, 102, 105, 138, 139, 153, 170, 197
Colorsport: 11, 34, 101, 168, 210, 217
Hulton Picture Company: 6, 16, 24, 27, 42, 48, 54, 64, 65, 72, 82, 83, 87, 92, 94, 98, 117, 119, 135, 137,
141, 142, 145, 147, 159, 161, 172, 179, 185, 192, 204, 206, 207, 212, 221
Liverpool Daily Post & Echo: 200
Popperfoto: 15, 21, 23, 113, 121, 191, 203, 223
Professional Sport: 45, 47, 76, 89, 115, 125, 155, 157, 175, 186, 188, 194, 198, 214
Sport & General: 29, 33, 37, 49, 60, 70, 73, 79, 96, 107, 151, 162, 165, 182, 220
Sporting Pictures: 132
Bob Thomas: 10, 56, 61, 67, 131

Front cover
Left: Jack 'Kid' Berg (Hulton Picture Company) *Right:* Muhammad Ali (Colorsport) *Below:* Sugar Ray
Leonard
Back flap
Henry Cooper (Hulton Picture Company)

Typeset, printed and bound in Great Britain by Butler & Tanner Ltd, Frome and London

CONTENTS

INTRODUCTION

The hardest task of all when making my selection for this book was not which boxers to choose but which to leave out. Ask 1,000 boxing experts to sit down and name their top 100 boxers and you can bet your boxing boots that you will get 1,000 different lists, with agreement on fewer than 60 of the names.

After hours of agonising I decided to go for my 100 personal *favourite* boxers. I am sure you can come up with cases for many whose names are missing from my list, but beauty, as they say, is in the eye of the beholder. I have been helped in the preparation of this book by writer Norman Giller, who was a reporter on the trade paper *Boxing News* when I first became British heavyweight champion back in 1959. The facts and figures have come from Norman, but the feelings are mine.

Not so long ago I appeared in a television series devised by Norman called *Who's the Greatest?* It was supposed to end the arguments as to who have been the greatest champions in all sports. The boxing programme featured Muhammad Ali against Rocky Marciano. Dennis Waterman put the case for Ali and dear old Eamonn Andrews argued for Marciano. A jury of 12 neutral members of the public listened to the debate and then voted for the man they considered to be the greatest. I was called as a witness for Marciano, although in my heart I rated Muhammad Ali the most complete champion of all time. Even though it meant a defeat for Eamonn and me, I thought justice had been done when the jury voted by nine to three for Ali.

So who *is* the greatest? Well, I have come up with my top 100 boxers but I have an idea my list will cause more arguments than it will settle. As well as focusing on the ring achievements of each of the great champions featured in the following pages, we have tried to provide at least a glimpse of their background. You will find it hard to believe the adventures that ring masters like Harry Greb, Stanley Ketchel, Jake 'Raging Bull' La Motta, Rocky Graziano, Mickey 'Toy Bulldog' Walker and Barney Ross had *outside* the ring. Their real life stories all make the *Rocky* film adventures seem tame.

Ever since I was a kid in short trousers and hero worshipped the likes of Joe Louis I have been an avid fan of boxing. As well as having been actively involved in the sport for a quarter of a century I have spent hour upon hour reading about the history of the great champions, listening to all the stories that have been handed down through the generations and, of course, I have been fortunate enough to have seen many of the great fighters in the flesh (and I've even been punched on the nose by a few of them!). Another great help in making assessments for this book has been the easy access to the scores of films of old champions that are now available thanks to the video revolution.

One point that recurs time and time again when you study the careers of the great champions is how boxing has saved so many of them from a life either in the gutter or behind bars. It is a sport that gives discipline, direction and hope to the lives of young men who would be lost without

Opposite: My most memorable moment in boxing. I have just buttoned the 'Louisville Lip' Cassius Clay in the fourth round of our 1963 contest at Wembley. The bell stopped me from trying to complete the destruction of the man who will always be number one in my book. He recovered to stop me with a cut eye in the fifth round. In his next fight he became the new world heavyweight champion before he changed his name to become the one and only Muhammad Ali.

it. Those abolitionists who argue against the sport on medical grounds should try to balance their outlook by taking into consideration the good that boxing does by helping people – the boxers and their families – to escape the poverty trap.

Before letting you loose on my top 100, I must explain that there are no Asian boxers featured. I appreciate that Japan in particular has produced some great champions in the past, but I hold up my hands and confess that I do not have sufficient knowledge of Asian fighters to be able to form a proper opinion of them. I also feel guilty about leaving out one particular heavyweight: Teofilo Stevenson, the Cuban who won three successive Olympic gold medals. He was never tested against professionals so we were unable to gauge his greatness, but I have a feeling he would have been able to stand up to the very best heavyweights of all time.

That's enough of my excuses about the boxers *not* included. I'm happy with the list I have compiled – see what you think.

Seconds out . . . come out reading.

MUHAMMAD ALI

Muhammad Ali should not, strictly speaking, come first in the alphabetical listing of my 100 boxers, but he will always be the number one in my book. The fight game has continually attracted colourful, controversial and entertaining characters, but they would all have to doff their caps to Ali as the greatest sporting showman of the 20th century. He transcended sport, and his face − and his voice − became just about the best known in the world, more often recognised even than those of presidents and kings.

The descendant of a slave and the son of a Kentucky signwriter, he had three boxing careers in one. First there was the brash, flash gaseous Cassius Clay who, after winning the Olympic light heavyweight gold medal, was launched as a professional by a syndicate of white millionaire businessmen under the expert eye of Miami trainer Angelo Dundee. Standing a beautifully-chiselled 6 feet 3 inches and weighing around 16 stone at his peak, he was dubbed the Louisville Lip as he drummed up box office business with a tongue that was even quicker than his fast fists. A lot of people thought he had a big head as well as a big mouth, but his boasts and rhyming fight predictions were calculated to boost ticket sales, and also to give himself a psychological advantage over opponents. It was all a big act with Clay. Once the microphones were turned off, the notebooks put away and the cameras pointed in a different direction, he became quietly spoken and a really nice bloke to be with.

I had the privilege of sharing the ring with him in two contests, the first a non-title fight at Wembley Stadium on 18 June 1963. That's a fight and a night that will stay in my memory for as long as I breathe. It was unbeaten Clay's 19th professional bout, and he saw me as a stepping stone to a world title fight. But I nearly threw a spanner − or rather a hammer − in the works when I whacked him on the whiskers with my favourite left hook near the end of the fourth round. He fell backwards into the ropes and on to his backside. I have often wondered how boxing history might have changed had I landed ten seconds earlier. As it was, young Cassius was up and at my mercy at four, but just as I was about to deliver the *coup de grâce* the bell rang. Some time-wasting chicanery by his wily cornerman Angelo Dundee helped give Clay precious seconds to recover. One of his gloves had split, and Dundee has since admitted making the tear worse so that they had to wait for a replacement glove.

Anyway, Clay had recovered his senses by the time the fifth round finally got underway and he hit me with a stream of long lefts and rights that worsened a cut over my left eye and forced the referee to stop the fight. Clay, who was into his poetic predictions period, had said before the fight: 'After all the jive, Cooper will fall in five'. He had got the round right, but he'd done the falling.

In his next contest, on 2 February 1964, he forced 'big, bad' Sonny Liston to retire at the end of six rounds to become world heavyweight champion. Following a highly controversial one-round knock-out victory over Liston in a return fight, he dropped his slave name of Clay and his white managers and started the second phase of his career with the Muslim name Muhammad

Muhammad Ali
(originally Cassius Marcellus Clay)
Born Louisville, Kentucky, 17.1.1942
Career span: 1960-81
World heavyweight champion 1964-67, 1974-78, 1978-79
Ring record: 61 fights, 56 wins, 5 losses (1 stoppage); 37 inside-the-distance wins

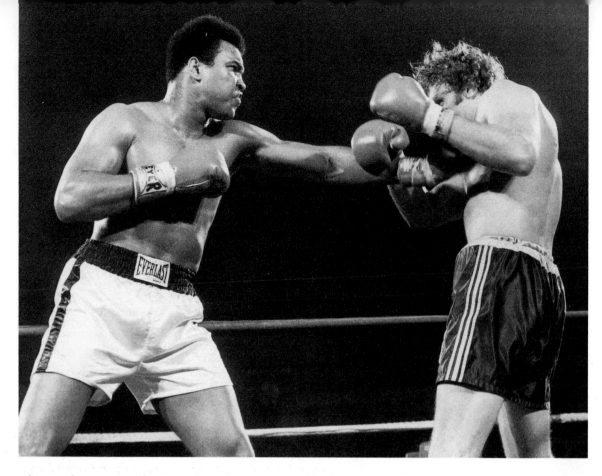

Ali at work, powering a left jab through Joe Bugner's defence . . .

Ali. He made ten successful title defences before being stripped of the championship in 1967 for refusing to join the US Army on religious grounds.

I was among his early title fight opponents. We met for the second time at Highbury Stadium on 21 May 1966. My old cut eye curse struck again and this time I was stopped in the sixth round. I had the satisfaction of knowing that in 11 rounds of boxing Ali had never once had me in serious trouble apart from the cuts. I'd had him down once and won more rounds than I had lost. I am really proud of the way I handled myself against Ali because there is no doubt in my mind that he was – as he continually told the world – 'The Greatest'.

The third stage of his extraordinary career came after a three and a half-year politically-forced lay-off which robbed him of his peak boxing years. Following the first defeat of his career in a classic contest with Joe Frazier, he regained his title with an incredible win over George Foreman in Zaire in 1974 when he introduced his rope-a-dope tactics. Ali allowed Foreman to punch himself to the edge of exhaustion while he rested on the ropes behind a gloved defence, catapulting himself forward in the eighth round to score a sensational knock-out victory.

He again defended the title ten times before losing it to relative novice Leon Spinks whom he outpointed in a return to become the first man in history to win the heavyweight crown three times. Ali went to the well once too often and was stopped for the only time when he retired at the end of ten rounds against Larry Holmes in 1980. He foolishly had one more fight, a meaningless affair against Jamaican-born Trevor Berbick in the Bahamas in 1981, which he lost on points over ten untidy rounds.

Since retiring Ali has suffered from ill health, and no doubt many of his problems are attributable to the fact that he wanted to conquer one mountain too many. He did me the honour of attending my 50th birthday party in London in 1984, and I would be lying if I did not admit to being shocked and saddened by his appearance. There was a slur to his speech, he had the movements of an old man and there were times when he could hardly keep his eyes open (maybe that was something to do with my boring company!). Obviously the punches he had absorbed over the years had taken their toll, but there were other factors that would need a doctor's diagnosis rather than mine. The boxing abolitionists would like to convince us that his poor health was all due to his ring career, but his problems with diabetes and Parkinson's disease could have afflicted him regardless of what he did for a living. And what he chose to do – boxing, at which he was better than anybody else in history – brought him the sort of fame, fortune and sheer satisfaction that he could not have found in any other field.

I prefer to remember him as the cocky yet likeable showman of the 1960s who brought a hurricane of fresh air to boxing with his quick wit, twinkling toes and fast fists. He was a master of long-range boxing, nearly always shooting for the head with a powerful left jab followed by overarm rights that had a jarring rather than a concussive effect. He avenged three of the five defeats in his 21-year career (by Frazier, Ken Norton and Spinks) and his setbacks against Holmes and Berbick came long after he should have dropped the curtain on what was arguably the greatest heavyweight boxing career of all time.

. . . and at play, clowning while he does some crafty holding against the destructive Earnie Shavers.

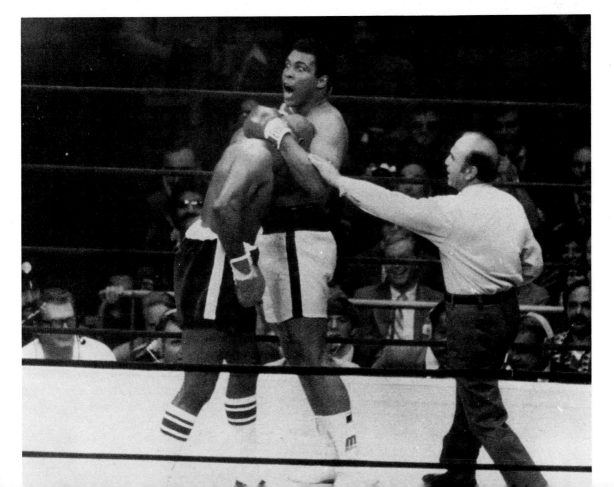

LOU AMBERS

*Lou Ambers
(originally Luigi Giuseppe
D'Ambrosio)
Born Herkimer, New York
State, 8.11.1913
Career span: 1932-41
World lightweight champion
1936-37, 1939-40
Ring record: 102 fights, 88
wins, 8 losses (2 stoppages); 27
inside-the-distance wins, 6
draws*

Lou Ambers was 18 when he came storming out of Herkimer on the Mohawk River in upstate New York to join the queue of Italian-American fighters trying to battle their way out of the slums by seeking fame and fortune in the boxing ring. One of ten children born to Italian immigrants, he was every bit as hungry as the city fighters from the East Side ghettos. His real name was Luigi D'Ambrosio, but he adopted the ring name of Lou Ambers to hide his true identity when boxing in illegal 'pirate' boxing shows before he became a legitimate professional in 1932.

He was more of a slugger than a scientist, and his hustling, bustling style of fighting earned him the nickname the 'Herkimer Hurricane'. New York was a 'lightweight jungle' in the 1930s, with dozens of fighters in the 9 stone 9 pounds division in championship class. Despite a procession of victories, it seemed that Ambers was going nowhere slowly with his career until he joined Al Weill, a well-connected manager who later piloted Rocky Marciano to the world heavyweight championship.

Ambers was chief sparring partner to former world lightweight champion Tony Canzoneri when Weill took over the reins of his career in 1934. Within six months he had manoeuvred him into a fight with Canzoneri for the vacant world lightweight championship, and although he was knocked down three times on the way to a 15-round points defeat he acquitted himself well enough to earn a return match.

He was two months short of his 23rd birthday when he became champion by outpointing Canzoneri in 1936, and he confirmed his superiority in a third battle that again went the distance in May 1937.

Ambers earns his place in my top 100 hit parade because of a peak performance in 1939 when he regained the championship from the great Henry Armstrong after having lost it to 'Homicide Hank' the previous year. Both contests were staged in New York City, and Lou's victory – on points over 15 rounds on 23 August 1939 – ended an astonishing 46-fight winning streak during which Armstrong had acquired the world featherweight, lightweight and welterweight titles. Their second bout was rated one of the roughest, toughest fights of the 1930s, which is saying something. The no-foul rule was in operation, and Armstrong had five rounds taken away from him for continually hitting below the belt.

It was the second time that Ambers had ended an incredible winning sequence. He was paid $82,500 – then a record for the lightweight division – to defend his title against Puerto Rican Pedro Montanez in New York in September 1937. Montanez was on a run of 61 fights without defeat, one of the longest winning records in boxing history. Among his victims was Ambers, who he had outpointed in a ten-round non-title fight five months earlier. But with his championship at stake Ambers was a more committed fighter, and he edged a split decision.

He retired in 1941 and joined the US coastguard after two inside-the-distance title fight defeats by Texan Lew Jenkins.

Opposite: Lou Ambers (right) slugs it out with Sammy Fuller under the watchful gaze of the referee, the one and only Jack Dempsey. Ambers was a 15-round points winner of this world lightweight title eliminator at Madison Square Garden, New York, in 1935.

ALEXIS ARGUELLO

Alexis Arguello
Born Managua,
Nicaragua, 19.4.1952
Career span: 1968-86
World WBA featherweight
champion 1974-77; WBC
junior lightweight champion
1978-80; WBC lightweight
champion 1981-83
Ring record: 86 fights, 80 wins,
6 losses (3 stoppages); 65
inside-the-distance wins

Alexis Arguello is the accomplished fighter who knocked Scotland's Jim Watt off my shortlist for entry in this parade of outstanding champions. I had a high regard for Watt, but saw him outclassed at Wembley in 1981 when Arguello knocked him down on the way to ruthlessly relieving him of his WBC world lightweight title with a convincing 15-round points victory.

It was Arguello's third world championship in what I call the 'alphabet era'. During my career there was generally one world champion for each weight division, and those were the good old days when you could reel off all the world title-holders. Nowadays it's like trying to learn the names in an international telephone directory. It's my personal opinion that world titles now come too cheaply. There are championships to be won with the World Boxing Association (WBA), the World Boxing Council (WBC), the International Boxing Federation (IBF) and, latest on the initial roundabout, the World Boxing Organisation (WBO). It's good news for promoters, of course, and for the boxers who can pick up golden purses for challenging for one of the alphabet titles, but it is totally confusing for fight fans and has devalued the meaning of world championships.

That's enough of my beefing. Now back to Arguello, who would have been good enough to have been rated championship class in the days when there was only one title for each division. He proved his quality in the 43rd fight of his eventful career when he knocked out Mexican ring master Ruben Olivares in the 13th round to win the WBA world featherweight crown.

Arguello, who had first started to punch for pay in his home town of Managua at the age of 16, made four successful defences of the 9 stone championship before increasing weight forced him to relinquish the title. He then won the WBC world junior lightweight crown (9 stone 4 pounds) by stopping Alfredo Escalera in 13 rounds in San Juan. After eight winning defences, he again found it difficult to make the weight and gave up the title to campaign in the 9 stone 9 pounds division, ripping the WBC championship away from southpaw Scot Jim Watt with a devastating display of box-fighting in which he combined clever ring skills with lethal combination punching. He was a smart boxer but could also be aggressive in a bulldozing manner if he felt a change of tactics necessary.

Arguello had amassed a huge fortune in the ring, but much of it was swallowed up during the political upheaval in his homeland of Nicaragua. He managed to escape to Miami but had to shelve a planned retirement as he tried to rebuild his bank balance. A magnificent 14th-round victory over American idol Ray Mancini, followed by two more successful title defences and a two-round stoppage of Kevin Rooney (later Mike Tyson's trainer), put him back on the road to riches.

Then he made the mistake of trying to become the first fighter in history to win world titles at four different weights. He was outpowered in two savage WBA junior welterweight championship contests against Aaron Pryor, losing the first in the 14th round and the second in the tenth.

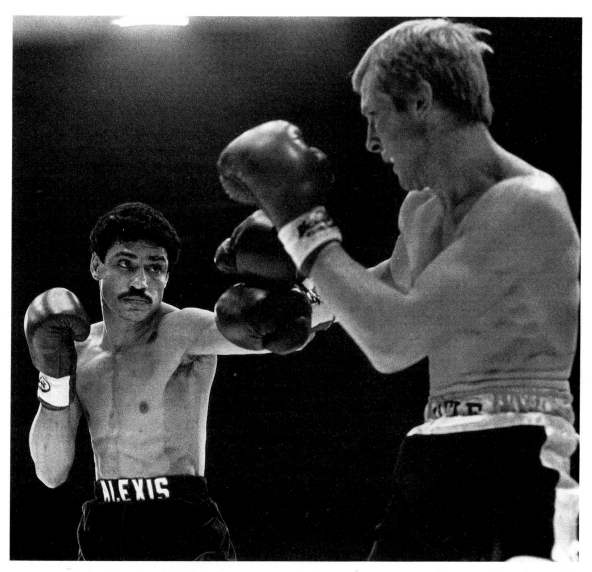

He retired after his second mauling by Pryor in September 1983, but US tax demands and a run of bad business investments pushed him towards the brink of bankruptcy and he was forced to make a comeback in 1985 that, inevitably, led him nowhere. At his peak, Arguello was – unarguably – one of the most formidable fighters ever to come out of South America, a view that I know would be echoed by Jim Watt!

Alexis Arguello on the prowl against southpaw Scot Jim Watt in a world lightweight title fight that he won comfortably on points in London in 1981.

HENRY ARMSTRONG

Henry Armstrong
(originally Henry Jackson)
Born Columbus,
Mississippi, 12.12.1912
Career span: 1931-45
World featherweight champion
1937-38; world lightweight
champion 1938-39; world
welterweight champion 1938-40
Ring record: 181 fights, 152
wins, 21 losses (2 stoppages);
100 inside-the-distance wins,
8 draws

Henry Armstrong is the only fighter in the history of boxing to have held three world titles simultaneously, and this was in the pre-alphabet days when every single championship had to be earned the hard way against the best men around. He won the featherweight, welterweight and lightweight titles in that order during an extraordinary run of 46 successive victories; and he made an audacious bid to make it four championships with a challenge for the world middleweight title, even though he rarely weighed more than 10 stone. His attempt to add the 11 stone 6 pounds crown to his collection ended with a draw against defending champion Ceferino Garcia.

Armstrong was, by all accounts, something of a miracle man outside as well as inside the ring. One of his trainers once revealed, 'Hank is a champion womaniser. I have to get him out of a different bed every day to train. I just don't know where he finds the energy'.

Perhaps the secret lay in the fact that he had an abnormally slow heartbeat that enabled him to fight at a relentless pace for 15 rounds. His

Henry Armstrong, aka
'Homicide Hank'.

perpetual motion style earned him the nickname 'Homicide Hank' and he used to swarm all over his opponents with both fists hammering away non-stop. Raised in a poor quarter of St Louis, Armstrong was the 11th of 15 children born to a husband and wife who had a rich mixture of negro, Cherokee Indian and Irish blood. With a cocktail like that, Henry just had to have fighting blood!

His real name was Henry Jackson, but he changed it to Armstrong to hide an early record that was dotted with defeats and draws from the days when he fought to the instructions of unscrupulous promoters. Al Jolson, the singing idol of the period, spotted his potential and advised influential manager Eddie Mead to take over the running of his career.

He gained his trio of titles in a ten-month period between October 1937 and August 1938. He stopped Petey Sarron in six rounds to win the featherweight title, and then made the mind-boggling decision to challenge for the welterweight crown which was in the possession of one of the ring's legendary heroes, Barney Ross. Armstrong gave Ross such a hammering over 15 rounds in May 1938 that battered Barney was forced to retire from boxing.

He captured his third championship three months later when he out-pointed Lou Ambers over 15 rounds to win the lightweight title. He then relinquished the featherweight crown and concentrated on the welterweight division after losing his lightweight title in a vicious return match with Ambers during which Henry was guilty of out-of-character roughhouse tactics.

What I find the most hard to believe when I study Armstrong's record is that in 1937 he had 27 contests, winning all but one of them inside the distance. The most fights I ever had in a year was nine, and even then I thought I was doing a bit too much!

Like so many of the old-timers Armstrong hung around for too long, and he had 49 more battles after losing his welterweight championship in his 11th defence in October 1940. The man who took his last prize away from him was Fritzie Zivic, a warrior of a fighter who outpointed him over 15 brutal rounds and then stopped him in the 12th in a bitterly-fought return match.

With the help of an army of hangers-on, Armstrong had managed to dispose of the fortune he had earned, and within months of finishing his career he was a prisoner of the bottle. But after becoming involved in a drunken brawl with a blind man he claimed he had had a message from God telling him to mend his ways. He was ordained as a Baptist minister in 1951 and travelled the world punching the Bible. When he died at the age of 75 in 1988 he was penniless, but he left behind rich memories of one of the greatest fighting machines of all time.

ABE ATTELL

Abe Attell
Born San Francisco, California,
22.2.1884
Career span: 1900-17
World featherweight champion
1904-12
Ring record: 171 fights, 124
wins, 19 losses (4 stoppages);
53 inside-the-distance wins, 24
draws; 2 no contests, 2 no
decisions

Abe Attell was the best of a fighting trio of brothers from San Francisco who between them helped to gain respect for the many Jewish boxers who were prominent in the fight game in the first half of the century. Monte and Caesar were both top-flight professionals, but it was Abe who put the Attell name on the map by hanging on to the world featherweight championship for eight years.

Just 16 when he started to box professionally, he learned his craft well and by the time he was 20 he was a seasoned pro who knew all the tricks of the trade. He was one of the elusive, now-you-see-me-now-you-don't brigade who was clever at feinting and then counter punching. Abe performed his tricks to such good effect against veteran George Dixon – probably the greatest of all Canadian-born fighters – that he was awarded a 15-round points decision following a 20-round draw in 1901. He claimed

Abe Attell sports his world
championship belt.

the world 9 stone title, but was not universally recognised as the champion until he knocked out Harry Forbes in the fifth round of a showdown in St Louis on 1 February 1904. Abe was a born gambler who thought nothing of putting his entire purse on himself to win, and he collected an extra $50,000 against Forbes by betting that he would stop him inside six rounds.

It looked as if he had lost the title in his first defence when he was knocked out by Tommy Sullivan in the fifth round, but he was able to prove that his opponent had come into the ring overweight and so retained it. He then had two narrow escapes against battling Brummie Owen Moran, rated by old-time Americans to have been the best British boxer ever to visit their shores. Their first contest, over 25 rounds, was adjudged a draw but neutral observers reckoned Moran had skated it.

Attell wanted the return over 20 rounds, but Moran's connections held out for 25. A compromise was reached and for the one and only time in boxing history a title fight was staged over 23 rounds. Again the result was a draw, and again Moran looked to have been robbed.

Abe did not seem happy against British opposition. In his first contest after the second draw with Moran he was outpointed by the 'Pride of Pontypridd', Freddie Welsh, in a 15-round non-title fight. Three months later he fought another Welshman, 'Peerless Jim' Driscoll, in one of the 'no decision' contests that were common in the United States in the first quarter of the century when official verdicts were prohibited. It was left to the newspaper ringside reporters to decide the winner, and they were unanimous in their view that Driscoll had won every one of the ten rounds.

But crafty Attell hung on to his crown, and went on to complete 20 successful defences until he lost on points over 20 rounds to Johnny Kilbane on his 28th birthday in 1912. He hung up his gloves in 1913, made a one-fight comeback in 1917 and then concentrated on running a bar on New York's Broadway. The one thing he did not give up was gambling, and he became involved in a betting scandal surrounding fixed baseball matches. He was one of Broadway's great characters who could have stepped right out of the pages of a Damon Runyan *Guys and Dolls* story, and he was still regaling anybody who would listen with stories about his colourful past right up until his death in 1970 at the ripe old age of 85.

CARMEN BASILIO

*Carmen Basilio
Born Canastota, New York
State, 2.4.1927
Career span: 1948-61
World welterweight champion
1955-57; world middleweight
champion 1957-58
Ring record: 79 fights, 56 wins,
16 losses (2 stoppages); 29
inside-the-distance wins, 7
draws*

Carmen Basilio was the sort of rough, tough slugger for whom every fight was a war. One of ten children who grew up on his father's onion farm just outside Syracuse towards the north of New York State, he was once asked why he stuck with boxing when it was obviously such a hard game for him. Carmen, who had a face that looked as if it had been quarried out of a slab of granite, replied: 'If you'd ever worked on an onion farm you wouldn't think boxing was that tough. Every day of my life I had to go down on my knees cutting the heads off onions with a knife. My brothers, sisters and me had to work like slaves at full speed and if you missed with the knife you gashed your thumb to the bone. Boxing ain't that hard after the onion farm, believe me'.

Basilio chose boxing as an escape from the onion farm after he had served in the US Marines. He was 21 when he made his professional debut, and he had been boxing for five years when he achieved the big breakthrough by outpointing Billy Graham for the New York State welterweight championship. This win earned him a crack at world champion Kid Gavilan, the 'Cuban Hawk', who had to call on all his considerable skills to edge a 15-round points victory after recovering from the shock of a second-round knock-down.

Carmen then put together a run of 11 fights without a defeat to force himself back into the title reckoning, this time against Tony De Marco in front of his own fans in Syracuse in 1955. His devastating two-fisted body attacks wore the champion down and he stopped him in the 12th round, a victory that he repeated in a championship return in Boston five months later.

After winning a three-fight series with Johnny Saxton 2-1, Carmen decided to relinquish his hard-earned title to have a crack at the middle-weight championship, which was in the keeping of the one and only Sugar Ray Robinson. They had two classic contests – no, that's not quite right – classic *battles*, neither of them conceding an inch in two 15-round bouts that are remembered as among the most exciting and explosive encounters ever witnessed. Basilio edged the first one on points, and Robinson won the return by a narrow margin. Iron man Basilio shed tears when he lost the title . . . and there was not an onion in sight!

*Opposite: Tears from the
'Onion Man'. Carmen Basilio
cries tears of triumph after
taking the world welterweight
title from Johnny Saxton on a
ninth-round stoppage in
Syracuse in 1956.*

Neither Basilio nor Robinson were quite the same force after their wars, which took a hell of a lot out of both of them. Carmen found the energy to make two more challenges for the world middleweight title against Gene Fullmer, but his power was fading and he was stopped in the 14th round and in his second attempt in the 12th round by the Mormon 'bull fighter' from Utah. The ex-Marine then went to war for the last time, retiring after losing on points over 15 rounds against Paul Pender in Boston on 21 April 1961. Suddenly the onion field did not seem such a tough place after all.

WILFRED BENITEZ

Wilfred Benitez
Born Bronx, New York,
12.9.1958
Career span: 1973-86
WBA world light welterweight
champion 1976-77; WBC
world welterweight champion
1979; WBC world light
middleweight champion 1981-
82
Ring record: 58 fights, 51 wins,
6 losses (4 stoppages); 30
inside-the-distance wins, 1
draw

Wilfred Benitez was a phenomenal prodigy who became the youngest world champion of all time at the age of 17 years and six months, and he was the first of a procession of modern boxers to win world titles at three different weights. His father, Gregorio, was a leading manager in Puerto Rico and from his schooldays Wilfred was a regular visitor to the top San Juan gymnasium where he sparred with some exceptional fighters.

Born in New York and raised in Puerto Rico, Benitez made his professional debut two months after his 15th birthday and was quickly knocking over men twice his age. The boxing world looked on in amazement when a boy who had hardly started shaving was matched with the formidable Antonio Cervantes for the world light welterweight title in 1976, and the reaction was one of even greater astonishment when Wilfred outboxed the Colombian to become the new champion.

Benitez was mean, moody and magnificent. He was mean in the vicious way he treated outgunned opponents; moody with his handlers, who complained about his lack of commitment to training, and there was no doubt that he was a magnificent fighting machine. Perhaps it all came a little too easily to Wilfred, who was a naturally gifted boxer. Throughout his career he exasperated those around him with his attitude to training and his love of the good life.

Benitez made three successful defences of his world title before being stripped of the championship for failing to go through with a return match against Cervantes. He moved up into the welterweight division and again proved his class by taking the WBC world title from Carlos Palomino, respected in British circles for his impressive victories over John H. Stracey and Dave 'Boy' Green. It was clearly going to take a remarkable fighter to beat Benitez, and he arrived in the shape of Sugar Ray Leonard. They met at Caesar's Palace, Las Vegas, on 30 November 1979, where the champion collected a purse of $1.2 million and the challenger $1 million. They earned every penny as Benitez battled his way back into the fight after taking a count in the third round and sustaining a jagged gash on his forehead in a sixth-round clash of heads. There was less than a minute to go to the final bell when Leonard dropped Benitez with a sweeping left hook. His legs had been reduced to rubber when he got up at eight and referee Carlos Padilla rightly rescued him as Leonard moved forward menacingly to finish it.

Benitez was back in business at Caesar's Palace in May 1981, challenging for the WBC light middleweight title held by British southpaw Maurice Hope. Wilfred was now a battle-hardened 'veteran' of 22, and the contemptuous way he dealt with the extremely capable Hope showed just what a vast divide there is between the 'good' and the 'great'. Swaggering and scornful, Benitez taunted and teased Hope in the pre-fight preliminaries, during which he showed good sportsmanship was not on his menu. He ended a brave defence by Maurice with a stunning right in the 12th round that knocked the man from Hackney cold.

He made two winning defences of the world title, the first against Carlos

Santos and the second against the mighty Roberto Duran. But Benitez, who had become the fifth boxer in history after Bob Fitzsimmons, Tony Canzoneri, Barney Ross and Henry Armstrong to win titles at three different poundages, met his match in Thomas Hearns, who hammered out a 15-round points victory in Texas on 3 December 1982. With that defeat Benitez, the boy who had got too much too soon, was suddenly a spent force at championship level. During a four-year retirement from 1986 he managed to get through what was left of the estimated $8 million he had earned in the ring and, at the age of 31, he was forced into a comeback in 1990.

Wilfred Benitez takes it on the nose from Roberto Duran, but he finished a nose in front for a points victory in their WBC welterweight title fight in Las Vegas in 1982.

NINO BENVENUTI

*Nino Benvenuti
(originally Giovanni
Benvenuti)
Born Trieste, Italy, 26.4.1938
Career span: 1961-71
World light middleweight
champion 1965-66;
world middleweight champion
1967-70
Ring record: 90 fights, 82 wins,
7 losses (3 stoppages); 35
inside-the-distance wins, 1
draw*

Nino Benvenuti composed one of the longest winning sequences of modern times as he presented a powerful argument to be recognised as the greatest Italian boxer of all time. As an amateur he won 120 contests, culminating in a wildly popular victory in the welterweight final in the 1960 Olympic Games in Rome. He then turned professional, and on the way to winning 65 fights without a hint of defeat collected the world light middleweight championship.

Benvenuti — his name means 'welcome' in Italian — captured the world title by knocking out his great local rival, Sandro Mazzinghi, with a classic sixth-round right uppercut in Milan in 1965. It was his 57th contest. Born in Trieste, where he became a city councillor for the Italian Socialist Party, Benvenuti was not always popular with Italian fans. He had an acid tongue and a confident manner that sometimes spilled over into arrogance.

Tall, handsome and stylish, both in and out of the ring, he won over all his detractors with his performances inside the roped square. In October 1965 he captured the vacant European middleweight championship by blasting Spaniard Luis Folledo in six rounds before outpointing Mazzinghi in a return match for the world light middleweight title. He then participated in his first ever contest outside Italy, stopping German challenger Jupp Elze

in 14 rounds in Berlin. This gave him the confidence to travel further afield, and for his 66th fight he went to Seoul to defend his world championship against South Korean Ki-Soo Kim. It was an unhappy trip for Nino. He came home bruised and battered and claiming that he was robbed of a points victory, his unbeaten record and his title in a brutal 15-round battle.

He decided to concentrate full-time on the middleweight division, and in 1967 he travelled to New York to challenge the redoubtable Emile Griffith for the world 11 stone 6 pounds title. In a thrilling three-fight saga he won, lost and won again in viciously-contested bouts that all went the scheduled 15 rounds. Neither fighter was ever quite the same force again after their savage battles.

Benvenuti made successful title defences against Don Fullmer and Fraser Scott, but lacked his old snap and sparkle. Dick Tiger outpointed him over ten rounds in a non-title fight in New York, and he came from behind to knock out Cuban Luis Rodriguez with a thundering left hook in the 11th round of a world championship contest. A measure of Nino's dwindling stamina came in Melbourne when he was battered to an eighth-round defeat by an ordinary American middleweight called Tom Bethea, who had lost his four previous fights.

He beat Bethea in eight rounds in a return fight in Italy when his title was on the line, but he was clearly past his peak and was no match for Argentinian Carlos Monzon, who stopped him in 12 rounds and then in three rounds to start his seven-year reign as king of the middleweights. It was all over for Benvenuti, who then concentrated on saying 'benvenuti' to visitors to his smart restaurant in Rome. He had given Italian boxing fans a feast, but had been in danger of outstaying his welcome.

Opposite: Nino Benvenuti (right) rocks Spaniard Luis Folledo with a right to the head shortly before stopping him in the sixth round to become the new European middleweight champion in Rome in 1965.

JACK 'KID' BERG

Jack 'Kid' Berg
(originally Judah Bergman)
Born Whitechapel, London,
28.6.1909
Career span: 1924-45
World light welterweight
champion 1930-32
Ring record: 192 fights, 157
wins, 26 losses (8 stoppages);
57 inside-the-distance wins, 9
draws

Jack 'Kid' Berg was a have-gloves-will-travel fighting man who gained the distinction of becoming as big a drawing card in the United States as he was in Britain. He has remained a great character since settling back home in London after an incredible 21-year career, and with his sharp brain and total recall of all his contests he has proved – in his 80s – just about the best of all walking, talking advertisements for boxing.

Jack's life and career has been like something out of a Hollywood movie. Born Judah Bergman into a poor Jewish family in Whitechapel, he disobeyed his parents, who hated him boxing, and was fighting professionally at the age of just 13 at the famous Premierland, an East End venue at which he fought almost exclusively until 1928. He adopted the name 'Kid' Berg because he wanted to follow in the footsteps of his idol Ted 'Kid' Lewis, who was the great East End Jewish boxing hero when Jack was at school. After just a handful of defeats in 59 fights Jack despaired of ever getting a crack at the British title and set sail for the United States.

The Americans took immediately to the all-action style that earned him the nicknames the 'Whitechapel Whirlwind' and the 'Whitechapel Windmill'. He earned quite a reputation as a playboy, and among scores of wild adventures he was once threatened by a pistol-packing mobster for making a pass at the girlfriend of notorious gangster boss 'Legs' Diamond. But Jack took his boxing seriously and he was, pound for pound, unquestionably one of the most outstanding of all British fighters. Among the opponents he beat at the start of his 70-fight campaign in the States was Mushy Callaghan, and they were matched in a return contest for the world light welterweight title at London's Royal Albert Hall in 1930. He forced Callaghan to retire at the end of the tenth round for a victory that brought him world title status in the United States, but not in Britain where the weight division was not recognised.

Berg returned to the States where he lost two world lightweight title battles against the all-time great Tony Canzoneri, the first on a third-round knock-out and the second on points over 15 rounds. He still claimed the world light welterweight crown, but conceded that it was no longer his when he lost on points to Sammy Fuller in New York in 1932. Two months later he scored probably the finest victory of his career when he outpointed legendary Cuban Kid Chocolate over 15 rounds in what eye-witnesses claimed was the most exciting fight ever.

Jack came home to London in 1934 to get his long-awaited crack at a British title and beat Harry Mizler – another outstanding Jewish fighter from the East End – on a tenth-round stoppage. He held the title until 1936 when he was stopped in nine rounds by Jimmy Walsh in Liverpool. That would have been enough for most people, but the man with atomic energy boxed on until 1934, continuing his globe-trotting with bouts in such stopping-off points as Johannesburg, Bermuda, Brooklyn, Dublin and Paris.

After a short-lived marriage to an American heiress, Jack found the woman of his dreams back home in London while serving as an RAF corporal during the Second World War. He married Miss Moyra Smith in

1943 and he has gone the distance with her for more than 40 happy years. They have a daughter who lives in France and is one of Europe's most respected women artists. 'Kid' Berg – there will never be another like him.

ERIC BOON

Eric Boon
Born Chatteris,
Cambridgeshire, 28.12.1919
Career span: 1935-48
British lightweight champion
1938-44
Ring record: 122 fights, 93
wins, 23 losses; 64 inside-the-
distance wins, 5 draws; 1 no
decision

Eric Boon gave a whole new meaning to the 'on yer bike' phrase re-popularised by Norman Tebbit. He cycled from his home in Chatteris, Cambridgeshire, to seek his fortune as a fighter in London after battling for shillings in local shows. Within months of arriving in the big city wearing his bicycle clips he was nicknamed the 'Golden Boy' of British boxing.

Boon was just 16 when he made the 72-mile bike ride that was to change his life, and I remember Jack Solomons telling me about how he reacted when he first saw him: 'I was the matchmaker at the Devonshire Club, and I was just locking up my office one day when an untidy boy pushing a bike called me. "Oi, mister," he shouted in a country yokel accent, "are you the man what makes the matches?" I was in a hurry, and told him, "Sorry, son, can't stop. I'm on my way to the gym". He said, "Let me come, and I'll show you what I can do". When he got to the gym he stripped off and I couldn't believe my eyes. The puny kid suddenly looked like a pocket Hercules, and when he started sparring he more than held his own with seasoned professionals. I put him on the next bill and he became an overnight star. But he still insisted on cycling everywhere because he reckoned it was good for strengthening his legs'.

'Boy' Boon, who stood just 5 feet 5 inches tall, owed his superb upper body physique to the fact that since the age of ten he had helped out in his father's blacksmith's forge. It gave him abnormal strength, and his opponents used to say that his right hand punch was like a donkey kick. He made a phenomenally quick rise to the top and became the youngest ever British champion when, trailing on points, he knocked out the highly regarded Dave Crowley in the 13th round of a lightweight title fight at Harringay Arena on 15 December 1938. The new champion was 13 days short of his 19th birthday.

Boon's first defence of the championship was a classic that is still talked about in awe by those lucky enough to have seen it. He came from behind to stop Bethnal Green hero Arthur Danahar in the 14th round of a sell-out contest at Harringay in 1939, the first title fight televised and also shown on a revolutionary closed-circuit link-up with three cinemas. Boon was a national hero after this dramatic victory, and he knocked out Crowley in a return match to win a Lonsdale Belt outright in what was then a record 11 months 24 days.

Boon, who was unlucky to lose his peak years to the Second World War, had weight problems when defending his lightweight crown against Welshman Ronnie James in Cardiff in 1944 and his famous strength deserted him. He was knocked out in ten rounds. In 1947 he challenged Ernie Roderick for the British welterweight championship, and put up a gallant show before losing on points.

Boon, who died on 19 January 1981, remained a popular character in Cambridgeshire, and was a regular at the ringside when Dave 'Boy' Green – from the same neck of the woods – was trying to emulate his ring performances in the 1970s. But there will only ever be one Eric Boon, the 'Golden Boy' of British boxing who got on his bike to find fame.

Opposite: Eric Boon (right) jolts Dave Crowley with a right to the jaw moments before knocking him out in the seventh round of their British lightweight title fight at Harringay in 1939.

JAMES J. BRADDOCK

James J. Braddock
Born New York City,
6.12.1905
Career span: 1926-38
World heavyweight champion
1935-37
Ring record: 86 fights, 46 wins,
23 losses (2 stoppages); 27
inside-the-distance wins, 4
draws; 11 no decisions

James J. Braddock became, as every schoolboy in my day knew, the 'Cinderella Man' of boxing because he arrived so late for the brawl. He deserves his place in my top 100 club if only for the fact that his rags-to-riches fairytale inspired an army of youngsters – yours truly included – to dream of following in his footsteps.

A 29-year-old dockworker, Braddock had been on the breadline in the Depression years and was in semi-retirement when he got his world title chance. He came off the dole queue to snatch the world's greatest sporting prize from playboy champion Max Baer, who failed to take his challenger seriously and was clearly outpointed over 15 rounds at Long Island on 13 June 1935.

Suddenly, the disbelieving world had a heavyweight champion who had won only 46 of his previous 83 contests. Braddock, who had boxed mainly as a middle and light heavyweight, had failed in a bid for the 12 stone 7 pounds title in 1929 when he was outpointed over 15 rounds by Tommy Loughran. He lost his appetite and his ambition, and in his next 30 contests he was beaten 19 times. It was hardly the stuff of which world heavyweight

title challengers are made, but Baer's handlers were looking for an easy defence and, on paper, they looked no easier than Braddock.

Jimmy was a neat, orthodox boxer but he lacked the punching power to make a real impact in the heavyweight division – that is until he got his chance against Baer, who believed along with the rest of the boxing world that he had been selected as 'strictly an opponent'. The challenger adopted hit-and-run tactics, and stole the title from Baer with snapping left jabs and jolting rights that pulled big-hitting Max up in his tracks every time he set himself to try to land his own feared right.

Braddock should have met former champion Max Schmeling in his first defence, but he was bribed into putting his title on the line against Joe Louis by being guaranteed ten per cent of his challenger's purses as title-holder if the championship changed hands. It was as smart a piece of business as any boxer ever did. Schmeling was, to put it mildly, upset at being side-tracked. On the date originally agreed for his fight with Braddock he went through the routine of a weigh-in and turned up in his boxing kit in an empty stadium to try to lay claim to the title. But this was in the days when Hitler was getting into his stride with his anti-semitism, and the Jewish promoters in the United States were in no mood to put themselves out to help a German battle for the world crown. Schmeling would get his chance, but first he had to wait for Braddock and Louis to settle their argument. Despite grounding the 'Brown Bomber' for a brief count in the first round, Braddock was no match for his young challenger, who blasted him to a knock-out defeat in eight rounds to start the greatest reign of any champion in the history of boxing.

Braddock had one more winning fight – a points win over British heavyweight hero Tommy Farr – and then retired. Jimmy's money, boosted by regular payments from the Louis camp, was wisely invested and he became a prosperous businessman. The 'Cinderella Man' finished up having a ball.

Opposite: James J. Braddock is short of the target with this left against Welsh hero Tommy Farr. The 'Cinderella Man' won this 1938 contest at Madison Square Garden, New York, on points over ten rounds and then announced his retirement.

JOE BROWN

Joe Brown
Born New Orleans, Louisiana,
18.5.1926
Career span: 1943-70
World lightweight champion
1956-62
Ring record: 161 fights, 104
wins, 42 losses (9 stoppages);
47 inside-the-distance wins, 13
draws; 2 no contests

Joe Brown was too good for his own good in the early stages of a career that stretched over more than a quarter of a century. The managers of world-rated lightweights heard on the boxing grapevine about his skill and punching power, and they wisely decided to avoid the flashy fighter from the jazz city of New Orleans. He had been a professional for more than ten years before he was at last given a shot at the lightweight title, and he not only won it but clung on to it for six years through 11 defences and late into his 30s.

Brown made his professional debut at the age of 17 in 1943, but after just one fight he was called up for wartime service during which he captured the all-services lightweight championship. He resumed his professional career after the war, and during the next ten years he strung together 61 victories and nine draws in 87 contests, numbering top-quality fighters of the calibre of Virgil Atkins (twice), Arthur Persley (twice), Teddy 'Red Top' Davis and Isaac Logart among his victims.

A whisker under 5 feet 8 inches, Brown was tall for a lightweight and he used his reach advantage to good effect, keeping opponents on the end of loose yet jolting left jabs before following up with powerful looping rights. During his long, hard apprenticeship he learned every trick of the trade and he was well equipped in every department when he finally got his chance of a championship fight against Wallace 'Bud' Smith in his home town of New Orleans on 24 August 1956. He had already outpointed Smith in a non-title fight, and he produced a superlative display of boxing to outmanoeuvre the champion and relieve him of his title.

It seemed to Brown that his hungry-fighter days were over when he proudly took his championship belt home to show to his wife and four children. But even though he had the title he was still struggling to gain full recognition from the fans. Then he read a quote from Sugar Ray Robinson's manager, George Gainford, who said: 'How can anybody with the name of plain Joe Brown expect to capture the imagination of the public?'

The message registered with the new champion and he picked up on a publicity man's idea to bill himself for future fights as Joe 'Old Bones' Brown. This little promotion trick, combined with his outstanding ability as a boxer, won him a place in the hearts of fans as over the next six years he made a dozen defences of his title.

Britain's very handy Dave Charnley went down to him twice, and his other title fight victories were against Bud Smith (rsf 11), Orlando Zulueta (rsf 15), Joey Lopes (rsf 11), Ralph Dupas (ko 8), Kenny Lane (pts 15), Johnny Busso (pts 15), Paolo Rosi (rsf 8), Cisco Andrade (pts 15), Bert Somodio (pts 15). It was Carlos Ortiz, a smart boxer from Puerto Rico, who finally ended Brown's reign with a 15-round points victory in a magnificent duel in Las Vegas in 1962, during which the challenger's ten-year age advantage was a decisive factor.

Joe just did not know how to give up the game that had been his life. He travelled the world boxing for any promoter prepared to pay his asking

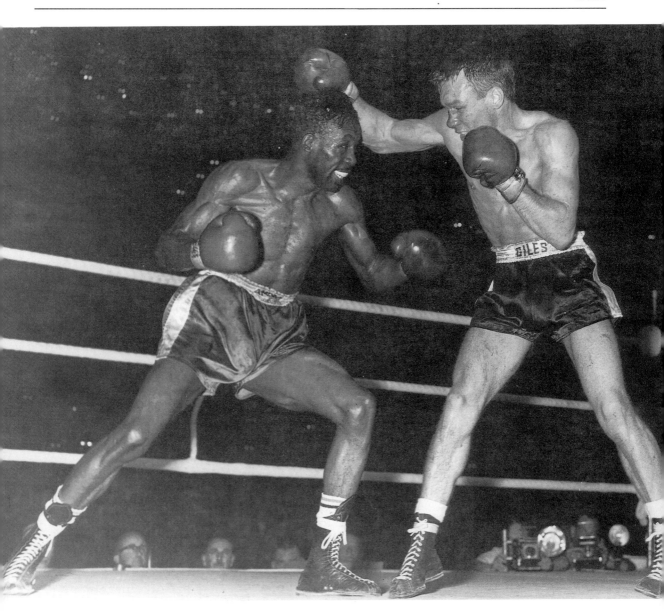

price, making up for all the hungry years when he had been forced to fight for peanuts. There was, sadly, little pride left in his performances and he lost 23 of his last 45 fights before at last hanging up his gloves in April 1970 at the age of 44. By then, he really *was* 'Old Bones' Brown.

Joe Brown slips inside Dave Charnley's southpaw lead and launches a two-fisted counter attack.

KEN BUCHANAN

*Ken Buchanan
Born Edinburgh, 28.6.1945
Career span: 1965-83
World lightweight champion
1970-72
Ring record: 70 fights, 62 wins,
8 losses (1 stoppage); 34 inside-
the-distance wins*

Ken Buchanan has a lot of supporters, particularly north of the border, who insist that he has been the best of all Britain's post-war champions. I rate him unfortunate in three respects. First, so many of his early fights were tucked away behind the closed doors of private sporting clubs that the general public were unable to appreciate his outstanding ability. Secondly, his winning of the world title coincided with the arrival on the scene of Roberto Duran, one of the finest fighting machines of them all; and thirdly, private financial disasters outside the ring forced him to fight on when his talent was diminished, which made him seem little more than ordinary in the latter half of his career.

There is no doubt that at his peak Buchanan was a master of the boxing arts. He was incredibly quick on his feet, punched with lightning speed – particularly with his ramrod left jab – and had a strong chin. Evidence of his ability to absorb a punch is that in 70 professional fights over a period of 17 years he was stopped only once.

I first noticed Buchanan's outstanding potential when he won the ABA featherweight title in 1965 as a member of the Sparta Amateur Boxing Club in his home town of Edinburgh. Within three years he was British professional lightweight champion, grabbing the championship from Maurice Cullen with an 11th-round knock-out victory.

*Ken Buchanan drives Al Ford
to the ropes on his way to a
ten-round points victory at
Wembley in 1972.*

A winning run that stretched to 33 fights came to an end in Madrid in 1970 when he was adjudged to have been outpointed over 15 rounds by Spaniard Miguel Velasquez, a decision that was hotly disputed. Buchanan, managed by former British welterweight champion Eddie Thomas, was suffering for his early lack of exposure to the British public and was unable to command the sort of purses his talent deserved. He decided to gamble everything on winning a world title, and accepted a token payment of £5,000 for the opportunity to challenge Ismael Laguna for his WBA lightweight crown in San Juan. Ken boxed out of his skin in intense heat and in front of a fiercely partisan crowd to steal the title from Laguna on a split points decision. It was a mighty performance, but the British Boxing Board of Control were unmoved and refused to recognise him as champion because they were affiliated to the WBC. There's loyalty for you!

Even the Board had to accept that Buchanan was the best in the world when he outpointed Ruben Navarro for the undisputed title in Los Angeles on 12 February 1971. He retained the championship with another points victory over Laguna, and then made the mistake of his life by agreeing to fight a relatively unknown fighter called Roberto Duran. He had a war in New York with the fighter who was to become a legend of the ring, losing in the 13th round after being knocked down with blows that seemed recklessly low. Duran did not give Ken the courtesy of a return, and later admitted that Buchanan had been one of the finest opponents he had ever met.

Back in Britain, he narrowly outpointed the relatively inexperienced Jim Watt to regain the British title and then put himself back into the world title picture by winning the European title. He went to Tokyo in 1975 to challenge Ishimatsu Suzuki for the WBC championship, but was outpointed.

Buchanan announced his retirement as undefeated European champion in 1975, but money problems forced him into a comeback four years later when he was like a poor imitation of the fighter who had proved himself one of Britain's greatest exports in his peak years. His career finished with the ignominy of appearing on an unlicensed 'pirate' promotion. It was as sad as hanging a Goya in a brick outhouse.

TOMMY BURNS

Tommy Burns
(originally Noah Brusso)
Born Chesley, Ontario,
17.6.1881
Career span: 1900-20
World heavyweight champion
1906-08
Ring record: 60 fights, 46 wins,
5 losses (1 stoppage); 36 inside-
the-distance wins, 8 draws; 1
no decision

Tommy Burns was not only the shortest man ever to hold the world heavyweight title, but also the shrewdest. Standing just 5 feet 7 inches and never more than a light heavyweight, he was the thinking man's champion. He developed a counter punching boxing style in which he was able to achieve maximum effect with minimum effort; he also developed a business sense that made him a fortune out of his reign as world heavyweight champion.

Burns became champion in 1906 by winning on points over 20 rounds against pretender to the throne Marvin Hart, who had claimed the vacant championship after stopping Jack Root in a fight refereed by retiring title-holder James J. Jeffries. It was Jeffries who had nominated Hart and Root to fight for his old title!

There was only one outstanding contender for the championship: Jack Johnson. But he was barred from fighting for the title in the United States because he was black. Burns knew that the time would come when he would have to defend the title against Johnson and, realistic enough to appreciate he did not stand an earthly, decided to cash in on the championship against a queue of virtual no-hopers before going into the ring with the 'Galveston Giant'. Johnson trailed Burns around the world throwing out challenges, but the canny Canadian kept one step ahead of him. He successfully defended the title 11 times in his own version of a 'bum-of-the-month' campaign. For such a short man, he had an extraordinarily long reach and he used to draw in opponents like a spider luring a fly and then knocked them senseless with carefully pinpointed punches to the most vulnerable parts of the head and body.

Burns had a finger in the promotion of most of his fights, and his sharp business brain amazed the British boxing fraternity when he made two defences in London. At one stage in his early career he was chiselled out of his purse, and he swore it would never happen again. He decided to manage himself and used to insist on receiving his money before throwing a punch in anger. When he fought British champion Gunner Moir at the aristocratic National Sporting Club he demanded that his £3,000 purse be paid to him in notes in the ring before the fight. The money was counted out in front of him, and then he handed it over to his second before getting on with the business of having Moir counted out in the tenth round. Two months later he declined a purse for defending against Geordie Jack Palmer at the Wonderland stadium in London's East End. Instead he chose to take 50 per cent of the takings. Spectators arriving to buy their tickets on the day of the fight were amazed to find Burns sitting in the box office. He waited until all the tickets had been sold and then put half the money in a bag that he locked in his dressing-room before climbing into the ring to knock out Palmer in four rounds.

Burns was then part-promoter of easy defences in Dublin and Paris before sailing for Australia, with Johnson in pursuit. To drum up interest in the inevitable showdown with Johnson, Burns made two defences in nine days against outgunned Australian challengers. Then, at a specially-built stadium

Opposite: Tommy Burns, short on height but long on reach.

at Rushcutter's Bay in Sydney, Burns put his title on the line against Johnson in the first black versus white world heavyweight title fight. He collected an enormous purse of £6,000 but had to earn every penny as the giant Johnson battered him around the ring in a fight that was staged on Boxing Day 1908 with the promoter, Hugh McIntosh, in the ring as referee. Johnson toyed with the champion and hit him with a stream of insulting words as well as injurious punches before police jumped into the ring and stopped the savagery in the 14th round.

Burns had five more contests before retiring, but then – in return for a £4,000 purse – made a one-fight comeback at the age of 40 against British champion Joe Beckett, who stopped the veteran in seven rounds at the Royal Albert Hall in 1920. He invested his money in pubs in Britain and in a speakeasy in New York, but later this extraordinary man 'got religion' and was ordained as a church minister in California in 1948. When he died of a heart attack in Vancouver in 1955 at the age of 74 boxing lost one of its most remarkable characters.

TONY CANZONERI

Tony Canzoneri rose from shoeshine boy to become America's greatest boxing idol of the '30s. He contested world championships at four different weights, winning three of them, and was the first man in history to lift the world lightweight title twice. There has rarely been a more exciting performer than Canzoneri, who seemed to grow a foot taller than his 5 feet 4 inches the moment he climbed into the roped square that he considered a second home.

Having moved to Brooklyn from Louisiana while still in short trousers, he used to shine shoes during the day and hand out shiners at night as a flyweight and bantamweight amateur who cleaned up a fistful of titles before turning professional at the age of 16. Canzoneri's aggressive style and flailing fists made him a favourite with the fans, who could relate to somebody obviously fighting his heart out in what were tough Depression days when every day was a battle.

At the age of 17 he made two unsuccessful attempts to win the world bantamweight crown, but in 1928 he captured the first of his world titles when he beat Johnny Dundee for the vacant featherweight championship.

Tony Canzoneri
Born Slidell, Louisiana,
6.11.1908
Career span: 1925-39
World featherweight champion 1928; world lightweight champion 1930-33, 1935-36; world light welterweight champion 1931-32
Ring record: 175 fights, 141 wins, 24 losses (1 stoppage); 44 inside-the-distance wins, 10 draws

Tony Canzoneri (left) in typical two-fisted action against Jimmy McLarnin in New York in 1936. Tony won on points over ten rounds but was himself outpointed in the return five months later.

Battling with the scales, he lost the title seven months later but then entered the most productive period of his career in the lightweight division. He won the world championship in sensational style in 1930, knocking out title holder Al Singer in just 66 seconds. Barney Ross wrested the 9 stone 9 pounds championship from him in 1933 after two wars, but giant-hearted Canzoneri was back as the king of the lightweights in 1935 when he reached down into his memory to produce all his vintage moves to outpoint Lou Ambers.

In between time, while averaging 12 contests a year, Canzoneri had a thrilling three-fight serial with Britain's Jack 'Kid' Berg. He lost the first on points over ten rounds, won the return on a knock-out in the third round and the third on points over 15 rounds. Perhaps the outstanding performance of Tony's career came in 1936 when he outpointed Belfast-born world welterweight champion Jimmy McLarnin in a non-title fight. But he was taking too much out of himself with his tearaway tactics, and in his next two contests he lost his lightweight championship back to Ambers and lost to McLarnin on points.

There was then a downhill run for Canzoneri, who could not accept that his best was far behind him. He fought on until 1939 when his career was finished by a lethal left hooker called Al 'Bummy' Davis, who destroyed him in three rounds.

The Canzoneri story after his retirement is, sadly, a familiar one with too many ring heroes after the final bell has sounded. He ran into problems with his businesses and his marriage, and in no time at all he had gone through the $300,000 he had built up during his astonishing boxing career. He was reduced to playing the straight man to a comedian on stage, and the sight of him being slapped around as part of the act reduced his former fans to tears.

He had a connection with a Broadway restaurant that carried his name, but when he died of a heart attack in a New York hotel room at the age of 51 in 1949 he was as alone as he had been in the ring. It was 48 hours before his body was discovered. What a sad end for a hero used to having the cheers of thousands ringing in his ears.

GEORGES CARPENTIER

Georges Carpentier had an amazing career that bridged the First World War, during which he fought in every weight division from flyweight to heavyweight. The 'Pride of Paris' dominated the European circuit for more than a decade while winning European titles at welterweight, middleweight, light heavyweight and heavyweight as well as every French championship from lightweight to heavyweight. He also crossed the Atlantic to capture the world light heavyweight crown and to play a supporting role in the first million-dollar gate fight against the legendary Jack Dempsey.

The son of a miner, he started boxing for pay before he was 14 and perfected the art of box-fighting, mixing skill with devastating punching power, particularly from his long right hand punch that was delivered straight from the shoulder and which accounted for a procession of opponents, including just about every top British boxer of the period. He was like a master fencer in the ring, feinting and then, after making his opponents miss, countering with thrusting attacks.

Carpentier had debonair style and charisma as well as boxing skill, and he was treated like a matinee idol. He was the first boxer to regularly attract women spectators to the ringside, and his habit of wearing an orchid in his lapel earned him the nickname the 'Orchid Man'. He became as popular in Britain as he was in France as he mowed down a queue of British opponents including Bombardier Billy Wells (twice), Bandsman Rice, Dick Smith, Joe Beckett (twice) and, in one of the most controversial of all contests, Ted 'Kid' Lewis, who claimed he was knocked out with an illegal punch on the break in the first round of their world light heavyweight title fight in London in 1922.

Carpentier won the world 'white' heavyweight championship when he beat American Gunboat Smith on a sixth-round foul at London's Olympia in 1914. He then lost five precious years of his career to the First World War, during which he was decorated for bravery while serving as a lieutenant in the French air force. Two years after resuming boxing he went to the United States to challenge Philadelphian Battling Levinsky – real name Barney Lebrowitz – for the American's world light heavyweight championship. The emphatic way in which he flattened Levinsky in four rounds prompted ace promoter Tex Rickard to line him up for a world heavyweight title showdown with the 'Manassa Mauler', Jack Dempsey. Rickard banged the publicity drum with such force that he attracted 80,183 fans to a specially constructed outdoor arena in Jersey City. They paid a total $1,789,238 to watch the contest, which lasted four rounds before the outgunned Carpentier was knocked out.

Four months after his headline-hitting victory over Ted 'Kid' Lewis, Carpentier lost his world light heavyweight title in dramatic fashion. He was matched with Senegalese Battling Siki, who had been brought to Paris by an aristocratic French lady who kept him in a splendour to which he was not accustomed in return for special favours. She even provided him with a French identity: Louis Phal, which she told friends with great amusement was symbolic! Siki, like Carpentier, had been decorated for

Georges Carpentier
Born Lens, France, 12.1.1894
Career span: 1908-27
World light heavyweight champion 1920-22
Ring record: 109 fights, 88 wins, 14 losses (8 stoppages); 56 inside-the-distance wins, 6 draws; 1 no decision

Georges Carpentier, the 'Orchid Man', with his influential manager Francois Descamps (left) and trainer Gus Wilson before his European heavyweight title defence against British champion Joe Beckett in London in 1919. Carpentier won by a knock-out in the first round.

bravery during the war after wiping out a German machine-gun post single-handed. As a publicity build-up for his boxing career he used to promenade through Paris with two tigers on the end of a leash.

He was a crude fighter who used to get by on a combination of raw power and blind bravery. Carpentier carried him through the opening three rounds after dropping him for a count in the first. He and his manager, Francois Descamps, had bought the rights to the film that was being made of the fight, and they knew a short-lived affair would have little commercial value. But it turned into a horror film for Carpentier. He had his nose broken by a thunderbolt punch from Siki in the fourth round and then took a fearful hiding as the African landed with wild swings that threatened to tear Carpentier's handsome head off his shoulders. A roundhouse right sent the Frenchman crashing to the canvas in the sixth round, and Descamps immediately threw in the towel. The referee kicked the towel out and waved his arms to signal that the fight was over. The ringside fans sportingly applauded what they thought was a new world light heavyweight champion. But their mood turned ugly when it was announced that the referee had disqualified Siki for allegedly tripping Carpentier. With a riot in prospect, the referee then allowed justice to prevail and changed the decision to a stoppage victory for the African. Siki then made the mistake of travelling to Dublin to defend the title on St Patrick's Day and was outpointed over 20 rounds by Irish hero Mike McTigue. He later based himself in the United States, where his career and life came to a brutal end when he was shot dead in a New York street.

Carpentier wound down his career by winning the French heavyweight title, beating British heavyweight Joe Beckett for the second time in the first round and making a final money raid on the United States, where he lost to Gene Tunney and Tommy Loughran in non-title contests. He then settled down to a long and happy retirement, running a bar in Paris where he remained an idol right up to his death at the age of 81 in 1975. If you asked boxing experts to list their top ten European boxers of all time, I reckon the name of Carpentier would head many of them.

MARCEL CERDAN

Marcel Cerdan
Born Sidi Bel-Abbes, Algeria,
22.7.1916
Career span: 1934-49
World middleweight champion
1948-49
Ring record: 109 fights, 105
wins, 4 losses (1 stoppage); 60
inside-the-distance wins

Marcel Cerdan's remarkable life came to a tragic end at the very pinnacle of his boxing career. He was flying to New York from Paris to prepare for a return world middleweight title fight with Jake La Motta in 1949 when the Air France plane crashed into the Azores, and 33-year-old Cerdan was among those who perished. His death made worldwide headlines, not only because of his prominence as a boxer but also because his well-publicised affair with the French singer Edith Piaf had occupied acres of gossip-column space.

Cerdan, who grew up in Casablanca, had won a place in the hearts of French fight fans with his rugged, two-fisted, American style of fighting. He was a month past his 17th birthday when he elected to follow two elder brothers into the professional fight game in preference to a possible soccer career. He felt more comfortable scoring with his fists than his feet, and after he had ripped through 28 fights without defeat in his first three years as a professional he was persuaded to base himself in Paris.

He won the French welterweight title in 1938, and it was not until the following year that his unbeaten run of 45 fights came to an end when he was disqualified against Harry Craster in the first of three visits to London. Swarthy and stocky, Cerdan threw punches from all angles and his occasional carelessness about where they landed had him in trouble with referees. His second defeat came in 1942 in his 69th contest, when he was disqualified against Victor Buttin, a loss that he later avenged with a third-round knock-out victory. He hammered his way into the world ratings in 1947 when he knocked out Leon Foquet in the first round to win the vacant European middleweight title.

Plans for a crack at the world championship were temporarily shelved when he surprisingly dropped a points decision to Belgian Cyrille Delannoit in a European title defence. He regained the championship and gained revenge with a clear-cut points victory over Delannoit in Brussels that cleared the way for a world title fight with Tony Zale. He met brute force with brute force when tackling Zale in Jersey City in 1948 and handed the American such a hiding before the referee intervened in the 12th round that he hung up his gloves. In a non-title fight before defending the world crown against Jake La Motta he returned to London to stop the very capable Dick Turpin in seven rounds. On his previous trip to England he had beaten Bert Gilroy in four rounds. He was handicapped by a first-round shoulder injury in his brawling battle with 'Bronx Bull' La Motta in Detroit on 16 June 1949, and was stopped for the first time in his career when forced to retire after ten brutal rounds.

The return match was all set for November 1949 when Cerdan took off on his fatal flight from Paris. When his plane went down it was the second time that he had been reported killed in an air crash. Tragically, this time the reports were true. His name lived on through his son Marcel Cerdan Junior, who was a good class professional in the 1960s. But he was never able to match the phenomenal performances that had made his father a legendary figure of French boxing.

Opposite: Marcel Cerdan (right) makes front-page news as he batters Tony Zale to a 12th-round defeat.

But CLUB

NUMÉRO SPÉCIAL

16 PAGES

VENDREDI 24 SEPTEMBRE 1948

CERDAN, CHAMPION DU MONDE

15 frs

Afrique du Nord - Avion

EZZARD CHARLES

Ezzard Charles
Born Lawrenceville, Georgia,
27.5.1921
Career span: 1940-59
World heavyweight champion
1949-51
Ring record: 122 fights, 96
wins, 25 losses (7 stoppages);
58 inside-the-distance wins, 1
draw

Ezzard Charles was never the most popular of world heavyweight champions, mainly because he committed the unforgivable sin of beating the legend that was Joe Louis. Charles, whose grandparents were cotton plantation slaves, had turned professional four months before his 19th birthday in 1940 after an illustrious amateur career in which he won all of his 42 contests, including the Golden Gloves final. He first of all campaigned as a middleweight and then as light heavyweight, and you can judge his ability by the fact that he beat experienced ring generals Archie Moore and Joey Maxim three times respectively.

In the first half of his career he was known as the 'Cincinnati Cobra' and was noted for the dynamite power of his punches as well as for the skilful boxing that brought him a string of inter-services titles while he was based in Europe as a GI during the Second World War. But following the death of one of his opponents in 1948 he switched moods in the ring, becoming a defensive boxer who seemed almost reluctant to let his heaviest punches go. Yet even with this cautious approach he still proved too much of a handful for most of his opponents when he moved up to the heavyweight division.

Charles rarely weighed much more than 13 stone, but he was so mobile in the ring that his bigger-built opponents could rarely make use of their weight advantage. He captured the championship that had been relinquished by Joe Louis when he outpointed Jersey Joe Walcott over 15 rounds in his 74th professional contest on 22 June 1949.

Louis, weighed down by financial problems, changed his mind about retiring and challenged Charles for the title that the public still considered Joe's property. The fight was staged on 27 September 1950 in New York, and Charles scored a points victory over a man who was just a shambling wreck of a once-great fighter. Ezzard had always idolised Louis and beating his hero gave him little satisfaction, and his win earned him only grudging respect from the fight fans who, to a man, had considered the 'Brown Bomber' the king of the ring.

Over the next two years Charles successfully defended the title eight times before running into a classic left hook in the seventh round of a third title clash with Walcott. He was outpointed by his old adversary Jersey Joe when he tried to regain the championship, and in 1954 lost two bruising title battles against Rocky Marciano.

Ezzard used every trick he knew to keep Marciano at bay in their first meeting, and although he was clearly outpointed he had the satisfaction of being the only challenger to take Rocky the distance. In a return three months later Charles was knocked out in the eighth round after inflicting a serious nose injury on Rocky that was to hurry Marciano's retirement from boxing.

Charles was never the same fighter after his two wars with Marciano, and lost 13 of his last 23 contests. One of his final appearances came in London in 1956 when he was matched with my old rival Dick Richardson. It was tragic to see Charles appear to lose his nerve in the ring, and he was disqualified for the only time in his career for some of the most blatant holding I have ever seen. He clung to Richardson like a drowning man hanging on to a lifebelt, and the referee had no option but to send him packing.

In all Ezzard took part in 13 world championship contests, yet somehow he managed to wind up broke and bitter. He hung up his gloves at the age of 38 when he was being beaten by opponents who would not have belonged in the same ring as him when he was at his peak. Sadly he finished up in a wheelchair, a victim of what was reported to be multiple sclerosis. He died on 27 May 1975 in a Chicago hospital, six days short of his 54th birthday. He is remembered warmly by the boxing fraternity for having been one of the finest of all ring technicians, and he was unlucky to have lived in the shadow of Joe Louis and to have stood in the path of Rocky Marciano.

Ezzard Charles (right) is out of range with a right against Jersey Joe Walcott. They met four times, winning two fights each.

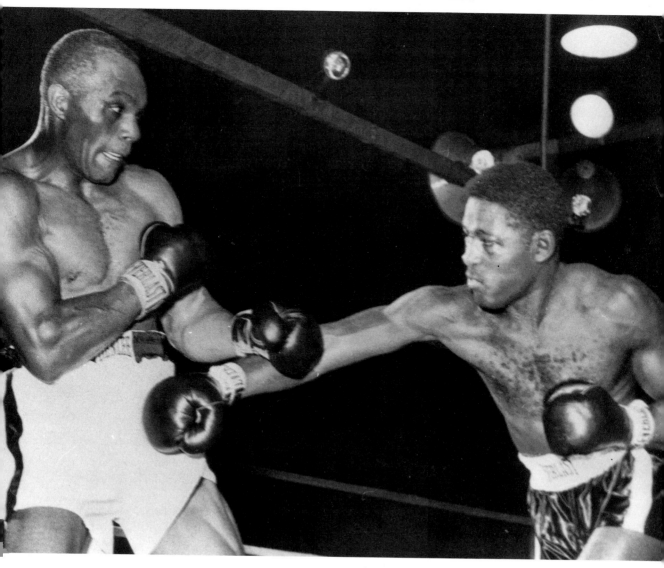

DAVE CHARNLEY

Dave Charnley
Born Dartford, Kent,
10.10.1935
Career span: 1954-65
European, Commonwealth and
British lightweight champion
1957-65
Ring record: 61 fights, 48 wins,
12 losses (2 stoppages); 30
inside-the-distance wins, 1
draw

Dave Charnley was, in my view, not only England's finest post-war light-weight but also the unluckiest. He failed by a whisker to take the world crown from Joe 'Old Bones' Brown, and if I had been the referee on the night he fought the veteran champion in London I would have had no hesitation in raising the arm of the man of Kent.

This was the second of three dramatic duels with Brown. Charnley first challenged him for the world title in Houston, Texas, in 1959. He was more than holding his own when a head clash left him with a jagged cut on his forehead that forced the referee to stop the fight in the fifth round. In the return at Earls Court on 18 April 1960 Charnley fought the fight of his life. He refused to concede an inch to one of the great world champions, and I

Dave Charnley, the 'Dartford Destroyer'.

reckoned that his non-stop aggression just about earned him victory. It was an opinion shared by many in the crowd of 18,000 who booed and jeered the decision for more than 30 minutes after British referee Tommy Little had raised Brown's hand at the final bell. It was British fair play gone mad. I am sure that in no other country in the world – apart from perhaps the United States – would Brown have got the nod. Charnley got some sort of revenge in 1961 when he had the satisfaction of knocking out Brown in the sixth round, but Joe had lost the world title by then and was very much on the slide.

Young Dave Charnley drops Neville Tetlow at Harringay in his seventh professional contest in 1955. Tetlow was counted out in the second round.

I followed Charnley's career from beginning to end. He grew up in Kent not far from my territory, and from when he first won the ABA feather-weight title in 1954 it was obvious that he was a class performer. Dave turned pro just a month after me, boxing under the banner of Arthur Boggis, a West London butcher who had been a good class boxer in his youth. In his early days Charnley was an apprentice blacksmith in his native Dartford, but he was quickly earning enough to become a full-time professional. Dave won 21 of his first 24 contests. He was outpointed and then held to a draw by cagey Welshman Willie Lloyd, and dropped a points decision to a very capable French fighter called Guy Gracia.

He stopped Lloyd in 12 rounds when they met for a third time to earn a tilt at the British title held by my stablemate Joe Lucy. It was an all-southpaw battle in which the chunky 'Dartford Destroyer' punched too hard for 'Mile End Joe' and had the champion down six times on the way to a comfortable points victory.

Charnley was one of the most compact fighters I have ever seen. It must have been daunting for opponents to try to find a way through his solid defence, particularly as he was a master of counter punching from a square-on stance. His punch-placing was always solid and accurate, and he packed heavy combination hooks and crosses in both hands to back up a powerful right jab. He mopped up the Commonwealth and European titles to go with his British crown. To get the Commonwealth championship he had to avenge a points defeat by Willie Toweel, who — along with his bantam-weight brother, Vic — was one of the finest fighters ever to come out of South Africa. Dave knocked Toweel out in round ten in the return.

He had a good chin to complement his ability, and he was stopped only once apart from when he lost on the cut against Brown. Possibly his one weakness was his caution early in fights, at least that was the belief before he defended his British lightweight title against David 'Darkie' Hughes at Nottingham Ice Rink in 1961. He knocked Hughes cold in just 40 seconds including the count, a record for British championship contests. Dave won a Lonsdale Belt outright by outpointing Maurice Cullen and then unwisely moved up among the welterweights after stopping a sadly past-his-best Peter Waterman. Dave gave a gallant performance against talented Swansea southpaw Brian Curvis before losing on points to add strength to the claim that a good big 'un will always beat a good little 'un.

In his final fight Dave was soundly beaten by world welterweight champion Emile Griffith, who forced him to retire at the end of nine painful rounds. He declared his career closed as the unbeaten British lightweight champion, and concentrated on a business career in which he has since amassed a fortune by showing the same conscientious effort and flair that he used to display in the ring.

JULIO CAESAR CHAVEZ

Julio Caesar Chavez has put together the longest unbeaten record of any modern fighter and is rated, pound for pound, the greatest boxer ever to come out of the boxing hotbed of Mexico. He is a heart-breaker of a fighter who wears opponents down with relentless two-fisted attacks, and the fact that 57 of his first 67 opponents failed to last the distance is positive proof of the power of his punching.

*Julio Caesar Chavez
Born Ciudad Obregon,
Mexico, 12.7.1962
Career span: 1980-
World super featherweight
champion 1984-87; world
lightweight champion
1987-89; world light
welterweight champion 1989-
Ring record: 67 fights, 67 wins;
57 inside-the-distance wins*

Julio Caesar Chavez, ready to get to work.

Chavez trod a tightrope in his light welterweight showdown with the marvellously skilled Philadelphian Meldrick Taylor in Las Vegas on St Patrick's Day 1990. He was just seconds from a points defeat when he unleashed a fusillade of punches to stop Taylor and preserve his unbeaten record. It was the only time in his ten-year career that he had looked second best, but a fight is not over until the final bell and his astonishing last-round rally added to the legend of his invincibility.

One of a family of ten children born and brought up in Ciudad Obregon, he followed three elder brothers into professional boxing and started punching for pay when he was just 17. Manager Ramon Felix brought him along carefully, and it was four years and 40 winning fights before he made a first challenge for a world championship. He stopped Mario Martinez in eight rounds in Los Angeles on 13 September 1984 to win the vacant WBC super featherweight title. He reigned supreme in his division over the next three years, powering through nine successful defences before moving up to lightweight to challenge Mike Tyson's stablemate Edwin Rosario for the WBA title. Many fight followers thought he was over-reaching himself against the rugged Rosario, but he was always in control of the fight and forced Rosario's corner to throw in the white towel of surrender in the 11th round.

Chavez got involved in some political shenanigans outside the ring with the powerful Don King organisation, but found time to unify the WBC and WBA lightweight titles when he outgamed his veteran countryman Jose Luis Ramirez, persuading him to retire after 11 rounds of non-stop bombardment.

There is not a weakness in the Chavez armoury. He has a chin of steel, can brawl, box or showboat and includes a potent knock-out punch among the vicious combinations that he has perfected over the years. In May 1989 he became a triple world champion when he repeated a previous win over the talented Roger Mayweather, knocking him out in the tenth round to capture the WBC world light welterweight championship.

He came within seconds of being parted from his latest title by Meldrick Taylor, but it was a further sign of his greatness that he was able to produce the finishing punches when all seemed lost. Chavez has a growing army of supporters who argue the case for him to be considered the best of all the modern fighters. Few will be able to dispute it while he remains unbeaten.

BILLY CONN

Billy Conn is best remembered for two stirring contests for the world heavyweight championship against Joe Louis, but it should not be overlooked that he was also an outstanding light heavyweight champion who might have reigned for years but for setting his sights on the crown of the 'Brown Bomber' and what he unashamedly described as 'a chance to win a million bucks'.

A remarkable fact about the Irish-American fighter nicknamed the 'Pittsburgh Kid' is that he turned professional without having fought a single amateur bout. He had just a handful of knockabout contests at high school where he showed exceptional promise as an artist with a brush rather than his fists. But he found that he preferred the canvas of the boxing ring and stepped straight into the professional ranks as an 18-year-old welterweight. After losing his debut on points, he learned the ropes by trial and error and had seven defeats on his record in his first 18 contests. Yet he had a natural gift for boxing and he started to perfect an orthodox, upright style in which his snapping left jab and powerful right crosses brought him increasing success. He was not an explosive puncher, but hit hard enough to earn respect and he had the sort of clever footwork that made him a difficult target to pin with a punch.

By the time he had developed into a middleweight he was a very good fighter indeed as he proved by beating former world champions Babe Risko, Vince Dundee, Teddy Yarosz, Young Corbett III and Solly Krieger. His hero was Gene Tunney, and he copied the way the former world heavyweight champion used to plot his victories by studying the strengths and weaknesses of every opponent. He used his artistic skill to draw pictures of the way he expected fights to end. Billy, tall, dark and handsome, enjoyed something of a playboy's life away from the ring, but he treated the build-up to each contest with deadly seriousness.

He had grown into a light heavyweight by the time he was 22 and after twice outpointing the then world middleweight champion, Fred Aspoli, he was nominated to fight Melio Bettina for the vacant world light heavyweight title that had been claimed in Britain by Len Harvey.

Conn outpointed Bettina twice in two world title battles, and then handed out the same treatment to the rugged Gus Lesnevich in two championship matches. He also twice got the better in non-title fights of a boxer trading under the name of Henry Cooper, but as I was only six at the time you can take it that it was not me in the opposite corner! Conn relinquished the light heavyweight crown in 1941 to concentrate on building himself up for a crack at the heavyweight championship which was in the safe keeping of Joe Louis. 'I enjoy being world light heavyweight champion,' he said, 'but my ambition is to earn a million bucks from boxing. The only way to do that is to beat Joe Louis. I honestly think I have the style to do it.'

He almost provided action to support his brave words in New York on 18 June 1941. For 12 rounds he boxed the 'Brown Bomber''s ears off, but then he got carried away with his success and went all out for a knock-out in the 13th round. It meant dropping his guard to try to land a pay-off

Billy Conn
Born East Liberty,
Pennsylvania, 8.10.1917
Career span: 1934-48
World light heavyweight
champion 1939-41
Ring record: 76 fights, 63 wins,
12 losses (3 stoppages); 14
inside-the-distance wins, 1
draw

Billy Conn prepares to snap out his left jab against 'Brown Bomber' Joe Louis in their return fight in 1946.

punch. It was just the opening Louis had been waiting for, and he knocked his young challenger cold with a single deadly left hook.

Army service delayed a return match until 1946 by which time Conn had lost a lot of his ambition and Louis a lot of his timing and sparkle. But they still produced eight exciting rounds of combat before Louis ended all arguments with a blitz of punches that sent Billy down and out.

Conn retired for 18 months, won two fights in a brief comeback and then hung up his gloves to concentrate on a lucrative used car business and an association with an oil company.

JOHN CONTEH

John Conteh had long, delicate hands that looked more suited to a classical pianist than a champion pugilist. They were so fragile that they gave the Merseysider problems right at the peak of his career when he most needed them at full power and strength. An even greater predicament for John was the perplexing web of boxing politics and finance, and he got involved in outside-the-ring disputes that were more damaging than anything that happened inside the ropes. All in all, the combination of the problems with his hands and the bitter friction over contracts and money prevented him from completely fulfilling his rich promise.

Conteh was just about to embark on his professional career when I dropped the curtain on mine in 1971. He had proved his undoubted class with a gold medal-winning triumph in the middleweight division in the Commonwealth Games in Edinburgh, but then threw shadows of uncertainty over his temperament when seeming to freeze in the European championships.

All went smoothly with the foundation-building to his professional career, and he looked to have the style, the punching power and the charisma to become the new idol of British boxing. There was only one hiccup in his first 18 fights when a journeyman American, Eddie Duncan, proved too cagey for him and won a points decision. John dabbled with the heavyweight division, but then accepted that his physique and power were best suited to the light heavyweight stage. It could be pointed out that John weighed as much as me in my peak years when he started campaigning as a heavyweight, but by the mid-1970s we were right into the era of the super-heavies who rarely hit the scales at less than 16 stone.

In his 19th contest he wrested the European light heavyweight title from West German Rudiger Schmidtke with a 12th-round victory. This set up a showdown with his great British rival, Chris Finnegan, the 1968 Olympic gold medallist who was in possession of the British and Commonwealth titles. They had two bitterly contested battles, the first — a nip-and-tuck classic — ending in a narrow points win for Conteh and the second in a sixth-round victory after a butt appeared to have caused a gash over Finnegan's left eyebrow.

Conteh's reward for his second win over the luckless Finnegan was a fight for the vacant WBC light heavyweight title against Argentina's iron-hard Jorge Ahumada at Wembley Arena on 1 October 1974. This was the night that Conteh reached down to his boots for the performance of a lifetime against an opponent who was a head-down slugger of the old school. John boxed beautifully behind an accurate jab, and continually rocked Ahumada with lightning-fast combination punches. Those who harboured doubts about John's commitment when the going got tough had them wiped away as he stood toe to toe with the bulldozing Argentinian in the late rounds when the pressure was at its peak. He thoroughly deserved his points victory, and everybody thought that this would be the start of a golden reign for the most naturally-gifted British boxer for years.

But then the troubles began. Conteh's career became cursed by hand

John Conteh
Born Kirkby, Merseyside,
27.5.1951
Career span: 1971-80
World light heavyweight
champion 1974-77
Ring record: 39 fights, 34 wins,
4 losses (1 stoppage); 24 inside-
the-distance wins, 1 draw

John Conteh prepares to launch a right against Chris Finnegan in their triple title fight at Wembley in 1974.

injuries and – worse still – promotional and managerial disputes. Suddenly it was more about what went on in the courtroom than the boxing ring, and following just three title defences in two and a half years John was stripped of his hard-earned title for refusing to go through with a contracted defence of the championship against Miguel Cuello in Monte Carlo.

He made three attempts to regain the title, losing on points in a hard slogging match with Mate Parlov in Belgrade and then to Matthew Saad Muhammad – formerly Matt Franklin – before taking a terrible four-round tanking in a return match. There were worrying rumours about John's lack of attention to his preparation for the second Saad Muhammad fight, and he retired in 1980 amid all sorts of stories about drug- and drink-related incidents. But by the late 1980s this good-looking and engaging character seemed more like his old perky, quick-witted self. He achieved a lot in boxing, but many people – no doubt including John himself – will always wonder just how great he could have become without all the hassle and distractions outside the ring.

HARRY CORBETT

Harry Corbett was a British featherweight champion in the bad old, good old days of the 1920s and 1930s when dozens of hungry fighters queued for the chance to punch for pay. They did not climb into the ring to get rich but just to earn enough pennies to be able to put food on the table. These brave fighting men were a breed apart, and I wanted them to be represented in my selection. In Harry Corbett I have picked somebody who was respected in the old school as a master exponent of the Noble Art.

Harry's real name was Henry William Coleman, but he turned professional as Young Corbett because he did not want his family to know that he was fighting for a living. When his younger brother – also a brilliant ring craftsman – followed him on the professional path under the name of Dick Corbett he dropped the 'Young' and became plain Harry Corbett. But there was nothing plain about him in the ring. He was an artist of a boxer who had such clever footwork that he could go through an entire contest without his opponent being able to land a worthwhile punch.

Born and raised in Bethnal Green in the East End of London, Harry was spotted as an amateur by Ted Broadribb, who later became famous as the manager of Freddie Mills and who, during a successful boxing career as Young Snowball, had once beaten the great Georges Carpentier. He persuaded Harry to supplement his meagre wages as an apprentice at an iron foundry by boxing regularly at the Premierland, a famous East End venue.

For more than a decade Corbett averaged around 16 fights a year, and in his second year as an 18-year-old professional in 1922 he squeezed in an incredible 35 contests, including two in one day on several occasions. Those days, thank God, are behind us, but Harry – along with scores of rivals – had the motivation of knowing that if he didn't fight he and his family would go hungry. During a career of more than 200 fights he fought two world champions, five European champions, ten British title-holders and dozens of top contenders. He never ducked a soul and while moving in top company was a winner on the majority of occasions.

He slogged away for four years before getting a title chance. His shot at the British bantamweight crown came just as he was outgrowing the division, and by boiling himself down to make the weight he left himself weak and was forced to surrender after 16 rounds against the very capable champion, Johnny Brown.

He was much more comfortable at featherweight, and became champion in 1928 by outpointing Sheffield's rugged Johnny Cuthbert. They played musical chairs with the 9 stone title in a series of eight fights, every one of which went the distance. In all they fought 118 three-minute rounds, and there was hardly a thing to choose between them at the end of each 20-round contest. The final score was Cuthbert four wins, Corbett two wins and two draws.

In 1932, after an undefeated three-fight trip to Australia and fattened into a lightweight, he was boxing Harry Vaughan at Edmonton when a loose lace hit him in the left eye. He lost the sight of the eye, which should have meant the end of his career. But somehow he fiddled his way through

Harry Corbett (originally Henry William Coleman) Born Bethnal Green, London, 14.2.1904 Career span: 1921-36 British featherweight champion 1928-29 Ring record: 219 fights, 141 wins, 50 losses; 54 inside-the-distance wins, 25 draws; 3 no contests

Harry Corbett. Note the cauliflower ear that was almost obligatory in the good old, bad old days when Harry was fighting.

medical examinations and continued boxing for another four years. This could not happen with today's strict medical supervision by the British Boxing Board of Control.

Harry, and his brother, Dick (who died a war-time hero when he was trampled on while trying to protect a baby whose mother had fallen going into an air raid shelter), both lived for their boxing. When Harry died in 1957 at the age of 53 the boxing world mourned the passing of an outstanding ring general whose rich talent never brought the financial rewards that he deserved. And, sadly, it's a story that could be told hundreds of times over about the brave fighting men of the 1920s and 1930s. We will not see their like again – and I hope we will not see those tough times again. Boxing should be exclusively for men who *want* to fight, not for hungry men who *have* to fight.

JAMES J. CORBETT

James J. Corbett was the first boxer to win the world heavyweight championship under the Marquess of Queensberry rules that demanded the wearing of gloves. 'Gentleman Jim' was also one of the pioneers of scientific boxing who practised and preached that the sport should be as much about avoiding punches as landing them. He was never a devastating puncher, but such a master tactician that he could nullify the aggressive work of more powerful opponents by clever footwork and smart defensive strategy.

It was a long time before the American public warmed to this former bank clerk as he beat their hero for all seasons, John L. Sullivan, who was used to fighting toe-to-toe sluggers and was outboxed and outsmarted by the fitter, younger challenger.

Like Sullivan, Corbett was the son of an Irishman but he was the complete opposite to the Boston braggart both in his style inside the ring and his behaviour outside. He was a dandy dresser, articulate and quietly spoken. His good manners earned him the nickname 'Gentleman Jim', which was the title of the biographical film in which Errol Flynn portrayed Corbett.

After proving himself an outstanding amateur, Corbett gave up his comfortable life in the bank to go in search of Sullivan. First of all he had to eliminate local San Francisco rival Joe Choynski, with whom he had three viciously-fought battles in 1899. The first was declared no contest, and the second – staged on a barge to avoid the police – ended with a knock-out victory for Corbett in the 27th round. He won the third encounter in four rounds.

He earned a crack at the champion by fighting a draw over 61 rounds with Peter Jackson, the black West Indian Sullivan had refused to fight 'on grounds of colour'.

Sullivan failed to take Corbett's challenge seriously enough, and despite a weight advantage of 40 pounds was unable to impose his immense strength on the fight. Corbett kept on the move against the out-of-condition champion and continually beat him to the punch. At 26, he was eight years younger than Sullivan and his fast pace exhausted the 'Boston Strong Boy'. Both men were wearing five-ounce gloves, and Sullivan was unable to wrestle his opponent to the floor as he had often done when fighting with bare fists. Corbett fought a textbook fight, gradually luring Sullivan into his trap. Once he had him puffing and blowing like an old bull he unleashed a stream of blows in round 21 to force the wind and the will out of the old champion, who was knocked out for the only time in his career.

In his first defence of the title, Corbett knocked out Englishman Charlie Mitchell in three rounds at Jacksonville in 1894. This was the one and only time Corbett lost his temper in the ring. Mitchell hurled a volley of abuse at him as the referee was giving his final centre-of-the-ring instructions. It was a deliberate ploy by Mitchell to goad Corbett and upset his concentration. But the plan backfired. The insults served only to turn the master of defence into a demon of attack, and he gave Mitchell the biggest hiding of his life before the referee counted him out.

After losing to Bob Fitzsimmons in his third defence following a three-

James J. Corbett
Born San Francisco, California,
1.9.1866
Career span: 1884-1903
World heavyweight champion
1892-97
Ring record: 19 fights, 11 wins,
4 losses (3 stoppages, 1
disqualification); 7 inside-the-
distance wins, 2 draws; 2 no
contests

'Gentleman' James J. Corbett.

year lay-off, Corbett made two attempts to win back the championship against James J. Jeffries, but each time he was bulldozed to defeat by his stronger, harder-punching opponent. Corbett never fought again after being knocked out in ten rounds in his second fight with Jeffries, but in a professional career spanning just 19 fights he had become a legend of the ring.

DON CURRY

Don Curry looked, pound for pound, the finest fighter around in the 1980s until he was sensationally stopped in six rounds by Britain's Lloyd Honeyghan. He deserves a prominent place in my personal hall of fame for all that he achieved before this sudden setback when, according to boxing village gossip, he was losing a battle with the scales.

Born in Fort Worth, Texas, Curry grew up in a boxing environment. One brother, Bruce, won the world light welterweight championship, and another, Graylin, was a good quality professional. But it was Don who was the real thoroughbred. He suffered only half a dozen defeats in more than 300 amateur contests, and he was a scorching-hot favourite for a gold medal in the 1980 Moscow Olympics until President Jimmy Carter knocked him out by ordering a boycott of the Games. Don won the gold medal in the 'alternative' Games, and then started a glittering professional career.

Don Curry
Born Fort Worth, Texas,
7.9.1961
Career span: 1980-
World welterweight champion
1983-86, world light
middleweight champion
1988-89
Ring record: 33 fights, 30 wins,
3 losses (2 stoppages); 22
inside-the-distance wins

Don Curry, the 'Cobra' who lost his venom.

Within two years he was number one in the welterweight ratings after ending the unbeaten run of Marlon Starling. When world champion Sugar Ray Leonard temporarily retired with eye trouble in 1983 it was Curry 'the Cobra' who took over as the new champion. He won the WBA version of the title by getting off the floor to outpoint Korean Jun-Sok Hwang, and he then stylishly mastered Starling again, Elio Diaz, Nino La Rocca and Welshman Colin Jones.

There were rumours that he was struggling to make the 10 stone 7 pounds limit as he campaigned with success among the light middleweights, but this gossip was silenced when he flattened WBC welterweight title-holder Milton McCrory in two rounds. Most people thought his fight with London-based Lloyd Honeyghan would be a routine defence, but he was never allowed to get into his rhythm by a peak-form Honeyghan, who forced his retirement and his first defeat after six rounds.

It was then confirmed that Curry had been losing a battle with the scales, and he moved up to light middleweight to challenge Mike McCallum, only to be knocked cold with a perfect left hook in the fifth round. It looked as if Curry had nowhere to go, but he pumped new life into his career by forcing Gianfranco Rosi to retire after a nine-round mauling, thus capturing the WBC 11 stone championship at San Remo on 8 July 1988.

Curry's power and timing seemed to desert him in his first defence at Grenoble on 11 February 1989, and he gave a sluggish performance on his way to a 12-round points loss against unheralded Frenchman Rene Jacquot. It was the first time he had been outscored in his career, and it added weight to my belief that he had never been able to get the defeat by Honeyghan out of his system. With his best behind him, it must have been galling for Curry to watch the rise of Marlon Starling – the opponent he had twice beaten – to the pinnacle of power that he had once held.

JACK DEMPSEY

Jack Dempsey was the first world superstar of the boxing ring whose fame transcended his sport. Only Mike Tyson might one day force me to reassess the view that there has been no more exciting and explosive heavyweight champion. William Harrison Dempsey, who took his ring name from a middleweight hero, developed great magnetism to go with his devastating power as he rose from bar-room brawler and hobo to become one of the most famous and fêted sportsmen in history.

After a string of unrecorded fights under the name of Kid Blackie, Dempsey teamed up with manager and publicist Jack 'Doc' Kearns. With Kearns beating the publicity drum and Dempsey beating all the opposition, the 'Manassa Mauler' forced himself into championship contention and ripped the title away from giant Jess Willard in three astonishing rounds. Dempsey was so confident that he could crush Willard that he bet his entire $27,500 purse at odds of 10-1 that he would win in the first round. He dropped the towering cowboy from Kansas seven times, and Dempsey climbed out of the ring to collect his winnings after the seventh knockdown. What he didn't realise was that the bell had sounded to save Willard, and he was recalled to the ring to continue the demolition. He finally forced the overpowered champion to retire on his stool at the end of the third round. Dempsey may have gambled his purse away, but six successful defences turned him into a millionaire before he lost the title to Gene Tunney in 1926.

Jack was the first fighter to attract a $1 million gate when he knocked out gallant Frenchman Georges Carpentier in four rounds in 1921, and his second title battle with Gene Tunney in 1927 drew the first $2 million gate. His championship clash with Argentinian Luis Angel Firpo has been acclaimed as the most thrilling fight of all time – and it was all over inside two rounds. Firpo was flattened seven times in the opening round, and then somehow found the strength to knock Dempsey through the ropes and out of the ring with a couple of crude swings. The champion was pushed back in by press men just before the bell, and he tamed the 'Wild Bull of the Pampas' by knocking him out in the second round.

Dempsey was also the champion who bankrupted a town. The local bank at Shelby, Montana, went out of business after it put up the townsfolk's money to stage Dempsey's defence against Tommy Gibbons. Dempsey won on points over 15 rounds before sneaking out of town on a train specially hired by manager 'Doc' Kearns, who had the takings safely tucked into a bag.

There was a falling out between Dempsey and Kearns after the Firpo fight, and the champion did not put the title on the line again for three years – avoiding, among others, outstanding black contender Harry Wills. Kearns disapproved of Jack's choice of film-star Estelle Taylor as his wife, and this caused a bitter argument and subsequent legal battles that led to the end of their profitable partnership.

Dempsey was anchored by worries about lawsuits and domestic problems when he finally returned to the ring to defend the title against Gene Tunney,

Jack Dempsey (originally William Harrison Dempsey) Born Manassa, Colorado, 24.6.1895 Career span: 1914-27 World heavyweight champion 1919-26 Ring record: 79 fights, 64 wins, 6 losses (1 stoppage); 49 inside-the-distance wins, 9 draws

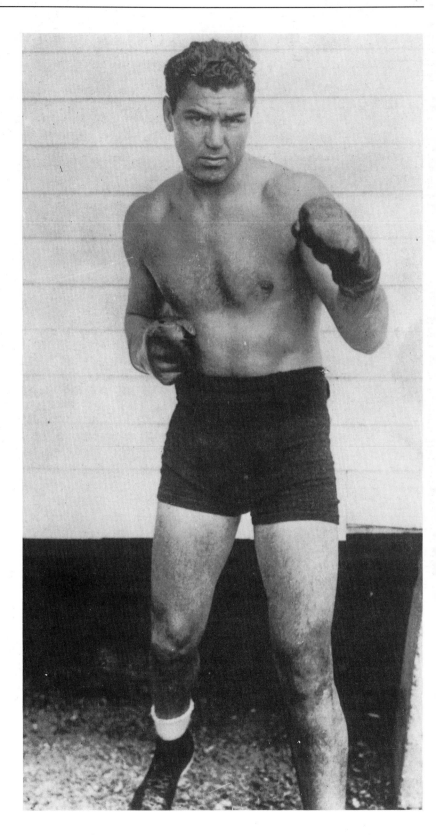

Jack Dempsey, the 'Manassa Mauler'.

Gene Tunney is down in 'the battle of the long count'. The referee tries to direct Jack Dempsey to a neutral corner.

who was the complete opposite to Dempsey in style. While Jack was a rugged, crouching swinger of a two-fisted fighter, Gene was a smart, upright technician, and he jabbed his way to a convincing ten-round points victory. The return was again over ten rounds, and Tunney retained the title with another points win in the famous 'battle of the long count' in Chicago in 1927.

Dempsey then hung up his gloves at the end of a career during which he had caused an eruption of excitement every time he climbed into the ring. His restaurant in New York became the place where big-fight matches were made and where old-timers gathered to remember the days when Dempsey was king. He died on 31 May 1983 aged 88. We won't see his like again.

TERRY DOWNES

Terry Downes
Born Paddington, London,
9.5.1936
Career span: 1957-64
World middleweight champion
1961-62
Ring record: 44 fights, 35 wins,
9 losses (6 stoppages); 28
inside-the-distance wins

Terry Downes may not have been the most skilled or elegant fighter Britain has ever produced, but I doubt if there has been anybody quite so colourful and entertaining. He was an unconventional mix of English jabber and American slugger, having learned his early technique in London amateur rings followed by a tough schooling in the US Marines.

Born in Paddington in 1936, he reached a Junior ABA final before emigrating to the United States with his family. Terry's love of adventure took him into the US Marines where — as a Cockney not frightened of pushing his opinions — he had to learn to look after himself in all sorts of challenging situations. He had 85 amateur contests in America, losing only five, and proved himself a knock-out member of the Marines boxing team.

His father brought him home for a look at 'the old country' in 1956, and Terry called into the offices of the trade paper, *Boxing News*, and asked where he could keep in trim. Tim Riley, then the deputy editor, had close connections with the Fisher club in Bermondsey and arranged for him to train there. With his fascinating background, Terry quickly made back page headlines and he started to box for Fisher in a blaze of publicity.

He chalked up a couple of quick wins, and then quit the amateurs in disgust after a referee stopped his third contest because of what Terry considered a tiny nick on his forehead. Turning professional under the joint guidance of Jarvis Astaire and Sam Burns, he started with two rapid victories and was then matched at Shoreditch Town Hall with an unheralded Liverpool-based Nigerian called Dick Tiger. Downes was decked twice in the first round, again in the second and was finally stopped with cuts in the sixth.

After his shock hiding, Terry revealed the quick-fire humour that was to make him a favourite with the sportswriters. 'Who would you like to meet next?' he was asked in the dressing-room. 'The b...... who made this match!' replied Terry in that strange, unique accent of his that is a cross between a Cockney twang and an American drawl. Perhaps he was only half joking.

Tiger moved to the United States where he became first world middle-weight champion and then world light heavyweight king. He and Downes had fought for a joint purse of £120. Efforts to get them back together in the ring some five years later at around 500 times that figure failed. Terry stayed in England and got on with the job of re-establishing himself after the shellacking from Tiger. He made himself the darling of the fans with his all-action style in which he seemed prepared to take two punches to land one of his own. His defence left a lot to be desired and he rarely ended a contest without some sort of facial damage. He used to entertain the crowd and intimidate his opponent by entering the ring with a leap over the top rope and then going through a form of Indian war dance as a warm-up to the battle ahead.

Few fighters gave better value for money than Downes, who battled and battered his way to title status in 1958 when he stopped Welshman Phil Edwards in the 13th round of a contest for the vacant British middleweight championship. He never seemed far from controversy, though, and lost his title in extraordinary circumstances when he dropped Scottish challenger John 'Cowboy' McCormack 11 times before being disqualified for low punching in the eighth round. In the return, he regained the championship with an eighth-round knock-out but at the expense of an horrific nose injury that required specialised hospital treatment.

In his first attempt to move up into world class company he was belted to an eighth-round defeat by a super fighter called Spider Webb, but he forced himself into the world ratings with a points victory over former

Terry Downes slugs his way to a fifth-round victory over American Mike Pusateri at Manchester in 1963.

world champion Joey Giardello in London in 1960. He then had a three-fight saga with Boston fireman Paul Pender for the world title. He lost the first contest on a cut eye stoppage in the seventh round in Boston, but made enough of an impression to earn a return in London six months later in July 1961. There was a dramatic finish to an uneventful fight when Pender suddenly quit on his stool at the end of the ninth round. It was not the most satisfactory of endings, and later that night two of Pender's connections were beaten up by angry London gamblers.

Terry travelled back to Boston to defend the title against Pender and was outpointed over 15 rounds in a fight in which he found it difficult to avoid Pender's English-style trombone left jab. An uninformed observer would surely have been convinced that Pender was the Englishman and the crashing, bashing Downes the American.

There did not seem much more for Terry to achieve after he had claimed the scalps of Don Fullmer and a fading Sugar Ray Robinson, but then he shocked us all by announcing his intention to go for the world light heavyweight championship. And the giant-hearted ex-Marine very nearly pulled off a stunning upset against Willie Pastrano in Manchester on 30 November 1964. He was well ahead on points and looked set for a memorable title victory until he walked into a right-hander from a close-to-exhausted champion in the 11th round.

The referee stopped the contest as Terry's legs betrayed him, and Downes wisely took this as a signal to get out of a game to which he had contributed 110 per cent in blood, sweat and tearaway action. He struck an oil gusher after his retirement when a betting shop chain in which he had a considerable interest was sold, leaving him a wealthy man. Downsey – as he was affectionately known – deserved every penny.

JIM DRISCOLL

Jim Driscoll was given the nickname 'Peerless', which suitably summed up his standing in the world of boxing. He was an immaculate boxer who was so clever that some of his outclassed opponents could not have hit him by throwing a handful of rice. 'Peerless' Jim turned boxing into a sweet science, and during an unbeaten ten-fight tour of the United States in 1908-09 the Welsh wizard was hailed as the 'Master'.

His tour of the States was during the 'no decisions' period when verdicts were left to the newspaper men. In every fight against the world's top featherweights he was voted the winner. He saved his greatest performance for his final appearance in America when he won every one of ten rounds against world champion Abe Attell, who was completely perplexed by Driscoll's clever counter punching, accurate jabbing and impregnable defence.

Driscoll claimed the world title after his devastating display against Attell, but achieved recognition only in Britain. Back home he underlined his supremacy in the 9 stone division by knocking out Frenchman Jean Poesy in 12 rounds to win the vacant European title, and he retained it with a 20-round draw against the globe-trotting Brummie Owen Moran.

Born in Cardiff, Driscoll learned to box while working as a copy boy in a local newspaper office. He used to wrap pages around his fists, and then spar with anybody who would take him on. His party piece was to challenge people to try to hit him while he had his hands down at his sides. Few landed on anything but his shadow.

He reversed his only defeat – a points loss to Harry Mansfield – in a remarkable run of 62 fights, but then lost his temper and his unbeaten run when he was disqualified for butting against his great Welsh rival, Freddie Welsh, in the tenth round of a needle match in 1910.

Driscoll retired as undefeated British, European and Commonwealth champion – and, he claimed, world titleholder – following his draw with Moran in 1913. He served in the army as a physical training instructor during the First World War, and was so hard up at the end of it that he made an ill-advised comeback in 1918 at the age of 37. He had none of the snap and sparkle of his peak years, and he was not in the best of health. But in those days there was no medical supervision, and he was allowed to resume his career. He stopped another great old-timer, Pedlar Palmer, in four rounds, drew over 20 rounds with Francis Rossi and then tackled outstanding French fighter Charles Ledoux, who was 11 years younger.

Driscoll had been in bed four days before the fight at London's National Sporting Club suffering from stomach pains, but he went through with the contest because he needed the money. He boxed rings round Ledoux for 14 of the scheduled 20 rounds, but then the strength suddenly left his body after the Frenchman had landed a succession of punches to his ulcerated stomach. He refused the pleas of his corner men to quit and came out for the 16th after being given a swig of champagne to pep him up. He was on the brink of being knocked out for the only time in his life when his corner threw in the towel to save him the indignity of taking the count.

Jim Driscoll
Born Cardiff, 15.12.1881
Career span: 1899-1919
World featherweight champion 1912-13
Ring record: 69 fights, 59 wins, 3 losses (1 stoppage); 35 inside-the-distance wins, 7 draws

The NSC members gave Driscoll a standing ovation, realising it was a farewell performance, and a hastily arranged collection at the ringside brought him a £1,500 bonus to help him in his retirement. He slipped into bad health and was dead within five years of this final fight, but his name will always live on in boxing legend because of his procession of 'peerless' performances.

ROBERTO DURAN

Roberto Duran used to be mentioned in the same breath as the likes of Muhammad Ali, Sugar Ray Robinson and Joe Louis as one of the greatest fighters that ever lived, but he stayed too long at the banqueting table and by the time the 1990s arrived his standing in the boxing world had been reduced to that of a mere mortal.

Duran fought as a professional from the age of 16, and revealed his thunderous punching power by winning seven of his first ten fights in the first round. They used to call him the 'Baby-faced Assassin' in his native Panama, where he grew up in abject poverty. Legend has it that while still a schoolboy he knocked over a horse with a single punch to win a bet.

When he started campaigning in the United States he acquired the new nickname of 'Hands of Stone' as he set out on a course of destruction against the world's leading lightweights. In 1972 he was matched with Britain's exceptionally talented Ken Buchanan for the world championship, and he overwhelmed the proud Scot, who could not come out for the 14th round, claiming he had been hit low.

Duran was unbeatable at lightweight over the next seven years, successfully defending the title 11 times, with only one opponent managing to stay around to hear the final bell. He stepped up to welterweight in June 1980 for one of his most memorable triumphs, luring the usually composed Sugar Ray Leonard into a brawl that he won on points. In an amazing return match five months later the 'invincible' Duran suddenly held up his hands in surrender in the eighth round and walked away declaring, 'No mas' (no more). The confused Roberto lost so much face over this public humiliation that he could not return home and he switched his base to Miami, from where he launched the second phase of his remarkable career.

He battered Davey Moore to an eighth-round defeat in 1983 to win the WBA world light middleweight championship, and then made an audacious bid to become the first fighter to win four world titles by challenging Marvin Hagler for the middleweight crown. He gave a brave account of himself against Hagler, but was beaten on points. His undisciplined lifestyle outside the ring started to catch up with him, and Wilfred Benitez and Britain's gifted but erratic Kirkland Laing were among the fighters who got the better of him as he started to lose his way. He was in the habit of blowing up to a cruiserweight in between fights, and his sudden reductions of weight started to have their effect in the ring. It seemed his career was all over when Thomas Hearns knocked him spark out for the first time in the second round of a fight for the vacant world light middleweight title in June 1984, but after a short retirement he came back fighting to take the WBC middleweight title from Iran Barkley with a split points decision in March 1989.

The publicists got the drums out and banged loud enough to earn Duran a megabucks showdown fight with Sugar Ray Leonard in Las Vegas on 7 December 1989, but 38-year-old Roberto had nothing left in his tank and was outpointed by a mile in an undignified contest that did nearly as much damage to his reputation as his 'no mas' performance ten years earlier.

Roberto Duran
Born Guarare, Panama,
16.6.1951
Career span: 1967-
World lightweight champion
1967-79; world welterweight
champion 1980; world light
middleweight champion 1983
Ring record: 93 fights, 85 wins,
8 losses (2 stoppages); 61
inside-the-distance wins

Overleaf: Roberto Duran traps
Sugar Ray Leonard on the
ropes during their first world
title fight in Montreal in 1980.

TOMMY FARR

Tommy Farr is best remembered for a single defeat, yet he recorded scores of outstanding victories which made him arguably the greatest of all British-born heavyweights.

The loss which earned Tommy Bach a permanent place in boxing folklore came against Joe Louis, when the 'Brown Bomber' was just beginning to build his legend of invincibility. Their contest was staged at New York's Yankee Stadium on 30 August 1937, and it was the champion's first defence of the world title after taking it from James J. Braddock nine weeks earlier.

Most people anticipated a quick victory for Louis, but they had under-estimated Farr's vast experience. He called on all the tricks and moves learned in hundreds of boxing booth matches to nullify the greater punching power of the champion. Louis was forced to dig deep to find the ammunition and the stamina to snatch a narrow points victory. A live ringside commentary on the fight was broadcast to Britain in the early hours of the morning, and thousands of fans stayed up to listen on their wireless sets. Farr's spirited and skilful performance made him a national hero, and for the rest of his life he was known as 'the man who nearly beat Joe Louis'.

Tommy Farr
Born Tonypandy, Wales,
18.12.1913
Career span: 1926-53
British and Commonwealth
heavyweight champion 1937-38
Ring record: 104 fights, 71
wins, 22 losses (3 stoppages);
23 inside-the-distance wins, 11
draws

Tommy Farr shows his famous crouch.

73

I got to know Tommy well in his days as a newspaper columnist, and whenever I used to ask about the fight against Louis he used to wince and say, 'Henry, bach, I wish you wouldn't talk about that fight. Just the mention of the name Louis makes my nose bleed!'

Tommy had a lovely sense of humour and was a great credit to the sport of boxing that was his life from the age of 13. Born in Tonypandy in 1913, he had come up the hard way and learned his boxing while punching for pennies in a touring fairground booth. He saw the fight game as his only route out of the coalmines where he used to slave during the day before dashing off to fight at night. 'It was easy in the ring compared with down the pit', he told me. 'Anybody who claims that boxing is a hard game should try working a shift at the coalface. The only things that kept me sane were my singing and my boxing.'

Tommy could sing like a bird, but it was being able to fight like a lion that brought him his fame. His hatred of the pits and his hunger for food took him to London – by foot! – at the age of 18, and he started to build on the foundation of his early experience in the rings of Wales. He had a crab-like style, boxing out of a crouch and deceiving his opponents into miscalculating the length of his reach. As they moved forward into attack they would find Tommy moving suddenly upright out of his crouch, and they were left hitting thin air while Tommy's counter punches rained in on them. He was not a devastating puncher but he was deadly accurate, particularly with a solid left jab that kept opponents off balance.

By the time he was 21, Tommy had won both the Welsh light heavyweight and heavyweight titles, and this was a stepping stone to a challenge for the British and Empire heavyweight championships which he won in March 1937 by outpointing South African-born Ben Foord over 15 rounds. It was a points victory over former world heavyweight champion Max Baer and a third-round knock-out defeat of German 'iron man' Walter Neusel that set him up for his world title challenge against Louis.

He gave up the British and Empire titles to concentrate on earning dollars in the United States after his magnificent performance against Louis. Points defeats by Max Baer, Lou Nova, Red Burman and James J. Braddock destroyed any hopes he had of another crack at the world championship.

Tommy returned to Britain to try to regain his national title, but then hung up his gloves when the war started. In 1950 – at the age of 36 – he surprised us all by making a comeback. Within three years he had battled his way back into championship contention, but a two-round knock-out defeat by Frank Bell and then a seventh-round stoppage by Don Cockell in a British title eliminator convinced him it was time to cancel his unwise comeback campaign. It is better that we remember him for his triumphs of the 1930s, with the narrow defeat by Louis taking pride of place.

BOB FITZSIMMONS

Bob Fitzsimmons was the first boxer ever to capture three world titles at different weights, and he is the only English-born winner of the world heavyweight crown. But, in all honesty, claims to Fitzsimmons being the 'one and only British boxer' to win the heavyweight championship are on weak ground. He was just a two-year-old child when taken by his Cornish parents to New Zealand where his father opened a blacksmith's business in the fishing port of Timaru.

From his schooldays Bob helped his father in the forge and developed an immense, heavily-muscled upper body that looked somehow out of place on what were spindly, freckled legs. He was introduced to boxing by Jem Mace, a master of the bare-knuckle boxing arts from Norwich, who toured New Zealand giving lessons and exhibitions. Fitzsimmons won a competition that he organised, and Mace was so impressed by his natural ability and punching power that he encouraged him to box professionally.

Fitz – variously nicknamed 'Ruby Robert', 'Freckled Bob' and the 'Lanky Cornishman' – never weighed much more than a middleweight, and with his prematurely balding ginger hair he was a strange-looking man. But he was a phenomenal puncher who could take out any man with a single hit.

I suppose because he just didn't look the part the Americans found it difficult to take him seriously when he arrived in California at the age of 28 to continue a career that he had started in Australia. He silenced the cynics by knocking out Jack the 'Nonpareil' Dempsey to win the world middleweight title in 13 rounds in 1891.

Fitzsimmons had already applied for American citizenship when he climbed into the ring for a crack at the world heavyweight title held by 'Gentleman' James J. Corbett at Carson City, Nevada, on St Patrick's Day 1897. It was the fourth time that promoters had tried to get the two of them together in the same ring, and Corbett was fuming because he thought Fitz had deliberately been messing him around.

At 35, Fitz was four years older than the champion who had arrogantly dismissed his challenger as 'an over-rated nobody'. His total confidence in his ability to win seemed justified in the first six rounds as he gave Fitzsimmons a boxing lesson, threading a procession of jabs through Bob's guard and flooring him for a count of nine with a slashing left hook in the sixth.

Conceding 20 pounds in weight, Fitz looked in terrible trouble, but from the seventh round on he switched his attack to the body and the champion suddenly started to run out of strength and stamina. At the end of the 13th round Fitz was so confident of scoring an upset victory that he told his wife Rose – sitting by his corner in the role of manager – to bet everything she could on him ending the fight in the 14th round.

As Fitzsimmons went out for the start of the 14th Rose shouted, 'Hit him in the slats, Bob'. This referred to the rib area, and early in the round Fitz followed her advice. He switched his stance to southpaw, feinted with a right to the chin and then threw a straight left that corkscrewed deep into Corbett's stomach and knocked the breath out of him. Fitzsimmons had

Bob Fitzsimmons
Born Helston, Cornwall,
26.5.1863
Career span: 1880-1914
World middleweight champion 1891; world light heavyweight champion 1903-05; world heavyweight champion 1897-99
Ring record: 62 fights, 43 wins, 12 losses (8 stoppages); 32 inside-the-distance wins; 6 no decisions, 1 no contest

Bob Fitzsimmons — British-born, New Zealand-raised.

invented what became known as the 'solar-plexus' punch. Corbett sank slowly to the canvas like a torpedoed ship and was fighting for air as the referee counted him out.

Fitz lost the title to James J. Jeffries in his first defence, breaking the knuckles on both his hands against the granite-hard challenger who outweighed him by 64 pounds. He was knocked out in the 11th round and caved in to defeat in the eighth round in a return match.

At the age of 41 he became the first boxer to win three world titles when he outpointed George Gardner to take the newly-introduced light heavyweight championship, losing it two years later in 1905 to 'Philadelphia' Jack O'Brien. Fitz found it hard to leave the game that he loved, and finally hung up his gloves in 1914 at the age of 52. Three years later this legend of the ring was finally beaten by pneumonia, and died in Chicago on 22 October 1917.

GEORGE FOREMAN

George Foreman stirred up the world heavyweight division in his 'second coming', but he had achieved enough the first time around to earn himself a place in my boxing hall of fame. I first became aware of Foreman when he won the gold medal in the 1968 Olympics in Mexico. They were the Games in which several American athletes staged 'black power' demonstrations at the victory ceremonies. George got himself noticed with a patriotic waving of the Stars and Stripes on the winner's rostrum. It was the way he waved his fists, however, that really took the eye as he launched his professional career with a series of stunning victories.

Foreman had lived on the wild side when growing up in Marshall, Texas, and he was steered towards boxing to help keep him out of mischief. It was his opponents who were in trouble as he clubbed them to defeat in a brutal fashion that owed little to the boxing textbook.

In the four years after the Olympics he knocked out all but three of his 37 opponents, but there was an almost novice-like rawness about his style that persuaded world champion Joe Frazier that he could handle him in what was intended as a warm-up fight to a re-match with Muhammad Ali. It is now history that Frazier made the biggest misjudgment in boxing history, and he was parted from his championship and a promised fortune in two rounds of unbridled savagery.

In almost any other era Foreman – magnificently built at 6 feet 4 inches and 16 stone – could have looked forward to a long reign, but Ali was waiting in the wings for *his* 'second coming'. After destroying Joe Roman and Ken Norton, George was talked into putting his title on the line against Ali in the 'rumble in the jungle' in Zaire in 1974. Ali psyched Foreman out of the fight and his championship, allowing him to punch himself into a state of exhaustion by adopting his famous rope-a-dope tactics. Then in the eighth round Ali came bouncing off the ropes to knock George out and end his unbeaten run of 40 fights.

Foreman was so shattered by the defeat that he has since admitted losing his way in life, going back to his bad old ways as the fortune he had made in the ring ran away from him like water. He returned to the ring for a gimmick night in Toronto when he took on five different fighters one after the other and knocked them all out. Then victories over Ron Lyle and Joe Frazier put him back in the title picture before an inexplicable points defeat by Jimmy Young in 1977 and the shock announcement that he was quitting the ring to become a preacher.

For ten years George pounded the Bible and set up a charity to help wayward youngsters in Texas where he himself had often been tempted to the wrong side of the law. Then, after ten years out of the ring and shortly before his 40th birthday, he stunned the boxing world again by announcing his comeback. Few took him seriously at first as he thumped his way to slow-motion victories over a procession of cruiserweights and unrated heavies, but there was no doubting that all his old power was still packed into his fists.

He was more than two stone heavier than in his championship days as

George Foreman
Born Marshall, Texas,
22.1.1948
Career span: 1969-
World heavyweight champion
1973-74
Ring record: 65 fights, 63 wins,
2 losses (1 stoppage); 61 inside-
the-distance wins

George Foreman, the second time around.

a 16-stone fighter, and his shaven head gave him a menacing appearance that was totally alien to the image he had fashioned outside the ring as a preacher spreading the word of God. As he entered the 1990s he looked capable of overtaking Jersey Joe Walcott's record of being the oldest world heavyweight champion at 38.

BOB FOSTER

Bob Foster was the delight of the headline writers. He held down a job as a deputy sheriff in the Albuquerque police force while boxing professionally, and his quick-on-the-draw style of punching gave the ringside reporters plenty of ready-made copy. I was proud of my old left hook, and watching Foster in action reminded me of the way I used to set myself just before throwing my favourite punch. He packed a cracking left hook – the best of all the text-book punches – and won many of his fights by the short route once that lethal hook had been brought into the argument.

Foster, who stood a gangling 6 feet 3 inches tall, was not all about punching power. He was also a stylish, precise boxer who could outsmart opponents with clever ring work and a long, snapping left jab that piled up the points. The only time he used to get into any sort of bother was when he stepped out of his weight division and challenged the big boys. His management rushed him too quickly into a fight with the dangerous Doug Jones in 1962 when his ring experience stretched to only nine fights, and he was stopped in eight rounds. Jones, you may recall, gave the young Cassius Clay a close call on his way to world title status.

Bob Foster
Born Albuquerque, New
Mexico, 15.12.1938
Career span: 1968-78
World light heavyweight
champion 1968-74
Ring record: 65 fights, 56 wins,
8 losses (6 stoppages); 46
inside-the-distance wins, 1
draw

He wisely elected to stay in the light heavyweight class after being stopped in seven rounds by the giant Ernie Terrell and then outpointed by my old rival Zora Folley, both of whom were exceptional heavyweights.

Foster made the world light heavyweight title his target but most experts reckoned he was reaching too high when he challenged Dick Tiger for the championship in New York in 1968. It was his eighth year as a professional and his 34th fight, while the Nigerian had been campaigning twice as long and had been the world middleweight champion before taking the light heavyweight crown from Jose Torres.

All those who thought Tiger was in for a comfortable defence were astonished to find him knocked out in the fourth round when the deputy sheriff exploded his left hook on the African's jaw. Foster ruled the light heavyweights with an iron fist, making 14 successful defences of the championship. But he could not get thoughts of the heavyweight title out of his mind. He was flattened in two rounds when he challenged Joe Frazier in 1970, yet he stubbornly refused to accept that he was out of his depth in the heavyweight division. Two years later he fought Muhammad Ali for the North American championship and was stopped in eight rounds.

Britain's Chris Finnegan made a brave bid to take the world light heavyweight title from him at Wembley in 1972, and was still in with a chance of victory until Foster unleashed his pet left hook punch in the 14th round to knock the fight out of the British bulldog.

The deputy sheriff decided to hang up his guns after Jorge Ahumada held him to a draw in 1974, but he was persuaded to make a comeback a year later when he was only a ghost of the great fighter he had been at his peak. He retired for good in 1978 after successive defeats by two unrated opponents who would not have given him any trouble during his days as world champion.

Foster was one of the all-time great light heavyweight champions, but he kept getting ideas above his station.

Previous page: Bob Foster knocks out brave Chris Finnegan in the 14th round of their world title fight at Wembley in 1972. The sheriff had got his man.

JOE FRAZIER

Joe Frazier became world heavyweight champion in the enforced absence of Muhammad Ali, who was stripped of the title for refusing to join the US Army. Those who dismissed him as just a pretender to the throne were silenced when he beat Ali on points in a magnificent battle in New York in 1971 that still rates as one of the greatest heavyweight fights I have ever witnessed.

Like so many great fighters before him, Frazier had used the boxing ring to escape the poverty trap. He was the seventh son in a family of 13 and worked on his father's run-down vegetable plantation from the age of seven. He followed his elder brothers to Philadelphia and got himself a job, perhaps fittingly, in a slaughterhouse.

Joe won 38 of his 40 amateur contests, his two defeats both being at the massive hands of Grand Rapids giant Buster Mathis. The second setback came in the US Olympic trials, but the victory cost the luckless Mathis a broken thumb and it was Frazier who went in his place to Tokyo where he won the gold medal.

Frazier fought like a black Marciano with a perpetual motion two-fisted style that earned him the nickname 'Smokin' Joe'. In his first 28 months as a professional he hurried through 19 straight victories, and then in 1968 he was matched with his old rival Buster Mathis in a fight that was billed for the heavyweight title vacated by Ali.

He gave Mathis quite a mauling before the referee stopped the fight in the 11th round. He eventually beat Jimmy Ellis for the undisputed championship and then, after outpointing comeback man Ali, he had easy-pickings fights against Terry Daniels and Ron Stander before agreeing to take on the unheralded George Foreman. It was one of the match making mistakes of the century. Frazier's handlers considered it no more than a warm-up fight for a megabucks return with Ali, but it proved not so much a warm-up as a roasting. Foreman had him up and down like a yo-yo before the referee stopped what had become a slaughter in the second round.

Frazier was never quite the same force again after this first devastating defeat of his career, but he motivated himself for two more storming fights with Ali. He was outpointed over ten rounds and then − in the 'thriller in Manila' − was stopped after 14 viciously-fought rounds that completely drained both fighters.

Poor old Joe could never get the defeat by Foreman out of his system. He tried to cancel it out in a return match in 1976, shaving his head bald in Marvin Hagler style in a bid to make himself look more menacing, but it is the punches not the looks that count in the boxing ring. Foreman again handed him a hiding, this time stopping him in five rounds.

He went through the motions of a comeback in 1981 when he fought 'Jumbo' Cummings over ten rounds, but 'Smokin' Joe' 's fire had gone out. He looked sluggish as he struggled to a ten-round draw − a pedestrian performance that convinced him that he should never fight again. Joe then switched to management, and under his guidance his son Marvis looked promising until he was rushed too quickly to title contention, suffering one-

Joe Frazier
Born Beaufort, South Carolina,
12.1.1944
Career span: 1965-81
World heavyweight champion
1968-73
Ring record: 37 fights, 32 wins,
4 losses (3 stoppages); 27
inside-the-distance wins, 1
draw

Smokin' Joe Frazier launches a two-fisted attack as Joe Bugner takes cover. Frazier won this non-title fight on points over 12 rounds in London in 1973.

round batterings against both Larry Holmes and Mike Tyson. Marvis had inherited his father's energy but not his chin.

Joe will go down in boxing history as a good rather than a great heavyweight champion, but he was unlucky to have lived in the shadow of Muhammad Ali, and even unluckier to find George Foreman such an insurmountable mountain. However, 'Smokin' Joe' did manage to set the heavyweight division alight with his all-action style.

LARRY GAINS

Larry Gains was an exceptional heavyweight unlucky to be born at the wrong time. He was at the peak of his powers in an era when black heavyweights were still paying for the arrogance displayed by Jack Johnson during his reign as world champion. They were frozen out of the title scene in the United States, so Larry came from his native Canada to try his luck in Europe after building a reputation in North America as a top-class amateur. He fought in France and Germany and returned home to Toronto to win the Canadian heavyweight title before finally settling down in Leicester, where he became one of the most popular performers of his time.

An indication of his ability is that while based in Cologne he knocked out young Max Schmeling in two rounds in 1925. Gains was a marvellous

Larry Gains
Born Toronto, Canada,
12.12.1901
Career span: 1923-41
Commonwealth heavyweight
champion 1931-34
Ring record: 146 fights, 116
wins, 23 losses (14 stoppages);
63 inside-the-distance wins, 5
draws; 2 no decisions

Larry Gains and Len Harvey
get to grips in their British
Empire heavyweight title fight
at Harringay in 1939.

83

advertisement for boxing. He had a magnificent physique, stylish skills and was a gentleman both in and out of the ring. I got to know Larry in the post-war years and found him to be a modest, likeable and articulate man who did not have an ounce of malice in him. Yet he experienced much that could have bred bitterness. Even in Britain he found the colour of his skin a handicap. White South African Ben Foord was allowed to fight for the British championship, but not black Canadian Gains. This was at a time when there was an obscene law that barred black fighters from challenging for British titles.

He captured the Commonwealth (then called the Empire) title by knocking out Phil Scott in the second round at Leicester in 1931, and then had to get special permission to defend the championship against South African champion Don McCorkindale at the Royal Albert Hall in 1932. Larry was the first black boxer allowed to fight there. He drew over 15 rounds with McCorkindale, won the return and then outpointed 'Ambling Alp' Primo Carnera over ten rounds at London's White City. Promoter Jeff Dickson tried to get him a shot at the world title held by Jack Sharkey. But the colour bar prevented the fight taking place and Carnera was given the chance instead, knocking out Sharkey to win the championship. It was enough to tear the heart out of any man, but Larry shrugged his shoulders and got on with his ring campaign in England.

The years were catching up with him quicker than his opponents, and after losing his Commonwealth crown to Len Harvey on points over 15 close-fought rounds in 1934 he was beaten by Jack Petersen, Ben Foord, Harvey again and Tommy Farr. He was into his 40s when he made an unsuccessful comeback during the war years, finally quitting the ring for good after three successive defeats by Jack London, an opponent he had flattened in two rounds in 1933.

It was a sad loss for boxing and for the human race when Larry passed on in 1983 at the age of 82. He was the nicest person you could wish to meet, and had he been born a few years later he would undoubtedly have contested the world heavyweight championship. I consider it a privilege to have known him.

JOE GANS

Joe Gans was known as the 'Old Master', and his performances over a span of more than 17 years were considered as near as anybody has ever got to perfection in the ring. In an era when black fighters were restricted to supporting roles he managed to break through the colour barrier to championship class, and after becoming the first black lightweight champion he stayed at number one for six years.

Gans first started to learn how to use his fists on the oyster wharves of Baltimore where he scraped a living selling oysters and fish, and he was fighting professionally before he was 17. Many of his early contests were in 'Battle Royals' in which he would share the ring with as many as six opponents. The last one standing would be named the winner.

He lost only three of his first 70 fights, his rare defeats coming when he was under orders from crooked promoters not to try too hard. Despite his obvious class he was ignored as a title challenger because of his colour and he was four months past his 26th birthday before he was at last allowed to fight for the lightweight championship in 1900. The title was held by Frank Erne, an interesting character who was the first and only Swiss-born fighter to win a world championship. Erne, based in New York, retained his crown when a clash of heads opened a cut over Joe's eye and Joe suddenly bent double and signalled his retirement. It was widely suspected that this was another contest in which Gans was under instructions not to win.

Another 32 fights with only one defeat brought demands for a return with Erne, and the champion agreed to put his title on the line out of the United States in Ontario. Gans landed a straight right to the chin after just 1 minute 40 seconds to record a spectacular knock-out.

Gans was noted more for his skill than his punching power, and was a master at drawing opponents on to his punches by clever shifts and feints. This tactic achieved a double impact as he drove home perfectly-placed counters. Joe made ten successful title defences over the next four years, but he was struggling to make the lightweight limit and excessive weight reducing started to affect his health. He made frequent excursions into the higher weight divisions, and he boxed a draw over 20 rounds when fighting world welterweight champion Joe Walcott and dropped a 15-round points decision to Sam Langford, who later became a top heavyweight contender.

In 1906 Tex Rickard staged the first of his many spectacular promotions by putting up a record $34,000 purse for Gans to defend against Battling Nelson, the 'Durable Dane' who was renowned for his strength and staying power. Although he was the challenger, Nelson's management insisted on their man taking two thirds of the purse money and they made Gans weigh in at the ringside just before the fight so that he had no time to put back precious pounds. Gans miraculously lasted 42 rounds under a blazing Nevada sun before Nelson was disqualified for continually hitting low.

Gans managed to make four more successful defences, but the fight with Nelson and his deteriorating health left him only a shadow of himself. In two subsequent contests with Nelson he was knocked out in first the 17th

Joe Gans
(originally Joseph Gaines)
Born Baltimore, Maryland,
25.10.1874
Career span: 1891-1909
World lightweight champion
1902-08
Ring record: 156 fights, 131
wins, 9 losses (5 stoppages); 90
inside-the-distance wins, 16
draws

Joe Gans, the 'Old Master'.

and then the 21st round. He had one more fight in 1909 before retiring, and a year later he was dead from tuberculosis.

According to boxing legend the 'Old Master' left his mark on our language. His family's favourite meal was bacon, and after each winning fight he would send his mother a telegram that always read: AM BRINGING HOME THE BACON — JOE. The press picked up on this, and 'bringing home the bacon' passed into everyday language.

KID GAVILAN

Kid Gavilan's name was bestowed on him by his first manager. Gavilan means hawk, and it was a name that accurately captured the way he used to swoop with his fists in the ring. He popularised the bolo punch, a hook-cum-uppercut that used to travel on a huge loop before being brought up and under the defence of his opponent. Gavilan perfected it while working on the sugar plantations as a boy in Cuba where he used to cut canes with a bolo knife, hence the name of the punch.

Born Gerardo Gonzales, he was the son of an impoverished sharecropper in pre-Castro Cuba where professional boxing – now outlawed – was a thriving business. He started fighting for pay in 1943, soon after his 17th

Kid Gavilan
(originally Gerardo Gonzalez)
Born Camaguey, Cuba,
6.1.1926
Career span: 1943-58
World welterweight champion
1951-54
Ring record: 143 fights, 107
wins, 30 losses; 28 inside-the-
distance wins, 6 draws

Kid Gavilan, 'the Cuban
Hawk'.

birthday, while still a bantamweight, but he had filled out to a welterweight by the time he based himself in the United States in 1947 with a record of 37 fights and just two defeats behind him. He had tested the water in the States a year earlier, winning three successive fights in New York with an all-action style that excited the fans and attracted the interest of the big fight promoters. The 'Keed' became one of the biggest draws on television, featuring in 46 nationally-televised bouts and topping the Madison Square Garden bill 22 times.

He beat former world lightweight champion Ike Williams 2-1 in a gripping three-fight series to set up a shot at the world welterweight title held by the one and only Sugar Ray Robinson. The great Sugar Ray had to produce his best form to outpoint Gavilan in a cracking contest. When Robinson moved up to the middleweight division Gavilan outpointed Johnny Bratton for the vacant title in 1951, and made seven successful defences over the next three years.

Gavilan then misguidedly stepped up to middleweight to challenge Carl 'Bobo' Olson, but was outgunned over 15 rounds. In his following fight he was robbed of the welterweight title when few people apart from the judges thought he had been outpointed by Johnny Saxton.

From then it was all downhill for Gavilan, who started to collect the bill for living too fast outside the ring. He was floored by lawsuits from managers, alimony demands from a former wife, unpaid tax bills and a recurring liver problem. He had to keep on fighting, and he went wherever promoters would pay him. Only nine victories in his last 25 contests showed that he had lost his way. Included in his travels were two visits to London to meet Peter Waterman, the late brother of actor Dennis. Peter was a top-quality welterweight who won the European and British titles, but his ten-round points victory over Gavilan in February 1956 was one of the worst decisions ever given in a British ring. Gavilan got his revenge two months later with a ten-round points win. I thought he had won the first fight even more clearly than the second.

There were few more exciting and entertaining boxers than Gavilan when he was at his best. As well as his bolo punch, he had flashy footwork that included the shuffle that became part of Muhammad Ali's repertoire. He would fight only in flurries, which made him a difficult man to judge, and he was often involved in tight decisions. His chin was like iron and he was dropped only three times during his long career, and was never ever stopped.

The 'Keed' was idolised in Cuba, but what a pity that when he finally went home at the end of his career in 1958 he was almost as penniless as when he left in search of fame and fortune.

ROCKY GRAZIANO

Rocky Graziano was, in his own words, on his way to a life behind bars until he was rescued by boxing. He was a hoodlum who ran wild in the slums of the East Side of New York, spending long spells in corrective centres and remand homes. They failed to tame him in the US Army and he was dishonourably discharged after serving a term in an army prison. He was persuaded to harness his liking of violence to the boxing ring, and it was the discipline of the fight game that at last brought him to his senses and gave shape and meaning to his life. After winning a Golden Gloves title as an amateur, he became one of the biggest of all American ring heroes in the immediate post-war years.

Graziano fought the way he lived, violently and with an aggressive, savage spirit that guaranteed packed crowds wherever he appeared. His three fights for the world middleweight title against Tony Zale – in 1946, 1947 and 1948 – have gone down in fighting folklore as among the most exciting ever seen. Both fighters were down in the opening round of their first contest before iron man Zale won by a knock-out in the sixth round to retain his championship. Graziano was on the verge of another sixth-

Rocky Graziano
(originally Rocco Barbella)
Born New York City, 1.1.1922
Career span: 1942-52
World middleweight champion 1947-48
Ring record: 83 fights, 67 wins, 10 losses (3 stoppages); 45 inside-the-distance wins, 6 draws

Rocky Graziano flattens Tony Zale in the sixth round of their second world title fight in 1947. The referee is Ruby Goldstein.

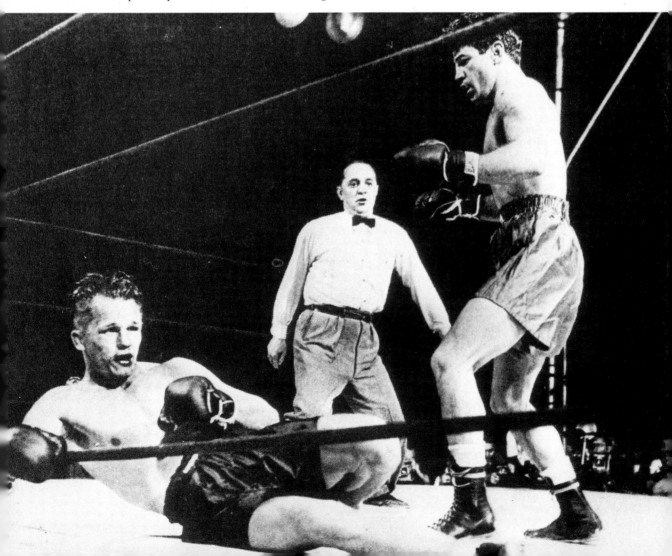

round stoppage in the return match, but suddenly unleashed a counter attack that reduced Zale to a helpless target. The referee had to rescue him as Rocky celebrated becoming the new champion. Eleven months later 35-year-old Zale produced the greatest performance of his career to regain the championship with a third-round knock-out victory.

By the time Graziano had got himself back into championship contention four years later there was a new king on the throne in the formidable shape of Sugar Ray Robinson, who was a definite class above Rocky. Graziano's reckless, walk-in style of fighting was made to measure for Robinson, who stood off and picked his punches. His lightning-quick combinations ripped through Rocky's defence and the New Yorker was counted out in the third round.

Even Graziano's most ardent admirers wanted him to hang up the gloves, but he insisted on one more fling. Chuck Davey outpointed him over ten rounds in Chicago five months after his shellacking by Robinson to convince him that there was no future left for him in the fight game.

Rocky then started a successful new career as a film and television actor. His life story – *Somebody Up There Likes Me* – became a bestselling book, and a popular film starring Paul Newman as Rocky.

Graziano never used to act in the ring. He used to fight for real, and there have been few more explosive characters in the history of world championship boxing. Rocky was walking proof that boxing is a sport that can save people who are lost on the wild side of life. As Rocky himself said: 'Boxing gave me dignity and discipline. Without it I was just a wild bum who was going to end up with a one-way ticket to Alcatraz'. With lines like that they just *had* to make a film of his life.

Rocky passed on to the great ring in the sky in May 1990, taking the final count at the age of 68 following heart and lung failure. He left us laughing at such priceless punchlines as: 'We stole anything when we were kids that started with an 'A' – A bicycle, A piece of fruit, A watch. If it wasn't nailed down it became a target' . . . 'I quit school in the sixth grade because of pneumonia. I didn't catch it. I just couldn't spell it'. His old boyhood chum, 'Bronx Bull' Jake La Motta, said of him: 'Rocky was one hell of a fighter and one hell of a man. They carved him out of the New York sidewalk. Everybody down here liked him'.

HARRY GREB

Harry Greb is probably the most remarkable character in my hit parade. He broke all the rules of boxing – both in and out of the ring – and had nearer 400 fights than the 299 that are on his record. Greb was considered the closest thing there has ever been to perpetual motion in boxing, and he chose to fight rather than train. He went to a gymnasium only reluctantly before a contest, and made no secret of the fact that he preferred the company of pretty girls to flat-nosed sparring partners. 'Give me broads before boxing any day', was one of the many colourful quotes attributed to him. According to legend it was commonplace for him to make love in the dressing-room before a fight, and it never seemed to affect his performance in the ring. From first bell to last he never stopped throwing punches, and he was known variously as the 'Pittsburgh Windmill', the 'Iron City Express', the 'Rubber Man' and – most appropriately of all – the 'Wildest Tiger'.

When 18-year-old Greb announced that he was going to box professionally after winning several local amateur titles he was literally thrown out of his home by his German-American father Pius Greb, who told him that boxers only ended up as bums. He spent the next 13 years trying to prove his father wrong, often fighting two or three times a week in a bid to make a fortune with his fists. But as quickly as he earned it he spent it on the bevy of beautiful girls who were always at his side.

He stood just 5 feet 8 inches tall and weighed only a couple of pounds over 11 stone, but he was frightened of no man and liked nothing better than to scrap with heavyweights. 'The bigger they are the slower they are, and the more target I've got to aim at', he said. There has rarely been a more ruthless fighter, but he punched too quickly to pack really devastating power. He concentrated on quantity rather than quality of blows and threw his punches in clusters, not caring where they landed. One of his nastier specialities was to thumb opponents in the eye, but this backfired on him during a 1921 fight against Kid Norfolk, who retaliated with a thumb in Greb's eye. For the rest of his career – more than 90 fights – Greb fought blind in his right eye, something that would, thank goodness, not be allowed in this day and age.

His most notable triumph came in 1922 when he was matched with unbeaten 'Fighting Marine' Gene Tunney for the vacant American light heavyweight title. He gave Tunney such a terrible hiding that even hard-hearted Greb was pleading with the referee to stop it, but Tunney's pride kept him on his feet and he lost on points. In four subsequent meetings Tunney got the better of Greb, all the fights going the distance. In their last meeting Greb's famous stamina deserted him and he was out on his feet in the last round. He pulled Tunney into a clinch and said, 'Gene, you've won it. Please don't knock me out'.

In all his fights he had been knocked out only once, by George Chip in his 13th contest. 'This was the highest compliment I had ever been paid', Tunney said later. 'Here was a great and game fighter having the guts to admit that he was laying down his shield, conceding defeat and then knowing I would not expose him. That took a very special kind of courage.'

Harry Greb
Born Pittsburgh, Pennsylvania,
6.6.1894
Career span: 1913-26
World middleweight champion
1923-26
Ring record: 299 fights, 264
wins, 23 losses (2 stoppages);
49 inside-the-distance wins, 12
draws

Harry Greb, the 'Pittsburgh Windmill'.

Greb was more interested in making money to fund his playboy lifestyle than in chasing titles, and he had fought more than 230 times before he got a crack at the world middleweight championship. Most of his contests were of the no decision variety, with newspaper men deciding the winner. It was the general consensus that he had been beaten by fewer than a dozen opponents before he took the world 11 stone 6 pounds title from Johnny Wilson with a 15-round points victory.

Greb successfully defended the title six times before losing it to Tiger Flowers, a church deacon from Georgia and the first black middleweight champion. Two months after a second defeat by Flowers, Greb – the 'Perpetual Motion Man' – was dead, at the age of 32. Despite failing sight in his one good eye he used to insist on driving everywhere at reckless speed. After the last of numerous crashes he was taken to hospital for an operation on a fractured nose and died on the operating table following a cardiac arrest. The one certainty is that there will never be another in anything quite like his mould.

EMILE GRIFFITH

Emile Griffith was one of the most heavily employed fighters of modern times, and packed into his 112 fights were no fewer than 22 world championship contests. He played a sort of musical chairs with world titles, winning the welterweight crown three times and the middleweight title twice. Emile, a workmanlike rather than gifted fighter, also won a European version of the world light middleweight championship that was not recognised in the United States, where he started his professional career in 1958 after winning a Golden Gloves title.

He was co-managed and trained by the fiery Gil Clancy, who added aggression to Griffith's compact boxing style. Sadly, he will always be most remembered for a series of savage fights with Benny 'Kid' Paret that overshadowed all else that he achieved in the ring and ended in appalling tragedy. He won the world welterweight title by knocking out Paret in the 13th round of his 25th fight in 1961. In a return bout five months later Paret won by a split points decision after 15 brutal rounds. Boxers often feign dislike of opponents outside the ring in a bid to drum up box office business, but the hatred that flared between Griffith and Paret was for real.

Griffith, who had moved to New York with his family from his native Virgin Islands, worked as a hat designer in a Manhattan millinery business owned by one of his managers. Paret claimed that this was no work for a man, and taunted Griffith with accusations of homosexuality. Emile's deep anger came to the surface during their third title fight in March 1962. He trapped Paret in a corner in the 12th round and unleashed a hurricane of blows. By the time veteran referee Ruby Goldstein had moved in and pulled off Griffith Paret was unconscious on his feet. The Cuban was rushed to hospital but never recovered, and the fight that caused his death – shown live on coast-to-coast television – brought an uproar of protests from the boxing abolitionists.

Griffith was heartbroken by the tragedy, and when he resumed his career four months later there was never again quite the same zip in his punches that he had shown before the fatal fight with Paret. He retained the welterweight championship by outpointing Ralph Dupas over 15 rounds in Las Vegas, and then won the European version of the world light middleweight title by outpointing Ted Wright in Vienna. On his return to the States he became involved in a three-contest saga with another Cuban, Luis Rodriguez, who he had beaten on points over ten rounds in a non-title fight to clinch his first crack at the championship.

Rodriguez won the first of their title fights on points over 15 rounds, but Griffith insisted that he was only borrowing the championship, and he outpointed the Cuban in their next two contests. Griffith then had two successive fights in London, beating Swansea southpaw Brian Curvis on points to retain the title and stopping Dartford's Dave Charnley in the ninth round of a non-title bout.

In 1966 Griffith relinquished the welterweight title after taking the world middleweight crown from Dick Tiger with a disputed points victory in New York. Yet again he became embroiled in a three-fight series, this time

Emile Griffith
Born St Thomas, Virgin
Islands, 3.2.1938
Career span: 1956-77
World welterweight champion
1961-65; world middleweight
champion 1966-68
Ring record: 112 fights, 85
wins, 24 losses (2 stoppages);
23 inside-the-distance wins, 2
draws; 1 no contest

Emile Griffith on the attack against British champion Brian Curvis at Wembley in 1964. Griffith won on points over 15 rounds.

against Italian Nino Benvenuti. Each contest went the full 15 rounds, Nino winning the first, Griffith the second to regain the championship and Nino the third.

Still Griffith was not finished with title hunting. He dropped back down to welterweight to challenge Jose Napoles, but was outpointed by the Cuban in Los Angeles in 1969. He was twice beaten by Carlos Monzon in world middleweight title fights, and then, in 1976, made his final appearance in a world championship contest, losing on points to West German Eckhard Dagge in a light middleweight contest in Berlin.

It was sad to see Griffith become a have-gloves-will-travel opponent late in his career when he won only seven of his last 23 fights. He finally bowed out after a points defeat by Alan Minter – his third British southpaw opponent – in Monte Carlo in 1977 when he was approaching his 40th birthday.

MARVIN HAGLER

Marvin Hagler ruled the world's middleweights with fists of iron for seven years, and in that time he accumulated sufficient evidence to convince many experts that he was the greatest middleweight of them all. I personally rate him a whisker behind the two Sugar Rays – Robinson and Leonard – and the astonishing Argentinian Carlos Monzon, but there is no question that at his peak Hagler was one of the most formidable fighting forces ever unleashed in the ring.

I first saw him on what was a night of shame for British boxing. He came to Wembley in 1980 to challenge fellow-southpaw Alan Minter for the world middleweight crown, and he was clearly proving himself the guv'nor when the referee stopped the fight in the third round because of worsening wounds on the face of the outgunned man from Crawley. What should have been one of the most glorious moments in Hagler's life was turned into a nightmare by football-type hooligans among Minter's supporters. They bombarded the ring with beer cans and screamed racist abuse at Hagler, who needed a police escort to get to the safety of the dressing-room before being announced as the new world champion. I had never experienced anything like it in all my years in boxing, and it left me feeling sick to the stomach and fearing for the future of my sport. It made me wonder whether British fair play was a thing of the past.

Over the next seven years Hagler proved himself to be a magnificent champion. He made 12 successful defences, ducking nobody and completely burying doubts about his ability under fire after defeats in his 27th and 29th contests by Bobby Watts and Willie Monroe, both of which were avenged in savage style.

Hagler made his first bid for the world crown in 1979, and most good judges thought he was unlucky only to draw with defending champion Vito Antuofermo. Ten months later he took the title from Minter, and he seemed to grow in stature almost overnight. With his shaven head and cold-eyed stare, Hagler looked a man of menace and many of his opponents seemed almost to freeze at the sight of him standing in the opposite corner waiting for the first bell. He had a square southpaw stance and threw clubbing punches, following powerful right jabs and hooks with long, raking lefts that had a cutting as well as a concussing effect. The American press dubbed him 'Marvelous Marvin' and he officially adopted this as his name outside as well as inside the ring.

His most devastating performance came against Thomas the 'Hitman' Hearns in a megabucks match in Las Vegas in 1985. Hagler was in trouble with a cut eye, but before the referee could call the ringside doctor he had ended the fight in the third round with a crashing salvo of punches that knocked Hearns cold.

A year later he outgamed and outfought the previously unbeaten Ugandan John the 'Beast' Mugabi before knocking him out in the 11th round of what was a war of attrition.

Hagler has a great sense of boxing history and desperately wanted to go down as the greatest middleweight of all time. To do that he knew he

Marvin Hagler
Born Newark, New Jersey,
23.5.1952
Career span: 1973-87
World middleweight champion
1980-87
Ring record: 67 fights, 62 wins,
3 losses; 52 inside-the-distance
wins, 2 draws

Marvin Hagler prepares to relieve Alan Minter of the world middleweight title at Wembley in 1980.

had to get out of the shadow of the flashier, more charismatic Sugar Ray Leonard, who was tempted out of retirement for a showdown that cost a record $30 million to stage.

The record book shows that Leonard won a fascinating 12-round contest on a split points decision. Hagler has never got over his bitterness at this verdict, and remains convinced that he won. It was his final fight, although he has often talked of a comeback. Regardless of whether he ever sets foot in the ring again he is guaranteed a lasting place in boxing's hall of fame. But the greatest middleweight of them all? That's open to a lot of argument.

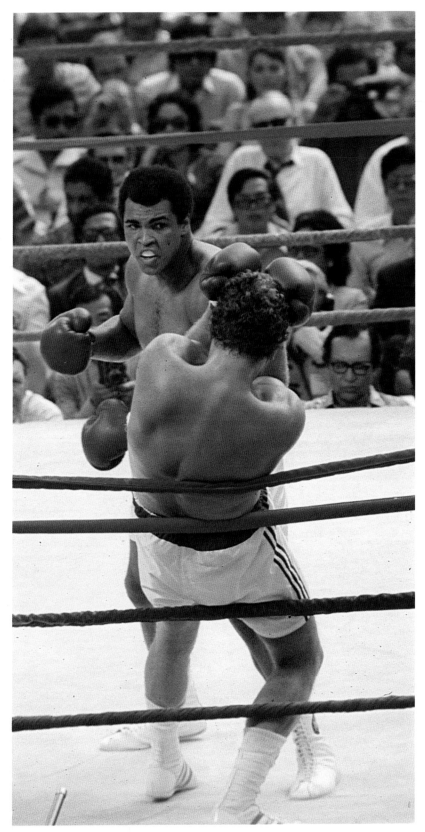

Muhammad Ali
Colorsport

Joe Frazier
Allsport

LEFT: *George Foreman*
Colorsport/Duomo

BELOW: *Pernell Whitaker*
Action Images

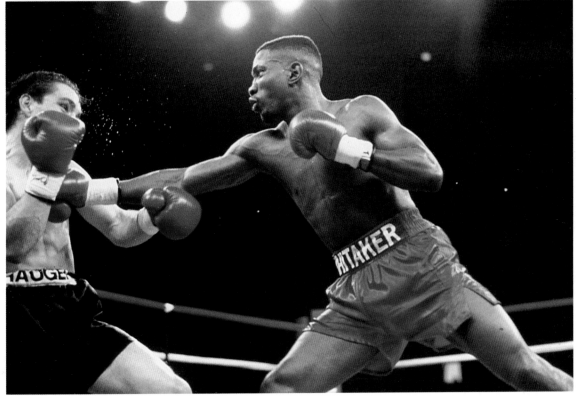

Marvin Hagler
Professional Sport

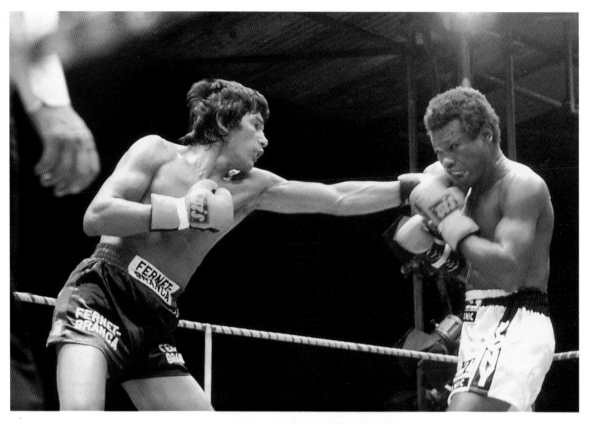

ABOVE:
Carlos Monzon (left)
Professional Sport

LEFT: *Barry McGuigan*
Allsport/Steve Powell

RIGHT: *Azumah Nelson*
Colorsport

BELOW:
Julio Caesar Chavez
Allsport/Holly Stein

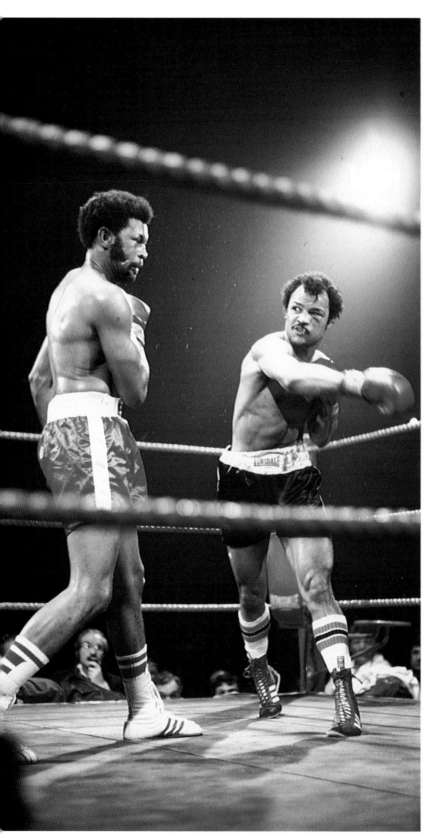

John Conteh (right)
Allsport/Steve Powell

Sugar Ray Leonard
Allsport/Mike Powell

Mike Tyson
Colorsport/Duomo

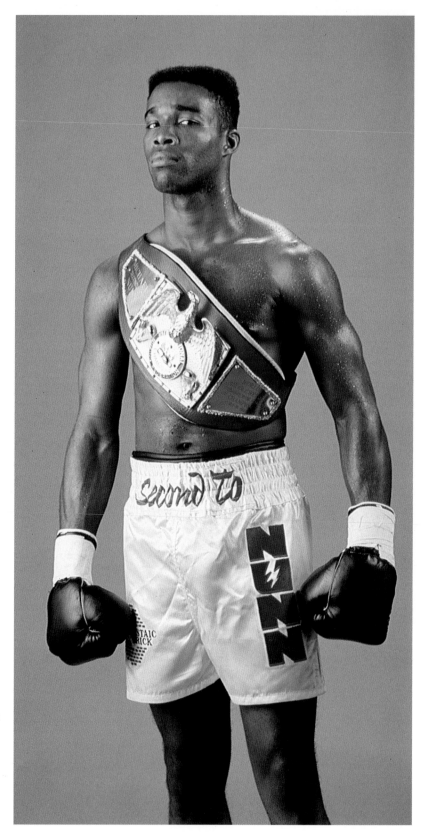

Michael Nunn
Colorsport/Duomo

TOP RIGHT:
*Joe Frazier, George Foreman
and Muhammad Ali*
Allsport/Gray Mortimore

BOTTOM RIGHT:
Evander Holyfield
Allsport/USA

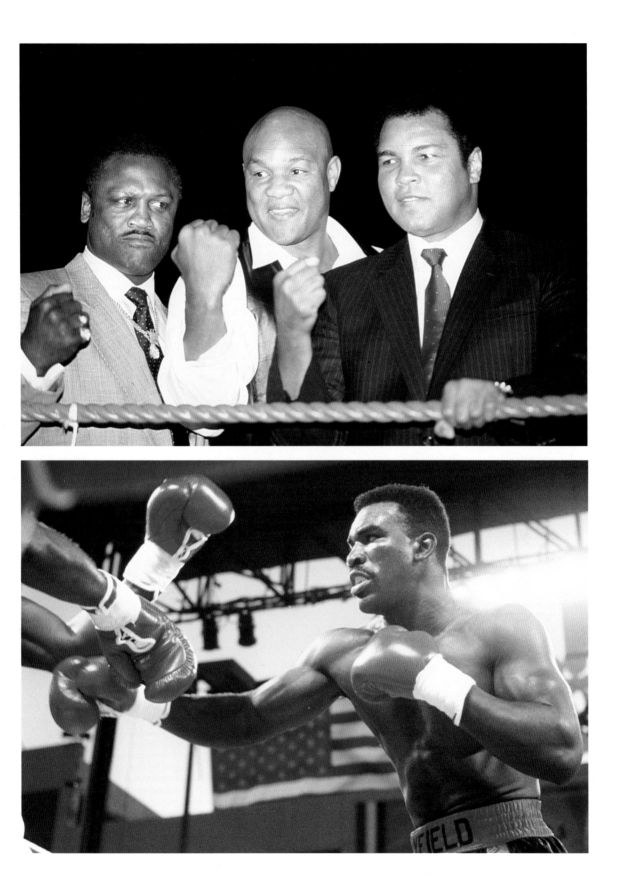

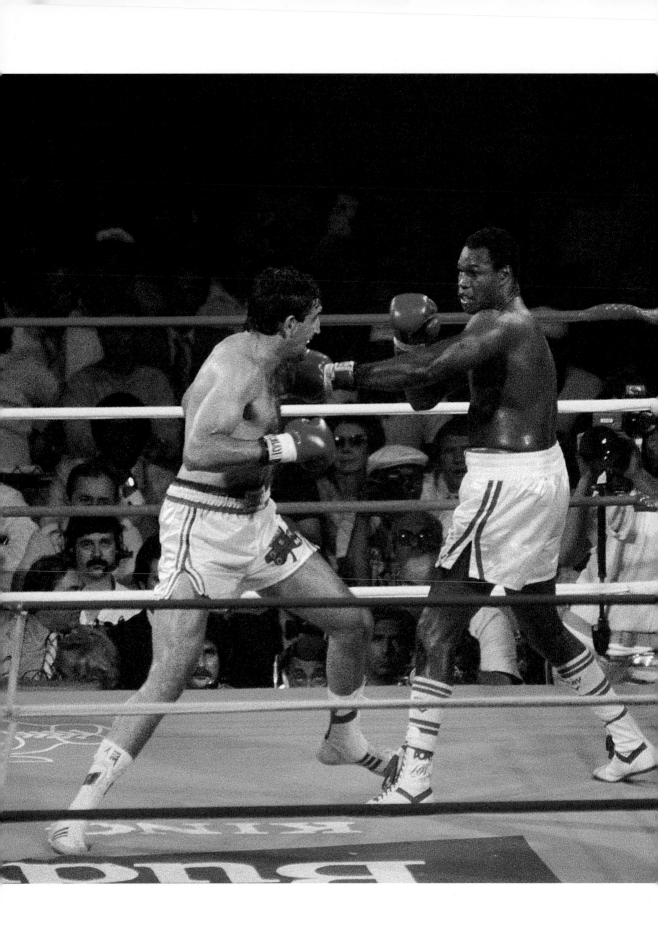

Michael Spinks
Colorsport/Sipa Sport

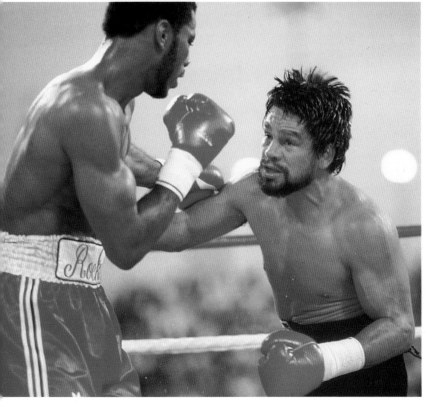

LEFT:
Roberto Duran (right)
Allsport/Mike Powell

FAR LEFT:
Larry Holmes (right)
Colorsport

ABOVE:
Thomas Hearns (right)
Allsport/Holly Stein

LEFT: *Lloyd Honeyghan*
Sporting Pictures (UK) Ltd

FAR LEFT: *Don Curry*
Allsport/Chris Cole

Bob Foster
Colorsport

LEN HARVEY

Len Harvey was arguably the most accomplished ring general produced by Britain, a master tactician whose lack of a 'killer' punch was all that stood between him and worldwide domination. He could tie opponents in knots with clever feints and smart footwork, and his defensive skills were good enough to nullify the power of the biggest hitters. His extraordinary professional career started when he was only 12 years old, scrapping for five bob a time during the hungry '20s. There are 133 fights on his official record, but during the many conversations I had with him in the post-war years he told me that at least another 250 contests had not been recorded.

Like his fellow-Cornishman Bob Fitzsimmons, Len collected titles like trading stamps and he remains the only fighter ever to have won the British middle, light heavy and heavyweight championships. He also went close to winning the welterweight crown, holding the highly-rated Harry Mason to a draw over 20 rounds when he was 18.

His first championship victory came in his 90th official fight in 1929 when he stopped Alex Ireland in seven rounds to take the British middleweight title from the Edinburgh fighter. He had three classic contests with Midlands master Jack Hood, winning the first and third on points with a draw in between.

Len tried his luck in the United States with three successive fights in New York in 1931, but his upright, typically British jab-and-move style was not appreciated across the Atlantic. He was twice outpointed by Vince Dundee and then lost on points again to Ben Jeby, and the American fight fans dismissed him as a spoiler who was not interested in giving them value for money. They did not share Len's outlook that boxing is as much about avoiding punches as landing them.

He resumed his career in Britain and retained his middleweight title against Jack Hood, Jock McAvoy and Len Johnson before being narrowly outpointed in 1932 in a bid for the world middleweight title held by aggressive Frenchman Marcel Thil.

Harvey admitted to me that he was never quite the same force after badly damaging both his hands trying to knock out Geordie Jack Casey, who was not nicknamed 'Cast Iron' Casey for nothing. He retained his British middleweight crown with a points win over Casey, but − still troubled by his hand injuries − lost it in his next defence against his great rival Jock McAvoy in Manchester in 1933.

Len moved up to light heavyweight and just two months later captured the vacant British title by outpointing Eddie Phillips. Before the year was out he added the heavyweight championship to his collection with a points win over Jack Petersen.

After taking the Empire title from Larry Gains, Len was paid £5,000 to defend his championships against Petersen. He fought with one eye closed from the seventh round and his corner threw the towel in during the 12th round − the only time in his career that Len was forced to surrender. In a third fight with Petersen he was knocked down in the first round on the way to a points defeat.

Len Harvey
Born Stoke Climsland,
Cornwall, 11.7.1907
Career span: 1920-42
World light heavyweight
champion 1939-42; British
middleweight champion
1929-33; British and Empire
light heavyweight champion
1933-42; British and Empire
heavyweight champion 1933-42
Ring record: 133 fights, 111
wins, 13 losses (2 stoppages);
51 inside-the-distance wins, 9
draws

He dropped back to light heavyweight and made the most of his role as matchmaker for promoter Arthur Elvin by importing American John Henry Lewis for a world light heavyweight title defence at Wembley in 1936. Len staged a storming finish but could not make up the points lost during a cautious start, and it was Lewis who had his arm raised after 15 rounds.

Harvey went back to accumulating domestic titles, taking the British light heavyweight championship from Jock McAvoy with a points win in April 1938, and then, nine months later, recapturing the British heavyweight title on a fourth-round disqualification against Eddie Phillips.

In March 1939 he stopped Larry Gains in 13 rounds to regain the Empire heavyweight crown, and then he signed for a return world title fight with John Henry Lewis. The champion arrived in London for the contest that was scheduled to be staged at the White City in July 1939, but was barred from fighting by the British Boxing Board of Control after they received a medical report from the United States about a serious eye problem affecting Lewis. Jock McAvoy was brought in as a substitute and the fight was billed as for the vacant world light heavyweight championship, but after outpointing McAvoy for the third time in four meetings Harvey was not recognised as the world champion outside Britain.

When war was declared two months later Len became a pilot officer in the RAF. After a three-year lay-off he was tempted into making a comeback in a light heavyweight title fight at White Hart Lane on 20 June 1942. At 35 and on legs that were no longer nimble, he was unable to slip out of the way of the crude but effective bulldozing attacks of 23-year-old RAF sergeant Freddie Mills. He was knocked out of the ring in the second round and was still trying to scramble back through the ropes when he was counted out for the one and only time in his incredible career. Len lost his title but he never ever lost his pride, and a light went out in the boxing world when he passed on in 1976.

Opposite: Len Harvey lands a right against Larry Gains in their British Empire heavyweight title fight at Harringay in 1939. Gains was forced to retire after 13 rounds.

THOMAS HEARNS

Thomas Hearns
Born Memphis,
Tennessee, 18.10.1958
Career span: 1977-
World welterweight champion
1980-81; world light
middleweight champion 1982;
world light heavyweight
champion 1987; world
middleweight champion
1987-88; world super
middleweight champion 1988
Ring record: 51 fights, 47 wins,
3 losses (3 stoppages); 38
inside-the-distance wins, 1
draw

Thomas Hearns is guaranteed a lasting place in the boxing history books as the first man to win four world titles. Although the feat has been made easier in modern times because of the overload of 'alphabet' championships, his performance is notable in that he joins Henry Armstrong and Bob Fitzsimmons in winning three of the traditional titles – welter, middle and light heavyweight. If we were judging my greatest boxers purely on punching power then Hearns would have a top ten place. He is known appropriately as the 'Hit Man' and can take the most durable fighters out with one punch, and as evidence I give you his sensational two-round knock-out victory over the redoubtable Roberto Duran in 1984. He exploded a right on Duran's jaw that poleaxed the Panamanian. It was the first ever knock-out defeat for Duran and the punch that did the damage is regarded as one of the hardest thrown in the ring outside a heavyweight contest.

Hearns has a superb upper physique, with the loose, supple muscles that I associate with big hitters. In boxing a punching muscle is long and sinewy, not a bunched muscle such as that of a weight-lifter or body-builder. Hearns was once described as 'a fighting machine that could have been built by committee'. He has a telescopic reach, good all-round boxing skills, a jarring jab that paves the way for the following heavy ammunition from either hand, and slimline legs on which he is fast and mobile. If he *had* been put together by a committee they would have strengthened one department: his chin started to let him down in the latter part of his career.

Born in the Deep South of the United States, he learned his boxing in the motor city of Detroit and signposted that he was destined for the top when he won the Golden Gloves welterweight title shortly before turning professional in 1977. He won 24 of his first 26 contests inside the distance, and became WBA welterweight champion in 1980 when he pulverised Pipino Cuevas in two rounds.

He successfully defended the title three times before a megabucks show-down against Sugar Ray Leonard in Las Vegas in 1981. Hearns looked as if he was going to maintain his unbeaten record until Leonard, an eye closed and behind on points, caught up with him in the 14th round.

Hearns regained world championship status in 1982 when he outpointed Wilfred Benitez to win the WBC world light middleweight title. After three winning defences, including the destruction of Duran, he moved up into the middleweight division for a battle with 'Marvelous' Marvin Hagler. He adopted suicidal tactics, choosing to stand and trade punches rather than using his footwork to keep out of distance. Hearns paid the price for his bold but foolish strategy by getting knocked cold in the third round after cutting Hagler's eye.

In March 1987 the king of the famous Kronk stable cheekily made a raid on the light heavyweight division, snatched the WBC title from Britain's brave but outgunned Dennis Andries and then dropped back to where he belonged among the middleweights. He made history in October 1987 by knocking out Argentinian Juan Domingo Roldan in four rounds to win the WBC championship, his record-making fourth world crown.

But it was becoming clear that Hearns was no longer a reliable force under pressure, and he lost his latest title to Iran Barkley in 1988 when he was knocked out in the third round. He gathered a *fifth* world title of sorts when outpointing James Kinchen for the newly-introduced WBO super middleweight title, but it is not a championship that was recognised worldwide in what has become an alphabet soup of boxing titles. He was unimpressive against Kinchen and it looked time for him to get out of the game he had graced with such style and power. But he was tempted into a return match with the remarkable Ray Leonard and forced a draw in a stunning duel in which fortunes swayed continually between two great fighters, both just past their best. One certain fact is that throughout his career Hearns has been a hit with fans and, spectacularly, with his opponents.

Tommy Hearns attacks Sugar Ray Leonard during their 12-round draw in Las Vegas in 1989.

LARRY HOLMES

Larry Holmes
Born Cuthbert, Georgia,
3.11.1949
Career span: 1973-88
World heavyweight champion
1978-85
Ring record: 51 fights, 48 wins,
3 losses (1 stoppage); 34 inside-
the-distance wins

Larry Holmes was never able to escape the giant shadow cast over him by his phenomenally popular predecessor Muhammad Ali. Even Holmes idolised Ali, for whom he used to work as a young sparring partner. It was one of the saddest days of Larry's life when he forced a tragically over-the-hill Ali to retire at the end of ten rounds in a championship contest at Las Vegas in 1980. 'I love that man and didn't want to see him getting hurt', said Holmes.

The only way Holmes might have closed the gap on Ali in the 'Who's the greatest?' argument was to equal or beat Rocky Marciano's record of 49 unbeaten fights. He was one away from drawing level when he dropped a disputed points decision to light heavyweight champion Michael Spinks and then lost the return match.

Holmes bitterly disputed both verdicts and announced his retirement in 1986 with a record of 48 victories in 50 fights. Two years later he was made an offer he could not refuse to stage a comeback at the age of 38 for

a crack at Mike Tyson's world crown. Even his £2 million purse seemed small consolation for the humiliation and pain he suffered at the hands of Tyson, who knocked him out in four rounds.

Larry had ascended to the WBC heavyweight throne in 1978 by narrowly outpointing Ken Norton in a classic 15-round contest. One of a family of nine brothers and three sisters, he was born in Georgia but it was in Easton, Pennsylvania, that he first started boxing in between earning desperately-needed cash as a shoeshine boy. He reached the finals of the United States Olympic boxing trials in 1972, but was disqualified for holding against Duane Bobick. The following year he made his professional debut, earning $63 in the fight that launched him on a career that was to net him more than $30 million.

Holmes always suffered in comparisons with quick-on-the-jaw Ali, but he was an outstanding fighter in his own right. His best performance in 21 championship contests came against 'white hope' Gerry Cooney, who was hammered into submission in 13 rounds at Las Vegas in 1982. In 1983 he surrendered the WBC heavyweight crown and accepted recognition from the newly-formed IBF as champion. Larry had an exceptional left jab, and he made the most of his 81-inch reach. He was not an explosive knock-out specialist, but evidence of the cumulative effect of his punches is that he stopped 34 opponents and equalled Tommy Burns' championship record of eight successive stoppages in title defences from 1978 to 1981. Standing 6 feet 4 inches tall and with wide, powerful shoulders, he had a strong chin and proved by getting off the floor to win against both Earnie Shavers and Renaldo Snipes that he had a big heart to go with his talent.

The only thing Holmes did not have was the recognition he craved as the greatest of all heavyweight champions. Any chances he had of that sort of rating disappeared with his defeats by Michael Spinks and Mike Tyson, which pushed him back deeper into the shadow of his old hero Muhammad Ali.

Opposite: Larry Holmes is close to victory against a fading Muhammad Ali in their 1980 world heavyweight title fight in Las Vegas.

EVANDER HOLYFIELD

Evander Holyfield
Born Atmore, Alabama,
19.10.1962
Career span: 1984-
World cruiserweight champion
1986-88
Ring record: 23 fights, 23 wins,
19 inside-the-distance wins

Evander Holyfield sat at the ringside for the Mike Tyson-Buster Douglas world heavyweight title fight and watched $12 million go out of the window. This was his guarantee for a summer showdown with Tyson, but 'Iron' Mike's shock defeat put at least a temporary end to the megabucks match. Holyfield had battled his way to the number one contender's spot with a sequence of impressive victories, winning his fights with style and precision in contrast to Tyson's bludgeoning ferocity.

It was obvious that Holyfield was destined for top honours from his earliest amateur days. Born and brought up in Alabama, he was persuaded to give up his ambitions for a military career to concentrate on boxing. He won a coveted Golden Gloves title at light heavyweight and seemed a certainty to collect an Olympic title in the 1984 Games in Los Angeles. He overwhelmed New Zealander Kevin Barry in the light heavyweight semi-final, but was then disqualified in controversial circumstances following a punch that unintentionally landed after the bell. A distraught Holyfield had to settle for a bronze medal, but he then started hunting for gold in the professional ring.

The only thing that seemed to stand between him and an eventual shot at the world heavyweight crown was a lack of real bulk. In this age of super heavyweights, he had to settle in as a cruiserweight, the 13 stone division that I suppose I would have campaigned in had it existed in my day (the likes of Rocky Marciano, Gene Tunney and Ezzard Charles were also 13-stoners).

Holyfield won his first ten professional fights with a flourish, but it appeared that he was being rushed up the ladder too quickly when he was matched with the vastly experienced Dwight Muhammad Qwawi for the world WBA title in only his 11th contest. Fears that he had taken too short a route to the top seemed well founded when Qwawi pounded him about the ring in the early rounds, but Evander proved he had the courage to match his skill and he battled back to steal a split points decision.

He defended the title three times, including in a seventh-round victory over his Olympic team-mate Henry Tillman, before accepting a re-match with Qwawi. Evidence of his improved power and confidence is that he bombed Qwawi to a knock-out defeat in four rounds. After adding the IBF and WBC cruiserweight titles to his collection he concentrated on pumping pounds on to his frame with a special diet and fitness programme, and he made his debut as a solid, 15-stone heavyweight in 1988 with a fifth-round victory over James 'Quick' Tillis.

He then hammered out spectacular victories against Michael Dokes, Adilson Rodrigues and Alex Stewart to put himself on target for a get-rich-quick showdown with Mike Tyson. Although 'Buster' Douglas beat him to the treasure chest, when the 1990s dawned most boxing experts rated Holyfield as the heavyweight with the finest all-round ability and the man most likely to one day succeed to the throne.

Opposite: Evander Holyfield (right) announces his arrival as a heavyweight with a fifth-round victory over James 'Quick' Tillis.

LLOYD HONEYGHAN

Lloyd Honeyghan
Born Jamaica, 22.4.1960
Career span: 1980-
World welterweight champion
1986-87, 1988-89
Ring record: 37 fights, 34 wins,
3 losses (3 stoppages), 22
inside-the-distance wins

Lloyd Honeyghan earns his place in my top 100 list thanks to one of the most astounding victories ever achieved in an overseas ring by a British boxer. He travelled to Atlantic City in October 1986 for what was considered a 'mission impossible' against undefeated world welterweight champion Don Curry. It was widely forecast that it would be 'Honey on toast' for Curry, who was rated the hottest thing around at the time. But Honeyghan dug down into his boots for the performance of a lifetime, and he stunned the outgunned Curry into a sixth-round retirement to take over as undisputed holder of the WBA, WBC and IBF titles.

I had rated Honeyghan a good box-fighter before this world championship victory, but now he was suddenly catapulted into the 'great' category. He lived up to his new standing in the fight game with victories over Johnny Bumphus, Maurice Blocker and then the destruction in just 40 seconds of highly-rated American Gene Hatcher. He surrendered the WBA title rather than defend it against a South African, but still had the WBC and IBF championships as his calling cards.

Lloyd, born in Jamaica and brought up near my old manor in Bermondsey, South London, was never far from controversy both inside and outside the ring. The father of children by three different girlfriends, he needed plenty of big purses to pay his bills, but it looked as if he had fallen off the gravy train when he was robbed of his titles by Mexican Jorge Vaca in October 1987. Honeyghan's first defeat since starting his career under the careful grooming of Terry Lawless and then the driving management of Mickey Duff followed an eighth-round clash of heads. Vaca was unable to continue because of a cut and the fight and the titles were awarded to him under a new who-is-ahead-at-the-time ruling (I wish that had been around in my cut-prone days!).

Honeyghan got his chance for revenge at Wembley five months later, and he took it with both hands as he knocked Vaca out in the third round. He then beat Korean challenger Yung Kil Chung in unsatisfactory circumstances — he was declared the winner when his opponent had been unable to continue after being floored by a low punch.

Cursed by brittle bones in his hands, Honeyghan knew he would only get into the megabucks league if he could beat his two outstanding welterweight rivals, Marlon Starling and Mark Breland. He made the mistake of thinking he could wade in without any defence against Starling and came badly unstuck in their title fight in February 1989. Honey was stopped in nine one-sided rounds.

Worse was to come when he made a bid to regain the WBA version of the world welterweight title against Breland at Wembley in March 1990. He was knocked down in the first round by what looked a conventional left jab from the gangling Breland, and then went through a nightmare before being rescued by the referee in the third round after six visits to the canvas. It was a night when he seemed hardly able to stand on his own two feet, and I was saddened to hear a British crowd turn on their former hero. Dejected Honeyghan left the ring with boos and choruses of 'what a

load of rubbish' ringing in his ears. No boxer deserves that sort of treatment. It looked to be the end of the road for Honeyghan, who will always be remembered for the way he knocked the seemingly unbeatable Don Curry off his perch.

Lloyd Honeyghan (left) searches for an opening against Maurice Blocker at the Royal Albert Hall in 1987.

JACK HOOD

Jack Hood
Born Birmingham, 17.12.1902
Career span: 1921-35
European and British
welterweight champion
1926-33
Ring record: 77 fights, 61 wins,
6 losses; 23 inside-the-distance
wins, 8 draws; 1 no decision, 1
no contest

Jack Hood was a master ring craftsman who was an idol in the Midlands during a 14-year career in which he came as close as anybody has ever done to turning boxing into a science. His impressive record might easily have included a world championship had it not been for the fact that he was continually handicapped by hand problems. Early in his career he was a devastating puncher, but after he had broken his right hand five times he accepted that he would have to rely purely on skill for his victories.

Jack had a style of boxing that was not far removed from that popularised by Muhammad Ali in the 1960s. He liked to hold his left hand low down by his hip, and as opponents came forward to hit at what looked an easy target he would whip in a left jab followed by a hook with the same hand.

Jack Hood, jacketless and with his artistic hands hidden in his pockets, watches American Dave Shade weigh in before their drawn contest in London in 1930.

He was beautifully balanced, could avoid punches with clever footwork and – even after all his broken bone problems – had a jarring right hand that earned respect.

Hood won the British welterweight title by outpointing Yorkshire's cultured Harry Mason in 1926, and won a Lonsdale outright by beating Mason in a return and then outpointing Alf Mancini. This was in the days of the 20-rounders, and nobody was better at pacing himself over the marathon course than Hood.

While supreme as a welterweight, he always had eyes on the more profitable middleweight crown, but it was just his luck that another out-standing ring general was at his peak at the same time. He had three marvellous British middleweight title fights with Len Harvey, losing two on points and drawing one. There was hardly a thing to choose between the two masters after 45 rounds of scintillating boxing.

His best performance in the middleweight division came when he was called in as a late substitute for an unwell Len Harvey to take on American Vince Dundee in London in 1931. Dundee, a future world middleweight champion, had twice outpointed Harvey in the United States that year and, with weight advantage, was expected to prove too hot for Hood. But the Brummie boxed brilliantly, and was rewarded with a draw by referee Ted 'Kid' Lewis, the old welterweight king.

Hood never quite had the power to make an impact in the 11 stone 6 pound division, but he was virtually unbeatable at welterweight. He knocked out 'Stoker' George Reynolds in nine rounds in a British title defence on 13 March 1933, and two months later he took the European title from Adrien Aneet when the Belgian was disqualified in the third round in front of Jack's adoring home town fans in Birmingham.

Finding it increasingly difficult to make the 10 stone 7 pound limit, Jack decided to quit the ring in 1935 at the close of a career in which he was one of the untouchables. There have been more powerful welterweight fighters, but rarely one to match him for proving that boxing really can be the Noble Art.

JAMES J. JEFFRIES

James J. Jeffries
Born Carroll, Ohio, 15.5.1875
Career span: 1896-1910
World heavyweight champion
1899-1905
Ring record: 23 fights, 20 wins,
1 loss (1 stoppage); 15 inside-
the-distance wins, 2 draws

James J. Jeffries started his boxing career as a sparring partner to James J. Corbett. 'Gentleman Jim' acted in something less than a gentlemanly manner and each day in training used to give the powerfully-built boilermaker from California via Ohio a painful hiding. After taking the world heavyweight title from outweighed and outgunned Bob Fitzsimmons in 1899, Jeffries gave Corbett two chances to regain the championship. Each time he gained revenge for all the punishment he had taken in training, although he looked on the verge of defeat in their first meeting at Coney Island in 1900. Corbett outboxed and outfoxed him for 23 rounds before being caught by a right that stretched him flat out. In the return in San Francisco in 1903, the old champion ran out of steam after building up an early lead and Jeffries knocked him out in the tenth round.

Jeffries, who had Scottish-Dutch ancestry, was renowned for his strength, and one of his nicknames – the 'Californian Grizzly Bear' – was well-earned. Before challenging Fitzsimmons for the title in only his 13th fight in 1899, he called into the champion's dressing-room pretending to want to wish him luck. When Fitz reached out to shake his hand Jeffries grabbed him in a bear hug and squeezed with all his might. It was his way of letting old Bob know that he could not match Jeffries' enormous strength. He battered Fitzsimmons to defeat in 11 rounds, but lost money because he had laid out $5,000 on Fitz to retain his title so that he would have consolation if beaten.

Trained by former world middleweight champion Tommy Ryan, Jeffries was taught to fight out of a crouch and his tucked-up style made him a difficult man to pin with any telling punches. The 'Jeffries crouch' was copied by many fighters of his era, but few could match the champion's success with it. He defended his title against Irishman Tom Sharkey (pts 25), Gus Rehlin (rtd 5) and Jack Munroe (ko 2) before announcing his retirement as undefeated champion in 1905. He had won 20 and drawn two of his 22 professional contests.

Six years into his retirement Jeffries allowed himself to be talked into making a comeback for a showdown with Jack Johnson, who was despised by many white American fans unable to come to terms with a black man holding the championship. Racial tension was stirred up, and James J. Corbett, brought in by the promoter Tex Rickard to help publicise the fight, was widely quoted as saying, 'The black boy has a wide yellow stripe running down his back, and Jeff is going to expose it'.

James, as they say in the American fight game, 'shoulda stood in bed'. At 35 and no longer a magnificent physical specimen, he was outclassed by Johnson, who battered him to a standstill in 15 rounds. There was a horrifying sequel when whites went on the rampage in the Deep South after hearing the result and nine blacks were killed in bloody riots.

Jeffries returned to his farm in California and maintained an interest in boxing by promoting amateur tournaments. He had fewer fights than any other world heavyweight champion this century until the brief reign after just eight contests of Leon Spinks. When he died on his farm in 1953, six

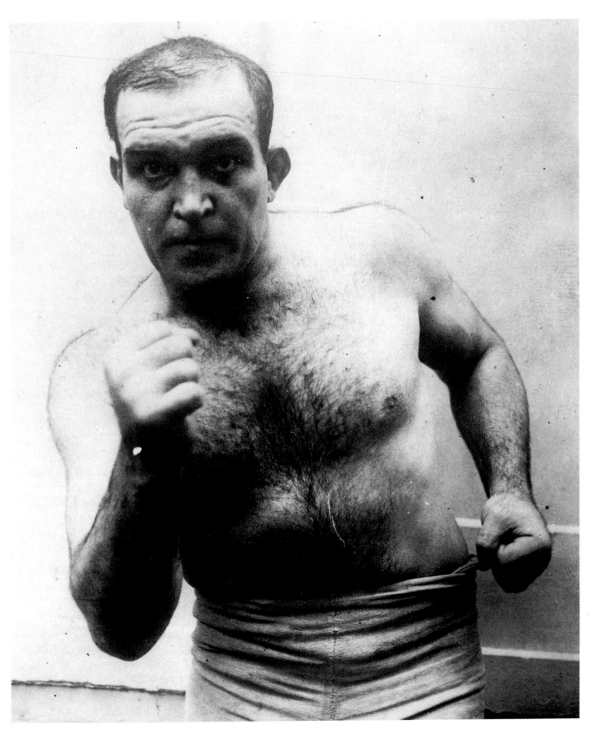

weeks short of his 78th birthday, his obituary writers spotlighted his enormous strength and durability. The only mistake he made throughout his boxing career was to allow himself to be talked into a comeback against the great Jack Johnson.

James J. Jeffries, the 'Californian Grizzly Bear'.

EDER JOFRE

Eder Jofre
Born Sao Paulo, Brazil,
26.3.1936
Career span: 1957-76
World bantamweight
champion 1960-65; world
featherweight champion
1973-74
Ring record: 78 fights, 72 wins,
2 losses; 50 inside-the-distance
wins, 4 draws

Eder Jofre was the first Brazilian boxer to win a world championship, and at his peak in the 1960s he was rated by many good judges the best pound-for-pound champion of his era. He was also unusual in that he was one of the few vegetarians to reign as a world title-holder. Jofre first came to my attention in 1961 when he fought Irishman John 'Cold Eyes' Caldwell for the undisputed world bantamweight championship. I rated Caldwell an exceptional fighter, and so I realised that Jofre was something extra special when he battered the Belfast man to a tenth-round defeat in his native Sao Paulo.

The referee for the contest was former world featherweight kingpin Willie Pep, and one of the judges was the highly respected newspaper columnist Peter Wilson – the Man they can't Gag, as he was tagged in the Daily Mirror. Peter was a good old pal of mine and of my manager, Jim Wicks. On his return from Brazil, Peter told us: 'Jofre is one of the greatest little fighters I've ever seen. He carries a bomb in both hands'.

He exploded those bombs on chins with such devastating effect that he was beaten only twice in 78 professional contests, and 50 of his victories came inside the distance. Both defeats were points losses against Japan's Fighting Harada at a time when, despite his vegetarian diet, he was struggling to make the 9 stone limit.

Jofre was born to box. His father, 'Kid' Jofre, had been a good class lightweight who moved to Brazil from Argentina and married an Italian girl (what a good judge!). He coached his son from the age of five, and taught him every trick in the book. Armed with all his knowledge and natural punching power, Eder won the Brazilian amateur title and represented his country in the bantamweight divison in the 1956 Olympics in Melbourne, where injury prevented him from progressing past the quarter-finals. He made his professional debut on his 21st birthday and won the American version of the world bantamweight title in his 38th contest. He then became recognised as world champion in most countries after stopping Italian Piero Rollo in ten rounds in Rio de Janeiro in 1961.

Tall, slim and with long limbs, Jofre was able to keep opponents at a distance before unleashing his two-fisted combination punches which invariably left them stretched on the canvas. He successfully defended his world title seven times, including his showdown with Caldwell, before losing it to Harada when weakened at the weight.

Jofre announced his retirement after losing the return fight with Harada in Tokyo in 1966, but three years later he made the surprising decision to resume his career as a featherweight. He was 35 when he made his comeback, and after 14 victories earned a title shot against Cuban Jose Legra, whom he outpointed over 15 rounds.

Another veteran, Mexican Vicente Saldivar, challenged him and was hammered to defeat in four rounds. Jofre was stripped of the title in 1974 for refusing to go through with a mandatory defence and hung up his gloves for good in October 1976 at the age of 40 after another seven successive victories.

Opposite: Eder Jofre receives the best sort of belting after knocking out Mexican Eloy Sanchez in six rounds to become the new world bantamweight champion in Los Angeles in 1960.

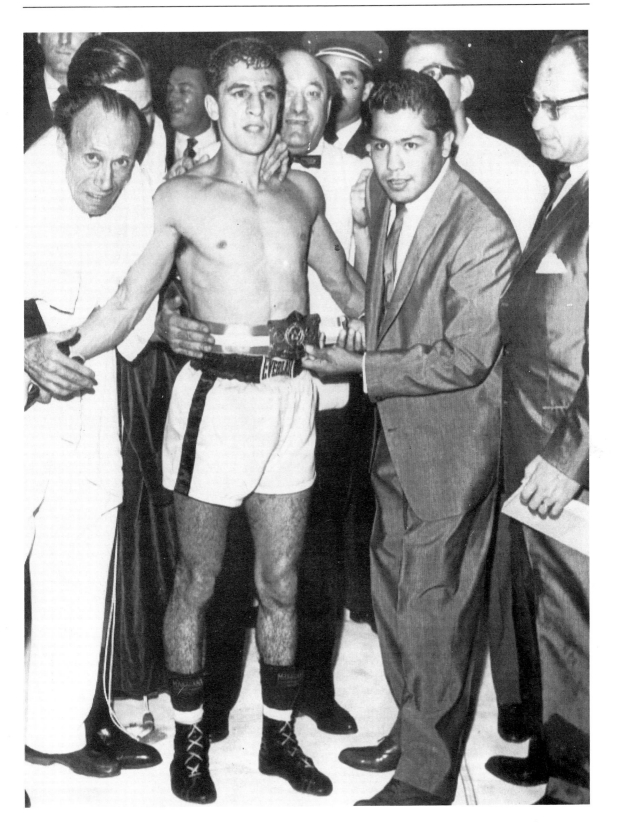

INGEMAR JOHANSSON

*Ingemar Johansson
Born Gothenburg, Sweden,
16.10.1932
Career span: 1952-63
World heavyweight champion
1959-60
Ring record: 28 fights, 26 wins,
2 losses (2 stoppages); 17
inside-the-distance wins*

Ingemar Johansson was a one-off as a world heavyweight champion. He was a handsome man with a big dimple in his chin, a winning smile and an almighty thump in his right hand. Nothing was ever allowed to stop him enjoying the good life, and he led a playboy existence even when training for major fights. It was the norm for him to go nightclubbing and dancing into the early hours during the build-up to his championship fights, and his beautiful 'secretary' Birgit — later his wife — used to stay with him at his training camps. Ingo cleverly exaggerated his playboy image while in the United States preparing for his title shot against Floyd Patterson at New York's Yankee Stadium in the summer of 1959, and he duped the press and Patterson into thinking he was more interested in fun than fighting.

I could have told Patterson that he was walking into a minefield when he agreed to defend his world title against the Swede. Along with a procession of European heavyweights I had felt the full weight of the mighty right hand that became known as 'Ingo's Bingo'. Johansson knocked me out in the fifth round of a European championship defence in an open-air promotion in Stockholm on 19 May 1957. I can't describe the path the punch took simply because I didn't see it. I was backed into a corner and was blinded by the sun. All I know is how it felt. It was as if somebody had whacked me across the jaw with a baseball bat. Bingo!

Patterson and his cautious manager, Cus D'Amato, like so many of us, completely miscalculated Johansson's ability. The Swede just didn't look a class fighter. His left jab was a pawing punch which from outside the ring seemed novice-like, but when you were in there facing him it quickly became apparent that this was just a range-finder for his 'say goodnight' right. Opponents used to think they could brush the left jab aside, which is exactly what he wanted them to think. As they forced their way forward he would be waiting to ambush them with a right hand that was used almost exclusively as a counter punch. So it is easy to see how the Patterson camp managed to underestimate him.

My first view of both Patterson and Johansson came during the 1952 Olympics in Helsinki when I was Britain's light heavyweight representative. Floyd won the gold medal in the middleweight division in impressive style, while Ingo reached the heavyweight final against American Ed Sanders. He suffered the humiliation of being disqualified for allegedly 'not giving of his best', a harsh decision that was quite rightly wiped out of the record books some 20 years later. Both Patterson and Johansson turned professional after the Olympics and when their paths crossed seven years later Ingemar was champion of Europe and undefeated in 22 fights.

The American press wrote Ingo off as a no-hoper after watching him in lethargic training sessions when the crafty Swede kept his right hand under wraps. He talked about his right as if it was something separate from the rest of his body. 'It is a gift from the Gods', he said. 'It is mystic and moves faster than the eye can see. I do not tell it when to go. Suddenly, boom! It lands like toonder.' Hard-bitten American sportswriters thought they were being given ticket-selling spiel, but they — along with Patterson — found it

*Opposite: Floyd Patterson hits
the deck for the seventh and
last time against Ingemar
Johansson in the sensational
third round of their first fight
in New York in 1959.*

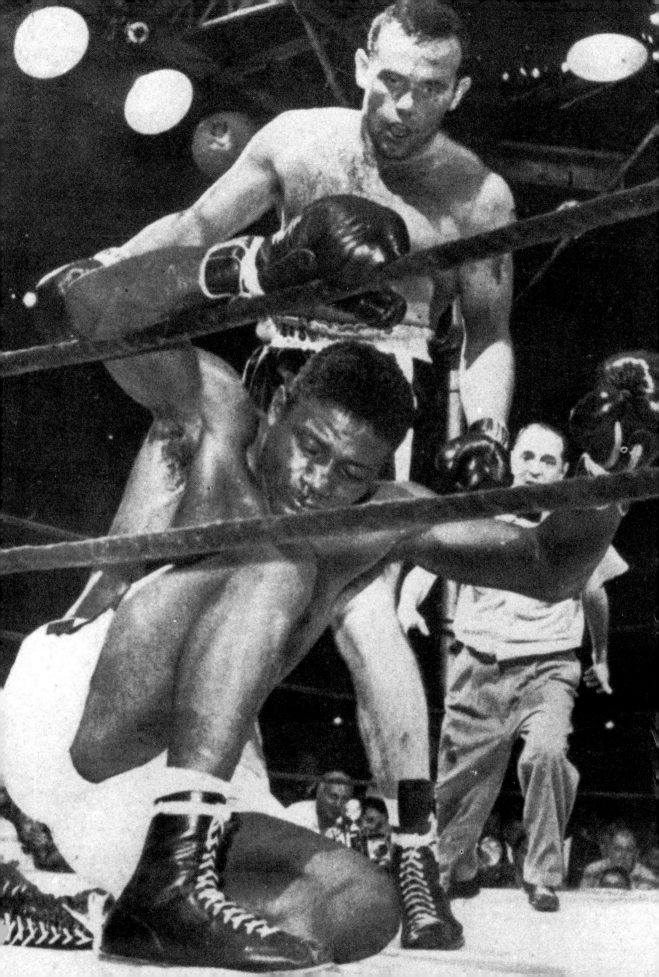

was no mere sales talk when the right exploded on the champion's jaw in the third round. Floyd was up and down like a yo-yo — seven times in two minutes — before referee Ruby Goldstein stopped the slaughter. Johansson was the first Swede ever to win the heavyweight crown and the first European holder of the title since Primo Carnera 25 years earlier.

Ingo and Floyd tied up the championship for the next two years, which all other contenders, me included, thought was a disgraceful monopoly. They met in a return at the Polo Grounds in New York a year later, and this time a grimly determined Patterson created history by becoming the first world heavyweight champion to regain the title. He knocked Johansson spark out with a cracking left hook in the fifth round after the Swede had been floored for a count of nine.

The 'decider' was staged in Miami on 13 March 1961. Patterson settled it once and for all by knocking out Johansson in the sixth round. Ingemar returned to Sweden nearly £2 million richer from the three battles with Patterson, but he was still hungry for another crack at the title. He got back on the championship trail by beating first Joe Bygraves and then detonating the old Ingo Bingo on Welshman Dick Richardson's jaw to regain the European crown that he had given up after winning the world championship.

He was being manoeuvred into a world title showdown with Sonny Liston when he took what he thought would be a routine fight with my old rival Brian London in Stockholm on 21 April 1963. But it didn't work out as planned. Johansson won on points over 12 rounds but he was the last person to know it. London landed a volley of punches in the dying moments of the fight, and Ingemar was flat on his back when the bell saved him from a knock-out defeat. It was too close for Johansson's comfort and he wisely decided to call it a day at the age of 31 after a career during which he caused some earthquaking shocks with his 'toonder' and lightning right. Ingo's Bingo pulled many a full house.

JACK JOHNSON

Jack Johnson was certainly the most controversial and possibly the most accomplished heavyweight champion of the first half of the century. It took Johnson ten frustrating years to reach the status of number one challenger for the world title in an era when the colour of your skin rather than your ability dictated matters. For at least five years Johnson was the best heavyweight fighter on earth, but he was a black man in a white man's world. Most of the leading white heavyweights dodged him by drawing what was known as the 'colour line'.

The son of a former bare-knuckle fighter, Johnson ran away from home at the age of 12 and worked in racing stables before starting to fight as a professional. He developed some of the finest defensive skills ever seen and was a master at picking off punches with open gloves and then throwing

Jack Johnson
(originally Arthur John
Johnson)
Born Galveston, Texas,
31.3.1878
Career span: 1897-1928
World heavyweight champion
1908-15
Ring record: 107 fights, 86
wins, 10 losses (6 stoppages);
40 inside-the-distance wins, 11
draws

Jack Johnson, the 'Galveston Giant'.

cutting counters. His right uppercut was a speciality punch that he used to deliver at close quarters, bringing it up from below his waist.

After ten years of learning his trade and being ignored by the top white heavyweights, he chased Tommy Burns halfway around the world before finally catching up with him and relieving him of the title in Australia. Johnson's 14th-round victory, coupled with his arrogant manner and controversial lifestyle, made him one of the most unpopular figures in the United States and a massive hunt was launched for a 'white hope' who could dethrone him. World middleweight champion Stanley Ketchel, the 'Michigan Assassin', was persuaded to try his luck. They struck a private agreement that Ketchel would be allowed to go the distance so that they could have a return match, but he finished with two of his teeth embedded in Johnson's right glove after being knocked cold in the 12th round following a sneak punch that briefly put Johnson on the canvas.

Then James J. Jeffries was wheeled out of retirement and was pounded to a 15th-round defeat. In 1912 Jack beat 'Fireman' Jim Flynn on a ninth-round disqualification in Las Vegas, and then he exiled himself to Europe for three years after being accused of 'transporting a white woman for immoral purposes'. Johnson jumped bail and had three fights in Paris before he was talked into defending his title against giant Jess Willard in the open air in Havana in 1915. He was well ahead on points until, on the edge of exhaustion under the boiling sun, he was knocked out in the 26th round.

Johnson later claimed that he had deliberately thrown the fight, but I have studied dozens of action replays of the finish on film and it looks a fair and square knock-out blow to me. Jack returned to the States to serve a one-year prison sentence and then carried on fighting until he was past 50. Right up until his death in a car crash at 68 he was still giving exhibitions.

There is little doubt that Johnson deserves a prominent place in the ratings of the greatest heavyweight champions of all time, and had he lived in more enlightened times he would have had the opportunity to underline his supremacy much earlier in his career when he was at his physical peak.

PETER KANE

Peter Kane had distinctive saucer-size Eddie Cantor eyes, the sort of punching power that could have knocked over a horse and, for a flyweight, incredible arm strength that had been built up during his days as an apprentice blacksmith in Golbourne. It was a defeat that first made Kane a household name. At the age of 19 and already a veteran of 41 professional contests, he challenged the legendary Benny Lynch for the world flyweight title at Shawfield Park in Glasgow. Kane fought on instinct after being knocked down by a savage right to the jaw in the first round, and he won the hearts of the Glaswegian fans by taking the home hero to the 13th round before being counted out.

They met in a return in Liverpool five months later when the world title was again supposed to have been at stake. But Lynch came in overweight and the fight was reduced to a non-championship 12-rounder which ended in a furiously-fought draw.

When Lynch was forced to surrender the championship because of his losing battle with the bottle, Kane was matched with American Jackie Jurich for the vacant flyweight crown at Liverpool Stadium on 22 September 1938. He dropped Jurich three times for counts of nine on the way to a convincing 15-round points victory, but at enormous cost. Kane so badly damaged the knuckles on his right hand that he had to have his little finger amputated. He later revealed he had first sustained the injury when taking

Peter Kane
(originally Peter Cain)
Born Heywood, Lancashire,
28.2.1918
Career span: 1934-48
World flyweight champion
1938-43; European
bantamweight champion
1947-48
Ring record: 102 fights, 92
wins, 7 losses (4 stoppages); 56
inside-the-distance wins, 2
draws; 1 no contest

Peter Kane throws a right uppercut against Spaniard Baltazar Sangchilli in 1939. Peter won on points over ten rounds.

a swing at a punchball on a Blackpool fairground, and from then on he was never quite the same fearsome puncher and had to rely on his considerable boxing skill for his victories.

The war intervened before Kane could cash in on his championship, and he became a part-time professional while serving in the RAF. He was no longer a natural flyweight and had to boil himself down to make the weight for a title defence against Jackie Paterson at Hampden Park in 1943. Seriously weakened, he was knocked out in just 61 seconds. A year later he was the victim of a freak accident that almost cost him his eyesight. As a colleague swung one of those heavy RAF coats on to a hook the hem caught Peter across the face and he was temporarily blinded. He was told in the military hospital that he should never fight again, and that seemed the end of a career that had officially started when he was 16 after early experience in fairground booths. But an operation seemed to clear the problem and he extended his career by moving up to bantamweight. After a succession of 11 victories in the immediate post-war years he took the European title from Frenchman Theo Medina in 1947 with a 15-round points win.

Kane lost the title to Italian Guido Ferracini in Manchester in 1948 and retired at the end of the year after a points defeat by Stan Rowan, one of four boxing brothers from Liverpool.

Peter's real surname was Cain but he changed the spelling after he had been wrongly billed as Kane for his official professional debut in 1934. There was a sad sequel to the incident with the coat when he became permanently blind in his right eye after his career was over and he had returned to his work as a blacksmith. Strangely, Peter never held a British championship during a career of more than 100 contests, but there is no question that he was one of the finest of all Britain's 'mighty midgets'.

PETER KEENAN

Peter Keenan was the only bantamweight to win two Lonsdale Belts outright, and he took part in 17 championship contests – a British record beaten only by Ted 'Kid' Lewis, 'Bombardier' Billy Wells, Len Harvey and yours truly. I managed to squeeze 20 title fights into my career, but I did not work as hard as Peter, who was a real tiger in the ring. He had superb boxing skills and could mix it when necessary, and the only honour that eluded him during a distinguished 66-fight career was a world championship.

He made a bold bid for the world title in 1952 when he travelled to Johannesburg to challenge South African ring master Vic Toweel. He gave Toweel all the trouble he could handle, but – weakened by the altitude – he ran out of steam and finished up the loser on points. After his defeat the promoters offered to pay Peter in diamonds, but he preferred conventional cash. 'For all I knew about diamonds they might have been made of glass', he said with good old Scottish caution. He was never able to get Toweel to give him a return fight in Glasgow, and I have often wondered how he might have fared had he enjoyed the sort of backing his fellow Glaswegian Jim Watt experienced in later years when he was able to get his world title opponents to take him on in his own backyard.

The son of a former Royal Navy flyweight champion, Keenan turned professional soon after his 20th birthday after finishing runner-up in the ABA flyweight final to H. Carpenter – no, not Harry but Henry. In his

Peter Keenan
Born Glasgow, 8.8.1928
Career span: 1948-59
European, British and Commonwealth bantamweight champion 1951-59
Ring record: 66 fights, 54 wins, 11 losses (7 stoppages); 23 inside-the-distance wins, 1 draw

Tiny terror Peter Keenan (right) on the attack against Jean Sneyers, one of the greatest ever Belgian boxers. Peter won this ten-round battle on points in London in 1950.

20th contest he outpointed brilliant Belgian Jean Sneyers. Promoter Jack Solomons was so impressed that he offered him a world flyweight title fight against Terry Allen, but Peter was sensible enough to know that he would be weak at the weight and declined the chance because he wanted to concentrate on the bantamweight division.

He played musical (or muscular) chairs with the European championship, taking it from Spaniard Luis Romero, losing it to his old rival Jean Sneyers and then winning it from Frenchman Maurice Sandeyron. Peter was never frightened to go into his opponent's territory, and he captured the vacant Commonwealth bantamweight championship by outpointing Australian Bobby Sims in Sydney. He successfully defended the Commonwealth crown against all comers, conquering Zulu Jake Tuli, Australian Kevin James, South African Graham van de Walt and Canadian Pat Supple. Keenan lost the British title on points to Irishman John Kelly in Belfast in 1953, and regained it in a return match with a sixth-round knock-out win in Paisley 11 months later.

Cursed by a recurring eye injury from early in his career, Keenan needed to develop an excellent defence that opponents struggled to pierce. But Ulster southpaw Freddie Gilroy smashed through it too many times for comfort in Belfast in 1962, and Peter announced his retirement in the ring after being floored six times before he was stopped in the 11th round of a British and Commonwealth championship defence. He kept his interest in boxing alive by becoming one of Scotland's most prominent promoters, but was never able to find a crowd-puller quite in his own class.

STANLEY KETCHEL

Stanley Ketchel rose from bar-room brawler to become a world title contender at welterweight when he was 20, middleweight champion of the world when he was 21 ... and was dead at the age of 24. He was one of the wildest and most fearsome fighters ever to climb into the roped square. His life ended as violently as he had lived it when he was shot in the back following a quarrel over a girl.

Born Stanislaus Kiecal of Polish parents, he ran away from his Grand Rapids, Michigan, home at the age of 12 because he wanted to become a cowboy. He was employed briefly on a ranch, and then started 'riding the rods' as a hobo. He became a pro fighter at 16 while working as a pistol-packin' bouncer in western saloons.

There is no question that Ketchel – nicknamed the 'Michigan Assassin' – was something of a head case. One of his managers, the writer and gambler Wilson Mizner, claimed that he was so vicious in the ring because he had a mother fixation. 'He could be a darling boy until a fight was due and then he used to convince himself that his opponent had insulted his mother and he would work himself up into a frenzy of hatred', he explained. 'If ever he had problems he used to run home to his mother and cry in her arms like a baby.'

Ketchel was no cry-baby in the ring and showed no mercy when he had opponents in trouble. He knew only one way to fight and that was as a two-fisted slugger who gave no attention to defence. He lost only four fights, two of them early in his career when he was twice outpointed by Maurice Thompson. His third defeat came in his 53rd contest in 1908 when he was defending his world middleweight title against the equally tough, equally mean Billy Papke. As they met in the centre of the ring for what in those days was a customary shake of hands after the first bell, Papke ignored Ketchel's outstretched gloves, crashed a left hook on to the champion's undefended jaw and then knocked him down with a straight right that closed his left eye. Ketchel dragged himself off the canvas four times in that crazy opening round, and somehow survived until the 12th round before the fight was stopped.

This was their second contest, Ketchel having won the first on points in his first defence of the world title that he had won by knocking out Jack Sullivan in the 20th round on 9 May 1908. Ketchel and Papke met twice more, Stan regaining the title by stopping him in 11 rounds and then outpointing him over 20 rounds.

Ketchel's fourth defeat came in an extraordinary fight for the world heavyweight title in 1909 against Jack Johnson, who towered over his challenger and had a 45-pound weight advantage. They agreed Johnson would win narrowly on points so that they could earn a bigger purse in a return match. Ketchel forgot the script in the 12th round and dropped the 'Galveston Giant' with a swinging right. Johnson got up immediately and threw a straight right with such force that he fell over as it thundered against Ketchel's jaw and knocked him senseless. Two of Ketchel's teeth were later found embedded in Johnson's right glove.

Stanley Ketchel
(originally Stanislaus Kiecal)
Born Grand Rapids, Michigan,
14.9.1886
Career span: 1904-10
World middleweight champion
1907-10
Ring record: 64 fights, 55 wins,
4 losses (2 stoppages); 49
inside-the-distance wins, 5
draws

Stanley Ketchel, the 'Michigan Assassin'.

A year later, on 15 October 1910, Ketchel was dead. He loved women, often those attached to other men, and he was shot in the back by a jealous ranch hand whose girlfriend he had been chasing while resting at the ranch recovering from a nervous breakdown. When Wilson Mizner heard the news, he said: 'That darling kid can't be dead. Start counting over him — he'll get up'.

JAKE LA MOTTA

Jake La Motta's life story could have come out of the pages of a Hollywood screenplay. It was no wonder, then, that a 1980 film of his life was a big box office hit for actor Robert de Niro, who won an Oscar for his performance as the 'Raging Bull'. Jake was carved from the same New York slums as his boyhood pal Rocky Graziano, and – like Rocky – he was rescued from a career in crime by the discipline and demands of professional boxing.

Jake was never able to escape completely from his criminal past, and he admitted after retirement that he had got mixed up with 'the mob' – the gangsters who controlled much of the American boxing scene in the

Jake La Motta
(originally Giacobe La Motta)
Born Bronx, New York,
10.7.1922
Career span: 1941-54
World middleweight champion
1949-51
Ring record: 106 fights, 83
wins, 19 losses (4 stoppages);
30 inside-the-distance wins, 4
draws

Jake La Motta, the 'Raging Bull'.

immediate post-war years. At first he refused to have anything to do with them, but he found himself frozen out after turning down the chance to be managed by one of their puppet managers. Frustrated after seven years as a professional without a sniff of a title fight, La Motta claims that he deliberately 'threw' a fight against mob-controlled light heavyweight Billy Fox in return for a guaranteed shot at the world middleweight title.

He then had to wait two more years for his championship chance, and when it finally arrived he had to pay the mob an advance of $20,000, which was money he had made by promoting his own fights.

La Motta had 87 fights on his way to the world championship contest, and included among his notable scalps were top-line fighters Fritzie Zivic, Tommy Bell, Robert Villemain and – the best of them all – Sugar Ray Robinson. He was the first fighter ever to get the better of Sugar Ray, but was beaten by him in five subsequent meetings.

He took the world middleweight crown from French idol Marcel Cerdan in Detroit on 16 June 1949, winning in the tenth round of a brawling battle. Cerdan had struggled since the third round with a dislocated shoulder after the wildly aggressive La Motta half threw him to the canvas.

La Motta outpointed Italian Tiberio Mitri over 15 rounds in New York in his first defence in 1950, and then knocked out French challenger Laurent Dauthille with just 13 seconds to go to the final bell and a certain points defeat.

He was not a devastating puncher, but used to swarm all over opponents and wear them down with non-stop, two-fisted attacks delivered from a crouch. His nickname – the 'Bronx Bull' – fitted him perfectly, but Sugar Ray Robinson was always too clever a matador for him, apart from in their first contest when La Motta squeezed to a narrow points victory. It was Robinson who took the world title from him in Chicago in 1951, the referee jumping in to save La Motta from further punishment in round 13. The date of the fight was 14 February, and ringside reporters, knowing of La Motta's past connections with the mob, delighted in labelling it 'another St Valentine's Massacre'. 'I mixed it with Sugar so often that I got diabetes', he used to joke in the nightclub act he started as a stand-up comedian after his retirement.

La Motta was struggling to make the middleweight limit, and when he realised he did not have the power to gatecrash the light heavyweight title picture he retired to a topsy-turvy domestic life that brought even more drama to the biopic that made compelling viewing for worldwide cinema audiences more than a quarter of a century after his retirement from the ring.

SAM LANGFORD

Sam Langford was prevented from fighting for the world heavyweight title because of the colour of his skin, but there is no doubt that at his peak he was as gifted and as explosive as any of the white world champions. His ring record is one of the most remarkable that I have ever studied. In 291 fights across a span of 24 years he stopped 116 opponents, and he won another 69 contests on points. Because he was forced to spend most of his career fighting only fellow blacks he became involved in an amazing marathon series of contests against Harry Wills (23 fights), Sam McVey (15), Joe Jeanette (14), Jim Barry (12) and Jeff Clarke (11).

A measure of his ability is that he gave Jack Johnson the fight of his life when the 'Galveston Giant' was at his peak in 1906. Johnson edged to a points victory, and from then on refused all offers for a re-match against the fighter known as the 'Boston Tar Baby'.

Sam Langford
Born Weymouth, Nova Scotia, Canada, 4.3.1883
Career span: 1902-26
World heavyweight championship contender 1907-12
Ring record: 291 fights, 187 wins, 50 losses (9 stoppages); 116 inside-the-distance wins, 47 draws; 4 no decisions, 3 no contests

Sam Langford, the 'Boston Tar Baby'.

Langford started out as a featherweight, outpointing former world light-weight champion Joe Gans in his second year as a professional. Even when campaigning as a heavyweight he rarely weighed more than 12 stone. He stood just over 5 feet 7 inches tall, but had a magnificent upper body and a reach of 73 inches. His favourite tactic was to draw opponents towards him and then catch them with long, looping counter punches that travelled at blinding speed.

When he was at last let loose on the so-called white hopes being lined up in the chase for the championship in the keeping of Jack Johnson he destroyed the title dreams of Sandy Ferguson, Jim Barry, Jim Flynn and Tony Ross. Langford came to London in 1909 to meet British champion Iron Hague and knocked him out in four rounds. He later travelled Down Under and in ten contests against fellow black Americans during a 14-month stay in Australia he was beaten just once.

The only championship he won in all his years in the ring was, unbelievably, the Mexican heavyweight title. He captured it in the 272nd fight of his career when he knocked out countryman Jim Savage in the first round in Mexico City on 31 March 1923. Langford was then 40 and way past the time when he should have hung up his gloves. He continued boxing for another four years, by which time failing eyesight forced him to retire.

Cataracts on both eyes brought complete blindness, and he was rescued from total poverty when friends got together in Boston and staged a benefit to gather much-needed funds for poor old Sam. He died on 12 January 1956 at the age of 75, just months after being elected to *The Ring*'s boxing Hall of Fame in which he had so deservedly won a place of honour.

BENNY LEONARD

Benny Leonard is generally considered the greatest of all the world light-weight champions. He retired as undefeated champion in 1924 after seven years as the idolised king, but then came his biggest defeat ... in the Wall Street Crash of 1929. The fortune he had made in the ring was wiped out and he was forced into a comeback that he had vowed he would never make.

The son of Jewish immigrants, he learned the art of fisticuffs on the sidewalks of New York City's tough East Side where he became known as the 'Ghetto Wizard'. He was described by one ringside chronicler of the time as having 'the footwork of a ballet master, the delicate hand skills of a surgeon and punching power like the kick of a mule'. This may sound like exaggeration, but nobody could match him for attracting society celebrities to the ringside in an era when boxing had such a bad reputation in New York that decisions were banned. Fights were limited to a maximum of ten rounds, and it was left to newspaper reporters to decide the winners.

Leonard did not need reporters to judge who had won his professional debut when he was 15 years old. He was stopped in three rounds by a boxer delighting in the name of Mickey Finn, but instead of losing his appetite for boxing Benny doubled his time in the gym where he perfected moves and punching combinations that have rarely been bettered. If ever his talent was letting him down, he would use his tongue to 'psych' opponents much in the way that Muhammad Ali did four decades later.

He fought two no decision contests with world lightweight champion Freddie Welsh in New York in 1916, and then a year later stopped the Welshman in nine rounds to become the new title-holder. Over the next seven years he was considered invincible in the lightweight division, coming off second best only when stepping up among the welterweights. He challenged Jack Britton for the world 10 stone 7 pounds title in 1923, and was disqualified for the only time in his career for hitting the champion while he was down in the 13th round.

Leonard announced his retirement in 1924, saying that he was keeping a promise to his mother never to fight again. He was offered fortunes to change his mind, but insisted that he would never again pull on the gloves.

When all his money disappeared in the Wall Street Crash he realised there was only one option left open to him. He waited until his mother had passed on and then gave up a promising acting career to make a ring comeback in 1931 at the age of 35 and after a seven-year lay-off. 'I know more about the sock market than I do the stock market', he told reporters.

Benny was a model of good clean living outside the ring and had kept himself in excellent condition by sparring with his brothers. He put together a string of 19 fights without a defeat to earn a title eliminator against top welterweight contender Jimmy McLarnin. But the years suddenly caught up with Benny, and the feet that used to seem winged were like lumps of lead as Irish-born McLarnin hammered him to a sixth-round defeat.

Benny knew the time had come to quit for good, but he stayed closely associated with boxing as a referee. After serving as a naval lieutenant

Benny Leonard
(originally Benjamin Leiner)
Born New York City, 7.4.1896
Career span: 1911-32
World lightweight champion
1917-24
Ring record: 213 fights, 180
wins, 21 losses (4 stoppages);
69 inside-the-distance wins, 6
draws; 6 no decisions

Benny Leonard, the 'Ghetto Wizard'.

during the war he resumed his refereeing, and he was in action as the third man in a contest in St Nick's Arena in New York on 18 April 1947 when he collapsed with a heart attack and died. His name lives on in boxing as an all-time great.

SUGAR RAY LEONARD

Ray Leonard has carried one of the greatest names in boxing – Sugar Ray – with pride and distinction, and there are even those who will argue that he is superior to the original Sugar Ray Robinson. I don't think I would go quite as far as that, but there is no doubt that he has proved himself one of the all-time greats of the ring.

His boxing story reads like something out of a *Boys' Own* adventure yarn, and he seems to have had nearly as many retirements as Frank Sinatra. His first farewell to the ring came after he had won the Olympic light welterweight title in the 1976 Olympics in Montreal. He claimed he had achieved all he had wanted to in boxing, but then his father and mother both became seriously ill and he announced his intention to box as a professional to help pay the family bills.

One of seven children born to Cicaro and Getha Leonard in Wilmington, North Carolina, he was given the first names Ray Charles after the blind jazz singer. But it was boxing rather than singing that attracted Ray, who followed one of his six brothers into the sport at the age of 14.

He was precociously talented, boxing in the style of his schoolboy idol Muhammad Ali, and was beaten only five times in more than 150 amateur contests. When he made his professional debut in 1977 he was paid a record

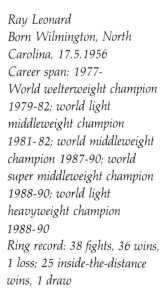

Ray Leonard
Born Wilmington, North Carolina, 17.5.1956
Career span: 1977-
World welterweight champion 1979-82; world light middleweight champion 1981-82; world middleweight champion 1987-90; world super middleweight champion 1988-90; world light heavyweight champion 1988-90
Ring record: 38 fights, 36 wins, 1 loss; 25 inside-the-distance wins, 1 draw

Sugar Ray Leonard, a master at the microphone as well as in the ring.

$40,000, but this was chickenfeed compared with the fortune he has since earned with his fists.

After 24 successive victories he won his first world title in 1979 when he stopped Wilfred Benitez in the 15th round to capture the WBC welterweight title. Then followed two spectacular contests with Roberto Duran. He was lured into an out-of-character brawl in the first contest and was narrowly beaten on points, but he gained full revenge in the return when he forced the famous 'no mas' surrender from Duran in the eighth round.

Leonard stepped up to light middleweight and relieved Ayub Kalule of the WBA title, and then became undisputed world welterweight champion by stopping Thomas Hearns in the 14th round of a dramatic duel. He was forced into retirement in 1982 because of problems with a detached retina, but the wonders of modern eye surgery enabled him to return in 1983. He was less than impressive in his comeback contest against Kevin Howard and again announced his retirement, having been knocked down for the first time in his career on his way to a ninth-round victory.

Leonard, an intelligent and engaging character, seemed content with a new career as a television commentator but was then drawn into yet another comeback for a middleweight title showdown with Marvin Hagler in 1987. He shook off the ring rust gathered in his three-year lay-off and boxed with style and courage to steal a remarkable points victory over Hagler.

He then added a record fourth and fifth championship to his collection when he got off the floor to knock out Donny LaLonde in the ninth round and win the WBC super middleweight and light heavyweight titles.

Leonard, the thinking man's champion, was surprisingly held to a draw by Thomas Hearns in a return match, and then confirmed his superiority over Roberto Duran with a one-sided points victory in Las Vegas on 7 December 1989. A shrewd businessman as well as a brilliant boxer, Leonard knows how to play on public support like an expert harpist plucking the strings, and he started strumming up business for another battle with Marvin Hagler. He seemed determined to go down in history not only as one of the greatest but also one of the wealthiest fighters of all time.

Opposite: Sugar Ray Leonard lures Marvin Hagler forward as he prepares to counter in their 1987 showdown, won by Leonard by a narrow points margin.

GUS LESNEVICH

Gus Lesnevich
Born Cliffside Park, New
Jersey, 22.2.1915
Career span: 1934-49
World light heavyweight
champion 1941-48
Ring record: 79 fights, 60 wins,
14 losses (5 stoppages); 21
inside-the-distance wins, 5
draws

Gus Lesnevich was born and raised in New Jersey, but used to refer to himself as the 'Old Russian'. His parents were immigrants from Russia, and he inherited from his powerfully built father tremendous strength and staying power. In Britain he will always be remembered for his two stirring battles with Freddie Mills for the world light heavyweight championship, while in America he was famous for his iron will and the determination that lifted him to victories over more gifted opponents.

Lesnevich turned professional as a middleweight at the age of 19 after winning an inter-city Golden Gloves title. He moved up to the light heavyweight division following a successful fighting tour of Australia, and on his return to the United States challenged Billy Conn for the world title. Though outpointed by the talented Conn, Gus gave such an impressive performance that they were re-matched six months later, with Conn again emerging the winner on points. Billy then elected to campaign as a heavyweight, and Lesnevich and Greek-born American Anton Christoforidis were nominated to fight for the vacant championship. Gus won on points to earn American recognition as champion in what was his 59th professional contest, and he then twice outpointed Tami Mauriello in 1941 to emphasise his right to the title.

America's entry into the war prevented Gus from cashing in on the championship, and during the next four years — at what would have been his physical prime — he had only two non-title contests, losing them both on points to heavyweights Bob Pastor and Jimmy Bivens. After serving in the US coastguard, Lesnevich resumed his ring career in 1946 at the age of 31 and was persuaded to come to London to defend his world title against Freddie Mills, who had claimed the British version of the world crown after knocking out Len Harvey in two rounds in 1942. Gus and Freddie had a real war that ended in the tenth round. Freddie was smashed to the canvas four times in the second round, but somehow managed to push himself back into the fight and looked as if he was about to pull off an amazing victory. Then the lion-hearted Lesnevich, with one eye completely closed, produced an all-out blitz in the tenth round and the referee had to step in to save a staggering Mills from a knock-out defeat.

After an eighth-round knock-out by British heavyweight champion Bruce Woodcock in London in 1946, Lesnevich made two successful defences of the light heavyweight crown against big-hitting Billy Fox. Gus, troubled for much of his career by eye problems, returned to London in 1948 for a return title battle with Freddie Mills and gave a sluggish performance on the way to a points defeat.

Lesnevich then fought Joey Maxim for the vacant US light heavyweight title, and he seemed to have nowhere to go after a points defeat. But promoters were looking for an opponent for world heavyweight champion Ezzard Charles. Lesnevich was surprisingly given the chance to win boxing's greatest prize, but was stopped in seven rounds.

Affectionately known as 'Old Muffin Face', Lesnevich became a referee and travelled the country with former world heavyweight champion James

Opposite: The calm before the
storm ... Gus Lesnevich (left)
and Freddie Mills at the weigh-
in for their first world title
battle in London in 1946.

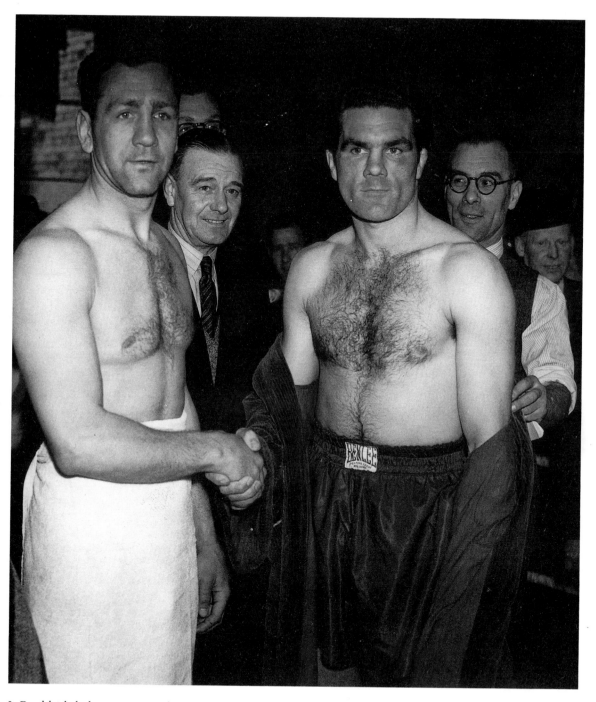

J. Braddock helping wayward youngsters get on the right road. He died following a heart attack in 1964, six days past his 49th birthday. Gus may not have been one of the most skilled fighters of all time, but he was certainly one of the strongest and a popular scrapper who never gave less than his best.

TED 'KID' LEWIS

*Ted 'Kid' Lewis
(originally Gershon Mendeloff)
Born Stepney, London,
24.10.1894
Career span: 1909-29
World welterweight champion
1915-16, 1917-19
Ring record: 281 fights, 170
wins, 30 losses (4 stoppages, 7
disqualifications); 68 inside-the-
distance wins, 13 draws; 68 no
decisions*

Ted 'Kid' Lewis was arguably the greatest fighting machine ever to come from British shores. His peak performances were witnessed by American audiences while he was on a barnstorming, 99-fight tour of the United States during which he twice won the world welterweight championship. He had an astonishing 20-fight series with his great New York rival, Jack Britton. They battled in 14 different cities between 1915 and 1921, Lewis winning three contests, Britton four. There was one draw and 12 no decision bouts, and the world title was at stake in six of their contests. All but one of their fights went the distance, and they were in the ring together through 222 rounds of boxing. Britton scored the one inside-the-distance victory when he stopped Lewis in nine rounds in their 20th meeting.

When I got to know Lewis late in his life I asked him about that serial with Britton. 'We used to play cards with each other in the dressing-room before most of the fights', he said. 'We'd put our card hands face down on the table when we were told to glove up. We'd then try to knock seven bells out of each other before returning to where we had left off in the card game. There were times when we lost or won more at the card table than we earned in the ring!'

Lewis, born Gershon Mendeloff in London's East End, started boxing as a professional at the age of 14. 'My first payment for a six-rounder was sixpence and a cup of tea', he told me. He began as a bantamweight, and before quitting the ring in 1929 was fighting light heavies and even heavyweights. His official ring record shows 281 contests, but Ted assured me that he had more than 400 bouts and often fought two and three times a week.

His all-action style earned him the nickname of the 'Crashing Bashing Dashing Kid'. He rarely took a backward step in a fight, and he would overwhelm opponents with two-fisted assaults that had a jarring effect. His relentless attacking brought him nine titles at weights ranging from featherweight to middleweight. In 1914 he travelled to Australia after winning the European, British and Empire 9 stone titles and engaged in five 20-round contests in nine weeks before moving on to the United States. During his five years in America he campaigned as a welterweight and in ten world title fights was a winner five times. Jack Britton was the only opponent to get the better of him in world championship contests.

Ted returned home to England after the First World War and proved himself too skilful and powerful for the home opposition. He added six more British and European titles to his collection, and was involved in a sensational world light heavyweight championship contest with Georges Carpentier in London in 1922. Ted was knocked out in the first round in controversial circumstances. He was turning to the referee to protest about Carpentier's holding tactics, and as he dropped his hands the Frenchman hit him on his unguarded chin with his lethal straight right.

Lewis was never quite the same force after the Carpentier setback and nine of the 24 defeats of his incredible career came in his last 32 contests. He trod the boards as the star of a revue called 'Hello Sweetie' and had a

spell in Austria as a boxing coach. In his later years he was a regular ringside spectator on big fight nights in London, and he was always given a tremendous reception by the fans, who acknowledged his standing as possibly the greatest British fighter of all time. Ted died in 1970, four days short of his 76th birthday.

SONNY LISTON

Charles 'Sonny' Liston
Born St Francis County,
Arkansas, 8.5.1932/4
Career span: 1953-70
World heavyweight champion
1962-64
Ring record: 54 fights, 50 wins,
4 losses (3 stoppages); 39
inside-the-distance wins

Charles 'Sonny' Liston was the meanest, moodiest and also the most mysterious world heavyweight champion of all time. And in the end he finished up as the most tragic of all the champions. He was painted as an out-and-out villain, a hoodlum heavyweight who ran with the gangsters and showed a flagrant disregard for the law. There is no doubt that he did keep dubious company, and many of his formative years were spent on the wrong side of the law; but I believe he deserves a charitable assessment of his career and his conduct, which need to be judged in the context of his early upbringing.

We're all of us shaped by the environment in which we grow up and Liston started life right at the bottom of the heap. He was one of 25 children fathered during two marriages by Tobe Liston, a poverty-stricken Arkansas farmer for whom Sonny had only contempt. His real name was Charles, but apparently his father called all his boys Sonny because there were so many kids around that he couldn't remember their names. How about that for creating an identity crisis?

At the age of about 13 Sonny ran away from home to St Louis and lived by his wits in the city streets, where he often stole so that he could buy

Sonny Liston, 'Old Stoneface'.

food and clothes. I say he was about 13 because he was never sure of his year of birth. The record books give it as 1934, but it was more likely to have been two years earlier. He had no schooling to speak of and he was unable to read or write. His reputation for being sullen and uncommunicative in later years was caused by an in-built suspicion and distrust because he'd had so many kicks in life.

Liston was continually in trouble with the police in St Louis and it was while serving a five-year prison sentence for robbery that he began to take an interest in boxing. He was paroled in 1952 on the understanding that he concentrated on his new-found sport and after winning a Golden Gloves title he turned professional in 1953. He won 14 of his first 15 fights, seven of his victories coming by the knock-out route. His one setback was an eight-round points defeat by Marty Marshall, who broke his jaw in the

Floyd Patterson down and out against Sonny Liston in their first world title fight in Chicago in 1962.

second round. In two re-matches Liston knocked out Marshall in six rounds and then outpointed him in March 1956. His career was just taking off in a big way when he got involved in an argument with a policeman over a parking ticket. The policeman finished up in hospital with a broken leg. Liston finished up back in prison for nine months. When he came out of jail he found he had more opponents than those in the ring. He was stopped and questioned by police more than 100 times and was arrested 19 times on charges that never led to anything but aggravation. Sonny was not the most popular person in St Louis as far as the police were concerned, and he moved to Philadelphia in a bid to make a new life for himself, but many of the dodgy acquaintances that he'd mixed with during his law-breaking days continued to cling to him.

He made his comeback after 20 months out of the ring on 29 January 1958 and took his winning streak to 33 out of 34 fights. There were several investigations into Liston's gangster connections and it was with some reluctance that he was given the go-ahead to challenge Floyd Patterson for the world title in Chicago in 1962. A powerhouse of a fighter with fists that he used like clubs, Liston flattened Floyd inside one round. He gave a repeat performance when they met again the following year. Sonny looked just about unbeatable, but then tamely surrendered the championship to chatterboxer Cassius Clay, retiring at the end of six rounds with a mystery shoulder injury. There was an even deeper mystery 15 months later when Clay knocked him out with a phantom punch in the first round. Liston won 14 out of 15 fights over the next five years, but was then found dead in his Las Vegas apartment on New Year's Eve 1970. He was said to have died of natural causes but there were strong rumours that mystery man Liston had been 'eliminated' by gangster associates. Sad Sonny took his secrets with him to the grave.

JOE LOUIS

Joe Louis was the *complete* champion, and like most kids growing up in the immediate post-war years I idolised him. He was the first fighter to capture my imagination and to fuel my dreams of one day becoming a champion of the ring. He was a composed and clever boxer, carried a knock-out punch in either hand and had strength and courage. His method was to soften up opponents with a textbook left jab and then follow up with short, murderous hooks and crosses that came in a blur of speed and power the like of which has rarely been seen in the ring before or since. The only opponent he could never beat was the tax man, and he finished up broke at the end of a career in which his ring earnings totalled nearly $5 million – the equivalent of at least ten times that by today's valuation.

Joe Louis
(originally Joseph Louis Barrow)
Born Lexington, Alabama, 13.5.1914
Career span: 1934-51
World heavyweight champion 1937-50
Ring record: 71 fights, 68 wins, 3 losses (2 stoppages); 55 inside-the-distance wins

Joe Louis, the 'Brown Bomber'.

Joe Louis knocks out Jersey Joe Walcott in the 11th round in 1948.

At his peak, Louis took on and beat all comers. They called it his 'bum of the month' campaign when he was bowling over challengers for his championship at intervals of just a few weeks. It wasn't so much that his opponents were bad as that Louis was in a class of his own.

Nobody could have had a more humble start in life than Joe, who was born Joseph Louis Barrow in a ramshackle cabin in the cotton fields of Lexington, Alabama. The seventh child of Monroe and Lily Barrow, he was of Cherokee Indian, Negro-white stock and he grew up in abject poverty. When he was ten his family moved to Detroit and Joe started playing truant from violin lessons to study boxing at a local gymnasium. He certainly never fiddled around in the ring and when he was 19 he won the coveted US Golden Gloves light heavyweight title before launching his professional career in July 1934.

There was only one scar on the Louis record when he captured the championship by knocking out James J. Braddock in eight rounds in Chicago on 22 June 1937: a 12th-round knock-out by Max Schmeling in the summer of 1936. But he soon reversed this one setback by smashing Schmeling to a sensational one-round defeat a year to the day after becoming champion. Louis survived a close call against brave Welshman Tommy Farr on the way to a record 25 successful title defences. He was champion – a great champion – for 12 years. After winning two memorable battles with Jersey Joe Walcott, Louis announced his retirement from the ring in March 1949. The 'Brown Bomber' was grounding himself as undefeated champion.

Sadly, his story does not end there. His tax troubles ran so deep that he was forced into making a comeback within two years and failed in a bid to regain the title from the skilful Ezzard Charles. The fight with Charles was the 'Brown Bomber''s 27th and last for the world championship, and the only one in which he finished a loser. Twenty-three of his title fight victories came inside the distance. Only Tommy Farr, Arturo Godoy and Jersey Joe Walcott stayed the full course with him, and both Godoy and Walcott were knocked out in return fights.

Though a shuffling shadow of his former self, he was allowed to be put up for slaughter against a rising young hurricane of a heavyweight called Rocky Marciano. The fight produced one of the saddest sights in sporting history, Louis being pounded through the ropes and stopped in eight one-sided rounds. 'I couldn't bring myself to count Joe out, so I stopped the fight', said referee Ruby Goldstein, capturing the supreme status that Louis had in boxing. There were a lot of friends ready to give Joe a helping hand when he finally retired, and even when his health deteriorated in his late years he continued to be employed as a 'greeter' in casinos and hotels in Las Vegas where he was revered by people from all walks of life.

Joe always carried himself with great dignity both inside and outside the ring and there has never been a more respected champion in sporting history. When he died in Las Vegas in 1981 a month short of his 67th birthday, the world mourned the passing of one of the most popular sportsmen of the century. I will always acknowledge him as one of my all-time heroes.

BENNY LYNCH

Benny Lynch
Born Clydesdale, Scotland,
12.4.1913
Career span: 1931-38
World flyweight champion
1935-38
Ring record: 122 fights, 90
wins, 15 losses (1 stoppage); 34
inside-the-distance wins, 17
draws

Benny Lynch could beat just about every opponent except the bottle. He was without any question the greatest fighter ever to come out of Scotland, but his addiction to alcohol destroyed him at what should have been the peak of his tragic career. Benny became a puppet of the evil drink from an early age, and he was encouraged to make many efforts to beat the habit by friends who recognised that he was wrecking his life. He went as far as to try shutting himself away from temptation in a monastery in Ireland, but he quickly fell off the wagon and into the gutter once he returned to Glasgow, where he was idolised for his achievements in the ring.

Benny showed exceptional boxing ability while at school and his first honours came at the age of eight when he weighed just 4 stone. He won 37 senior amateur contests, and toured with a travelling boxing booth before turning professional just after his 18th birthday. A complete master of boxing with knock-out power in both fists, Benny quickly rose to title status. He became Scottish 8 stone champion at 21 and in 1935 he drew with world flyweight champion Jackie Brown in a non-title fight. Six months later he ripped the world crown away from Brown in Manchester with a devastating display of controlled aggression. He knocked Brown down four times in the first round and six times in the second before the mesmerised Mancunian wisely surrendered his world and British titles.

Outside the ring Lynch was already leading a wildly undisciplined existence, and his ring record is peppered with defeats by opponents that he would have licked had he bothered to spend more time in the gymnasium and less in the pub. But he was at least still managing to get himself into shape for title fights. He stopped Pat Palmer in eight rounds and then boxed brilliantly to outpoint Filipino Small Montana, who had been claiming the world championship.

His defence of the title against Peter Kane on 13 October 1937 lured a record Scottish crowd of 40,000 to Shawfield Park, and they were rewarded with a classic contest that ended with a 13th-round knock-out victory for the Scot. It was to be his last moment of glory. Within a year his career was over and he was on the downhill run to a tragically early death.

He was less than 100 per cent fit when he met Kane in a return fight in March 1938 and many ringsiders thought he was fortunate to get a draw over 12 rounds. Three months later he arrived at the weigh-in for a title defence against American Jackie Jurich at Paisley looking as if he had spent the night on the tiles. He stepped on the scales and there was a gasp of astonishment when he was announced as being six and a half pounds overweight. He was stripped of his title, but there was still a great fighting man inside the bloated body and he stopped Jurich in 12 rounds.

Benny was now fighting on borrowed time. Three months later he was outpointed by an average American called Kayo Morgan, and then in his final appearance at London's Empress Hall on 3 October 1938 he took the only ten-second count of his career in the third round against Romanian Aurel Toma. He weighed 9 stone 12 pounds and was a pathetic figure as he was counted out without having landed a significant blow.

From then on Benny became lost in a sea of whisky. He pawned his boxing trophies and went back to fighting in booths for pennies to help support his drinking habit. He became homeless when his mother died and drifted to a slum lodging house in the Gorbals district of Glasgow. Benny was on a blind path of self-destruction, and he ignored all the efforts of well-intentioned friends to save him. In 1946 he was found lying in a Glasgow gutter. Scotland's greatest ever fighter was dead at the age of 33. What a tragic waste.

Benny Lynch shakes hands with Small Montana at the weigh-in before their world title fight in 1937. Benny won on points.

JOCK McAVOY

Jock McAvoy
(originally Joe Bamford)
Born Burnley, Lancashire,
20.11.1908
Career span: 1927-46
British middleweight champion
1933-39; British light
heavyweight champion 1937-38
Ring record: 97 fights, 74 wins,
17 losses (6 stoppages); 52
inside-the-distance wins, 6
draws

Jock McAvoy rivalled Len Harvey — some would say surpassed him — as Britain's outstanding middleweight champion of the 1930s. McAvoy and Harvey met four times in British championship contests, twice at middle-weight and twice at light heavyweight. Len won the classic series 3-1, with all the bouts going the distance and with hardly anything to choose between them at the end of each fight. McAvoy's one victory over his old rival came in their second middleweight match in 1933, and he reigned as British champion for the next six years.

After capturing the British middleweight championship, McAvoy nar-rowly failed in a bid to take the European light heavyweight crown from Frenchman Marcel Thil and then went to the United States where he hammered out victories over top Americans Al McCoy, Babe Risko, Jimmy Smith and Anson Green. His one-round destruction of Risko made him too hot to handle as far as the Americans were concerned. Risko, then recognised in the States as world champion, ignored Jock's demands for a return with the title at stake.

McAvoy, a natural middleweight, had to settle for a crack at the world light heavyweight championship held by an exceptional boxer called John Henry Lewis. Throughout his career Jock was troubled by bruised and swollen knuckles on his right hand. His world title fight with Lewis was, incredibly, his third contest in three weeks and he had to have painkilling injections in his right hand. This was no way to go into a major fight and he was outpointed over 15 rounds.

There was nothing conventional about McAvoy, whose real name was Joe Bamford. Born in Burnley, he grew up in Rochdale and came into boxing almost by accident. He got involved in a row with his foreman at the Corporation tramways where he was working as a labourer. After laying out the heavily-built foreman with a right hand he realised he had natural punching power. Within a year he became a professional and was paid just one pound for winning his debut in 1927 by a second-round knock-out. Jock bought a copy of a 'How to Box' book by his idol Jack Dempsey, and studied every page as if it were a Bible. His mother objected to him boxing, so when he made his second professional appearance he asked to be introduced as Jock McCoy. The MC misread the promoter's handwriting and accidentally gave him the name under which he was to fight for the next 18 years.

A mere five weeks after his world title defeat by Lewis, the 'Rochdale Thunderbolt' was back in action, challenging Jack Petersen for the British heavyweight title. Standing just 5 feet 9 inches, McAvoy conceded height, weight and reach and — troubled by bruised hands — he was clearly outpointed. He had a six-month lay-off before aiming for the British light heavyweight title that he took from Eddie Phillips with a 14th-round knock-out win on 27 April 1937.

Jock's father had run a small horse-drawn wagon haulage business, and he grew up with a love of horses. During his peak years when he was earning relatively high wages he owned a string of horses at the Rochdale

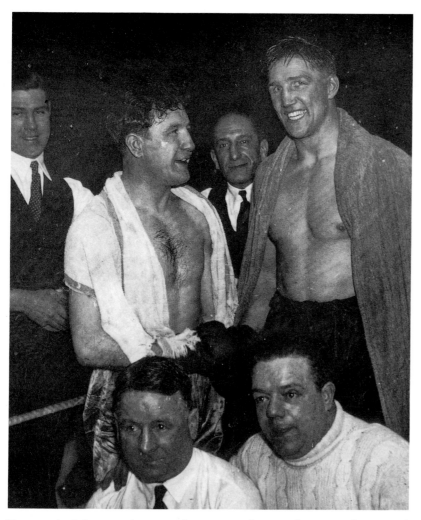

Hunt, and while out riding one day in 1937 he was thrown and sustained a broken vertebra in the neck. He had to wear a surgical collar, and it was feared that his boxing career was over. But in October of the same year he was back in the ring successfully defending his British middleweight crown with an 11th-round victory over Jack Hyams.

McAvoy lost his British light heavyweight crown to Len Harvey in 1938 and was then outpointed by the Cornishman in a fight billed as for the world title. In two wartime contests with Freddie Mills he was first outpointed and then retired in the first round with a damaged back muscle. It was heartbreaking to see this great fighter end his days in a wheelchair after contracting polio. When he died on his 63rd birthday in 1971 his old rival Len Harvey sent a wreath that read: 'I salute you, Mac — a great champion'. It was a fitting tribute from one master of the ring to another.

KID McCOY

*Charles 'Kid' McCoy
(originally Norman Selby)
Born Rush County, Indiana,
13.10.1872
Career span: 1891-1916
World middleweight champion
1897
Ring record: 105 fights, 81
wins, 6 losses (4 stoppages); 36
inside-the-distance wins, 9
draws; 9 no decisions*

Charles 'Kid' McCoy was a pioneer of modern boxing to whom I, along with a procession of other boxers, owe a great debt. He introduced a new style of punch in the 1890s during an era when nearly all blows were delivered as straight hits, crosses or swings. It was McCoy who first brought into play what he called his 'corkscrew' punch, a left thrown on a looping path around the outside of the opponent's defence and then hammered home with a powerful turn of the wrist. This was developed into what we now know as the left hook, and I was one of an army of successors to McCoy who adopted it as a pet punch.

McCoy has another place in ring history as one of the first globe-trotting fighters. He travelled the world in the pre-plane days taking on all comers and spreading the gospel of boxing on the continents of Europe and Africa. Legends surround McCoy, who started out in life as Norman Selby but changed his name when he ran away from home to become a prize fighter at the age of 18.

Tommy Ryan, the opponent he beat in 1896 to claim the world welterweight title, made an extraordinary allegation after his defeat. He said that McCoy had paid a private visit to his training camp and pleaded for a title shot to help pay for medical bills because he was dying of consumption. Ryan took him at his word and hardly bothered to train for his defence. He was the 'sick' one when McCoy knocked him out with his corkscrew punch in the 15th round of a championship contest that was not universally recognised. McCoy claimed the world middleweight title a year later after knocking out Dan Creedon in the 15th round.

He was involved in another major controversy in 1900 when he was alleged to have taken a dive in the fifth round of a non-title fight with James J. Corbett. There was such uproar that public boxing matches were temporarily banned in New York City where the 'fight' had been staged. It is claimed that when the unpredictable McCoy produced his best form the ringside fans immortalised the phrase 'that's the real McCoy'.

During his first visit to England in 1895 McCoy was surprisingly outpointed by former British amateur champion Ted White. But he more than lived up to his reputation for being unorthodox during a return trip to London in 1901 (when he realised he was best off out of the United States following his dodgy contest with Corbett). He fought three opponents on the same night at the famous old Wonderland arena and beat each of them in a total of seven rounds. McCoy was so contemptuous of the three English boxers that he did not even bother to strip for action and fought in his street clothes.

In 1903 McCoy boxed Jack Root for the newly introduced world light heavyweight championship and was outpointed over ten rounds. At the end of his eventful 25-year career he went into films and became quite a successful supporting star in silent movies. This extraordinary character seemed determined to govern his own destiny at all times, and on 18 April 1940 he took his own life at his home in Detroit at the age of 67.

Charles 'Kid' McCoy, the man who introduced the corkscrew punch.

WALTER McGOWAN

Walter McGowan
Born Burnbank, Lanarkshire,
13.10.1942
Career span: 1961-69
World flyweight champion
1966
Ring record: 40 fights, 32 wins,
7 losses (4 stoppages); 14
inside-the-distance wins, 1
draw

Walter McGowan was, in my view, one of the most talented of all post-war British boxers and only the curse of the sort of cut eyes that bugged my career stopped him making an even greater impact on the world stage. Walter was taught to box almost as soon as he could walk by his father, a former professional who had adopted the ring name of old-time lightweight Joe Gans. He developed superb skills, and featured in his armoury a snapping left jab, heavy hooking combination punches, confusing switches from an orthodox to a southpaw stance and dazzling footwork. At the peak of his career he brought the world flyweight title back to Britain after an absence of 16 years, but it was a short-lived reign because of his eye problems.

McGowan put together a magnificent amateur record, losing only two of 124 contests. He was ABA flyweight champion in 1961 and turned professional in the summer of the same year after representing Scotland for the ninth time at international level. Walter, who was based in Hamilton, bore a striking resemblance to Norman Wisdom with gloves, but he was anything but a clown in the ring. Guided by his father, he did not hang about building a foundation to his paid career and in his third contest he was matched with title contender Jackie Brown from Edinburgh. He was outpointed over eight rounds, and Brown went on to win the British and Commonwealth titles four months later.

For months Walter itched for revenge and he got his chance at Paisley on 2 May 1963 when, in his tenth professional fight and aged just 20, he challenged Brown for his flyweight titles. He paced himself beautifully and in the last third of the 15-rounder stepped up the tempo and the power of his punches, knocking out Brown in the 12th round to become the new champion.

In April 1964 he travelled to Rome where the legend is that you have to knock out your opponent to get a draw. But he had no complaints about his points defeat by the vastly experienced Salvatore Burruni in a tough battle for the European flyweight title. The following year, after two defeats caused by cut eyes, he returned to Rome to challenge for the European bantamweight championship held by Tommaso Galli. He appeared to have scored a points win, but had to be content with a draw.

Six months later, on 14 June 1966, he was re-matched with Burruni in London, and this time the world flyweight championship was at stake. He produced the performance of a lifetime to score a clear-cut points victory over the rugged, bulldozing Italian. He was then involved in a classic contest with Liverpudlian Alan Rudkin for the British and Commonwealth bantamweight titles, and squeezed to the narrowest of points wins.

He ended the year on a sad note, losing his world title to Chartchai Chionoi in Bangkok on 30 December. Walter was ahead on points when the referee stopped the fight in the ninth round because of the Scot's cut eye and damaged nose. Nine months later Chionoi came to London to defend the title, and stopped McGowan in the seventh round – again with a cut eye.

Walter put his British and Commonwealth bantamweight titles on the

line in a return match with Alan Rudkin in Manchester on 13 May 1968, and this time was on the wrong end of a close points decision. He then won six successive fights against European opponents before surprisingly quitting the ring at the age of 27. Walter was honoured with the MBE, a fitting tribute to an excellent boxer and a gentleman of the ring who was always a credit to our sport.

Walter McGowan (right) on his way to a sixth-round victory over Frenchman Rene Libeer in his first professional fighting visit to London in 1962.

BARRY McGUIGAN

*Barry McGuigan
(originally Finbar Patrick
McGuigan)
Born Monaghan, Ireland,
28.2.1961
Career span: 1981-89
World featherweight champion
1985-86
Ring record: 35 fights, 32 wins,
3 losses (1 stoppage); 28 inside-
the-distance wins*

Barry McGuigan was, for a span of two or three years, as exciting and as explosive as any fighter in the world, and at his peak he transcended boxing as the best known and most popular person in the whole of Ireland. Even the Irish troubles were pushed into the background when Barry was preparing to fight, and his enormous support bridged the sectarian divides. He attracted such a huge following that it became economically viable for the famous King's Hall in Belfast to be re-opened for boxing for the first time in more than 20 years. He pumped the pride back into the Irish fight game, and the emotion he generated when walking to the ring behind a 'flag of peace' turned his contests into unforgettable occasions.

Brought up in the border town of Clones, he was encouraged to box as a youngster by his father, Pat, a dance-band singer who represented Ireland in the Eurovision Song Contest. Barry captured the hearts of everybody in Ireland when he cried his heart out on the victory rostrum after collecting the Commonwealth Games bantamweight gold medal in Edmonton at the age of 17. He won two more gold medals in multi-nation tournaments, and then turned professional under the banner of Belfast bookmaker Barney Eastwood after being eliminated in the second round in the 1980 Moscow Olympics.

Barry rose above the disappointment of a points defeat by Peter Eubanks in his third contest and then the devastation of the death of his 12th opponent, Young Ali, to become as powerful a featherweight as has ever been seen in British rings. He developed into a skilful pressure fighter, specialising in forcing his opponents on to the back foot and slipping their leads before banging in wicked left hooks to the body and then to the head. There were often times when his punches strayed below the belt, but I have seen few featherweights to match his body-punching ability. Sitting at the ringside, you could hear his rivals grunt and groan as his huge, shovel-size hands sunk in below the ribs.

He hammered Vernon Penprase to defeat in two rounds to win the vacant British featherweight championship on 12 April 1983, and then seven months later he captured the vacant European crown by stopping Valerio Nati in six rounds. Barry strung together a sequence of 18 successive inside-the-distance victories to climb high in the world ratings, and then he set up a world title shot by outpointing former world title-holder Juan LaPorte over ten rounds in a crackerjack of a contest in the King's Hall on 23 February 1984.

Barney Eastwood and promoter/matchmaker Mickey Duff camped on the doorstep of Panamanian world featherweight champion Eusebio Pedroza and talked telephone numbers until they found the right figure to tempt him to London to defend his title. A crowd of more than 25,000 — 75 per cent of them Irish — packed the Queen's Park Rangers ground at Loftus Road to see the veteran Pedroza make his 20th and final defence of his championship against the 'Clones Cyclone'. McGuigan fought the fight of his life, and swung the contest his way by dropping the champion with a stunning right to the jaw in the seventh round when the fight was evenly

*Opposite: Barry McGuigan
and his supporters celebrate his
world featherweight
championship victory over
Eusebio Pedroza at Shepherds
Bush in 1985.*

balanced. From then on nothing was going to stop Barry, and he was perpetual motion as he swarmed all over the once brilliant but now bemused Pedroza for the rest of the contest to clinch a magnificent points victory.

It should have been the start of great times for Barry, but there was misery waiting around the corner. He was less than his usual impressive self in winning title defences against Bernard Taylor and Daniel Cabrera, and then he made the gigantic mistake of allowing himself to be persuaded to go to Las Vegas to defend his championship against a late substitute called Steve Cruz. Stories leaked from the McGuigan camp about training injuries and squabbles between the champion and his manager. He needed to be at his best both physically and mentally to beat Cruz, but he wilted in the almost unbearable 120-degree heat and was dropped three times on the way to a heartbreaking points defeat.

During a long and acrimonious break-up with Eastwood McGuigan retired from boxing and tried singing, chat-show hosting and motor racing, but the call of the ring was too strong. He won three comeback contests under the guidance of promoter Frank Warren and was then matched with Londoner Jim McDonnell at Manchester in May 1989 in what was supposed to be a final warm-up before a crack at the world super featherweight championship. A sharp, determined McDonnell took full advantage of the fact that he was meeting a ghost of the fighter who had ruled the world three years earlier, and his ripping punches caused the referee to stop the fight in the fourth round because of a cut eye.

McGuigan was honest enough to admit that he could no longer meet the skyscraping standards he had set for himself, and he bowed out with dignity from a sport in which he had, at least for a spell, looked one of the great masters — at times in the class of his great ring hero Roberto Duran. There can be little higher praise than that.

ROCKY MARCIANO

Rocky Marciano remains the only world heavyweight champion to have retired without a single defeat on his record. Mike Tyson looked to be the nearest thing there has been to 'another' Rocky. Like Tyson, Rocky used his fists as if they were sledgehammers and launched his clubbing attacks in such a brutal manner that he was called the 'Twentieth Century Caveman'. He was world champion when I was starting out on my professional career, and I've often offered up a silent prayer of thanks that he had hung up his gloves before I had reached title-hunting status. He was a vicious fighter who had little respect for the rules of boxing and who rolled over opponents like a runaway bulldozer. I was privileged to get to know Rocky after his retirement and was never able to associate the gentle, quietly spoken, modest man that I met in London with the butcher who had terrorised and tamed the world's greatest heavyweights.

Marciano's rise to fame and fortune was like something out of a Holly-

Rocky Marciano (originally Rocco Marchegiano) Born Brockton, Massachusetts, 1.9.1923 Career span: 1947-55 World heavyweight champion 1952-55 Ring record: 49 fights, 49 wins; 43 inside-the-distance wins

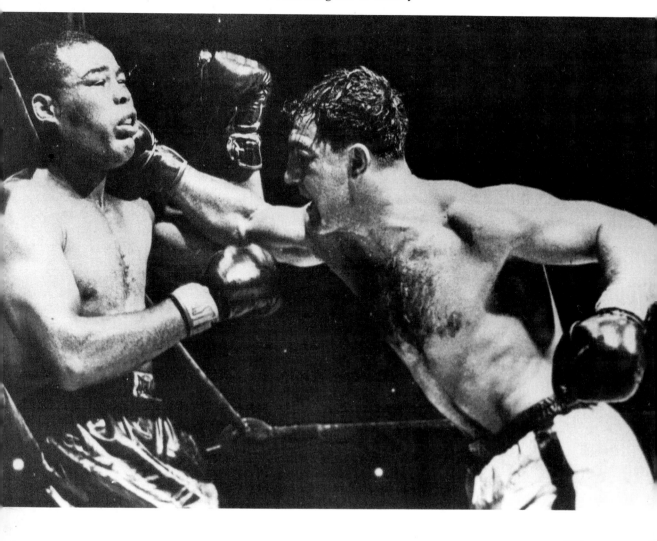

Previous page: Rocky Marciano launches the brutal attack that grounded 'Brown Bomber' Joe Louis in the eighth round of a non-title fight in 1951.

wood movie. Come to think of it, they could have called his life story Rocky! He was born Rocco Marchegiano in Brockton, Massachusetts, the eldest of six children of immigrant Italian parents who lived on the poverty line. After a brief amateur career, Rocky hitch-hiked from Brooklyn to New York for a gymnasium trial under the all-knowing gaze of Madison Square Garden matchmaker Al Weill. Most onlookers didn't know whether to laugh or cry at Marciano's clumsy attempts at sparring. But Weill noted Rocky's raw power and had the vision to realise he could be moulded into a fearsome force. He put him under the wing of veteran trainer Charley Goldman, an old-time bantamweight who knew every boxing trick in the book and a few that never quite got into print.

Rocky did not have the ideal build. His fists were small and his reach, at 68 inches, was the shortest of any world champion. But the tale of the tape doesn't give the overall picture of a man who simply oozed menace. Neither does it record that Marciano had the physical strength of a weight-lifter and a tough jaw that could withstand the hardest punches. Rocky was totally dedicated to his training and there has rarely been a fitter fighting machine. After battering an aged, over-the-hill Joe Louis to an eight-round defeat, he tore the world title away from Jersey Joe Walcott with a 13th-round knock-out victory in his 43rd fight on 23 September 1952. He knocked Walcott spark out in the first round in a return match and successfully defended his crown against Ezzard Charles (twice), Roland LaStarza, Britain's Don Cockell (crudely clubbed to a ninth-round defeat) and Archie Moore before retiring as the only undefeated world heavyweight champion in history. The 'Rock' is still held in awe by fight fans, particularly those of Italian origin. The day after Mike Tyson was knocked out by 'Buster' Douglas, London-based fight executive Denny Mancini voiced what many were thinking when he said: 'Rocky is walking six inches taller today. They *still* can't beat his record'.

There was an offer of a million dollars for Marciano to come out of retirement to fight his successor, Floyd Patterson, but he was happy with the $4 million he had made during his career (much of it allegedly buried away in sealed tins!). Rocky was a devoted family man and felt he had sacrificed enough time away from his loved ones in his lonely, punishing hours of training.

Rocky did have one more fight of sorts. He and Muhammad Ali faked their way through a computerised battle in 1969 in which they simulated seven different finishes for the benefit of the film cameras. Just two weeks before the film was released — with Marciano winning by a tenth-round knock-out — Rocky was killed when a private plane in which he was a passenger crashed in Iowa. He died on 31 August 1969 — the day before his 46th birthday. It was my great honour to read the lesson at a requiem mass at the Italian Church in Hatton Garden. Among the church ushers was his old rival Don Cockell.

Rocky Marciano and Don Cockell. We won't see their like again.

Rocky Marciano, the 'Brockton Blockbuster'.

FREDDIE MILLS

Freddie Mills
Born Parkstone, Dorset,
26.6.1919
Career span: 1936-50
World light heavyweight
champion 1948-50
Ring record: 97 fights, 74 wins,
17 losses (6 stoppages); 52
inside-the-distance wins, 6
draws

Freddie Mills was one of the bravest men ever to climb through the ropes. In fact he was, if anything, too brave for his own good. He learned his craft in the hardest school of all, the fairground boxing booths, in which he would sometimes have as many as half a dozen contests in a single evening. He used to take on all comers, and it was nothing for him to climb into the ring dwarfed by opponents two or three stone heavier. Freddie didn't know the meaning of the word fear.

Born in Parkstone near Bournemouth where he worked as a milkman, Freddie idolised Jack Dempsey when he was a kid and there was certainly some similarity in his fighting style, although he lacked the 'Manassa Mauler''s crushing knock-out punch. While boxing in the west country booths he teamed up with a wily old Welsh professional called Gipsy Daniels, a former British light heavyweight champion who, in his peak year of 1928, had gone to Germany and knocked out Max Schmeling in the first round. He was on the downhill run when he met up with Mills, but he passed on invaluable tricks of the trade during hundreds of rounds of sparring.

It meant that Mills was already a seasoned campaigner when he officially launched his professional career after winning a novice competition in Bournemouth in 1936. He squashed 72 fights into his first five and a half years as a professional and then sensationally established himself in the top flight by first outpointing and then stopping the exceptional middleweight Jock McAvoy in one round. Freddie followed this by knocking out ageing Len Harvey in two rounds in 1942 to win the British and Empire light heavyweight titles and the British version of the world championship.

Once he had finished wartime service in the RAF Mills continually agreed to take on opponents bigger and, frankly, better than himself, counting on his giant heart and all-out aggressive style of fighting to get him through. 'Fearless Freddie' was a formidable light heavyweight, but he was too often tempted to step into the heavyweight division where he had neither the physique nor the punching power to make his presence felt. In 1946 he unwisely agreed to fight giant Czech-American Joe Baksi on a Jack Solomons promotion at Earls Court. Baksi had a jutting jaw like Desperate Dan and punches in either hand that could have been measured on the Richter scale. There was no way Mills could give more than two stone away to a fighter of Baksi's calibre and he was hammered to a sixth-round defeat. Freddie sensibly dropped back into the light heavyweight class and became a hero of the nation on 26 July 1948 when he outpointed Gus Lesnevich to win the world championship, having been stopped in ten brutal rounds in their first contest.

But Freddie still wanted to prove that he was a good little 'un who could beat the good big 'uns. He stopped South African heavyweight champion Johnny Ralph in eight rounds in Johannesburg, and this convinced him that he should accept a return match for the British heavyweight championship against Bruce Woodcock, who had outpointed him just three weeks after his ten-round shellacking by Lesnevich. Bravery can take you only so far

Freddie Mills (right) pounds away from close quarters against Joey Maxim in their 1950 title battle. Maxim won in the tenth round in what was 'Fearless Freddie's' last stand.

in the ring, and in his return fight with Woodcock he was counted out on his knees in the 14th round.

Freddie was so ring-worn that he could manage only one more fight. He defended his world light heavyweight championship against American Joey Maxim at Earls Court on 24 January 1950, and all those hard battles of the previous five years weighed heavily on him. He was knocked out in the tenth round after a fusillade of punches had ripped three teeth out of his gums. A few months later happy-go-lucky Mills managed to cash in on this unsolicited dental work with a popular record called 'All I Want for Christmas is Me Two Front Teeth'.

The fight against Maxim was Freddie's last stand. He retired from the ring and invested what was left of the record £80,000 he had earned during his career in a restaurant, a nightclub and boxing promotions. Freddie had a lovely personality, and was always full of wisecracks and laughter that kept him in demand as a television and radio personality. But there was a sadness hidden behind the laughter, and few people knew his personal business problems. His tragic and mysterious death from a gunshot wound in 1965 shocked and saddened his army of admirers. It was described as suicide but those of us who knew him well just couldn't accept that Freddie would ever throw in the towel. I was a big fan of his and will always remember him for his extraordinary courage. They don't come braver than 'Fearless' Freddie Mills.

RINTY MONAGHAN

Rinty Monaghan
(originally John Joseph
Monaghan)
Born Belfast, 21.8.1920
Career span: 1935-49
World flyweight champion
1947-50
Ring record: 54 fights, 43 wins,
8 losses (1 stoppage); 19 inside-
the-distance wins, 3 draws

Rinty Monaghan was an entertainer both inside and outside the ring and he gave enormous pleasure and pride to his army of Irish fans. He was not the greatest flyweight champion of all time, but few could match his popularity. His supporters identified with his 100 per cent effort, and after bringing them to a pitch of excitement with a victory he would then soothe them with a beautifully sung ballad on the ring announcer's microphone.

Born John Joseph Monaghan in Belfast, he was one of 13 children and was nicknamed Rinty by his granny because he was as mischievous and as energetic as the Hollywood dog hero Rin Tin Tin. Encouraged to box by his father, who had been a Royal Marines lightweight champion, Rinty did not bother with the amateurs and became a professional the moment he left school at the age of 14.

He rushed through 21 straight victories before being knocked out in five rounds by Scottish southpaw Jackie Paterson in 1938. Rinty then notched up five more victories before his career was interrupted by the war. He first of all went to sea with the Merchant Navy, and then became an ambulance driver before joining the forces variety outfit ENSA as a singer and dancer. Rinty lost the three contests he had during the war because of lack of preparation, but he was soon back to his winning ways when he resumed his career full-time and in 1946 he avenged his defeat by Paterson, who had become world champion. They met in Belfast in an overweight match, and Monaghan was ahead on points when the champion was forced to retire with a cut eye. For once Rinty got his choice of after-fight song wrong and annoyed Paterson's fans as he sang 'Broken-hearted Clown'.

In March 1947 he made a dramatic London debut when he knocked out Terry Allen in the first round. Four months later Monaghan came in as a last-minute substitute for weight-troubled Paterson against Dado Marino in Glasgow and, paying the price for having eaten a late meal, he ran out of steam and was disqualifed for holding in the ninth round. Much to the undisguised disgust of Paterson, the world title was declared vacant and Monaghan and Marino were matched for the championship by London promoter Jack Solomons. Rinty got himself into the peak of condition and beat the Hawaiian on points, but Paterson was reinstated as champion after threatening legal action. The Scot then boiled himself down to below 8 stone for a title defence against Monaghan, but he was desperately weak at the weight and was knocked out in the seventh round on a memorable night in Belfast when Rinty spent nearly as much time in the ring singing as he did in clinching the title.

Among Rinty's stage impressions was one of Popeye, and he had something of the cartoon character's appearance in the ring. He had a nicely muscled upper body but spindly legs, and his pipestem arms used to be a blur as he attacked non-stop from first bell to last.

Rinty had only five more fights after becoming undisputed champion, two of them in defence of the title. He outpointed Frenchman Maurice Sandeyron to add the European crown to his world, British and Empire championships. He dropped a points decision to Terry Allen in a non-title

Rinty Monaghan – 'when Irish eyes are smiling'.

fight and then drew with him over 15 rounds in what was to prove the final fight of his career on 30 September 1949. Seven months later Rinty announced his retirement because of health problems, but he never lost his sense of humour and every time I saw him at the ringside or at boxing functions he used to have a wide grin on his impish face.

Shortly after releasing a record of his favourite song – 'When Irish Eyes Are Smiling' – Rinty died of cancer in 1984. Anybody who saw this great little scrapper and loveable sportsman will always have smiling eyes at the thought of him.

CARLOS MONZON

*Carlos Monzon
Born Sante Fe, Argentina,
7.8.1942
Career span: 1963-77
World middleweight champion
1970-77
Ring record: 101 fights, 89
wins, 3 losses; 61 inside-the-
distance wins, 8 draws; 1 no
contest*

Carlos Monzon was one of the untouchable modern masters in the ring, but he could not overcome problems in his private life. He finished up in prison when found guilty of murdering his third wife in 1988, 11 years after his retirement as undefeated middleweight champion of the world. My objective in this book is to judge boxers by their ability and achievements in the ring not their behaviour outside it, and assessed purely on his boxing record he was unquestionably one of the finest fighters of all time.

He started life at the bottom of the heap in the Argentinian city of Sante Fe where he worked as a shoeshine boy and newspaper seller. Monzon found the route to riches lay in the fight game, and after three early setbacks put together a sequence of victories almost unequalled in modern times. His first 82 fights were all in South America, and there was a cynical view

*Carlos Monzon, a master
middleweight.*

in the United States and Europe that he was being fed soft touches. Then he travelled to Rome to challenge Nino Benvenuti for the world middleweight crown and slammed the Italian idol to defeat in 12 rounds. In a return match in Monte Carlo Monzon won by a knock-out in the fifth round.

It was the start of a remarkable seven-year reign in what is probably the toughest of all weight divisions. He dodged no challenger and successfully defended the title 14 times, numbering outstanding former world champions Emile Griffith (twice) and Jose Napoles among his victims. Tall and slim, Monzon used his long reach to good advantage and softened up opponents with a jolting jab before unleashing two-fisted hooking combinations that knocked the resistance out of them. He lacked the style and charisma of a Sugar Ray Leonard and was not as hostile and aggressive as a Hagler or a Hearns, but there was not a weakness in his armoury. Throughout his 14-year career he was never once stopped.

Unlike many veteran fighters, he did not show any signs of deterioration at the back end of his career, and his victories over highly-rated South American rival Rodrigo Valdes in two classic contests in Monte Carlo in his last two appearances as a fighter were considered among his peak performances. He became a very wealthy man, although he missed out on the megabuck purses that came with the satellite saturation coverage of fights in the 1980s. But his money did not bring him happiness. His domestic life was, to say the least, often turbulent and his old friends and rivals in boxing looked on sadly as he pushed the self-destruct button once too often in 1988 and was sent to prison for the murder of his wife in the Argentinian resort of Mar del Plata.

ARCHIE MOORE

*Archie Moore
(originally Archibald Lee
Wright)
Born Benoit, Mississippi,
13.12.1913
Career span: 1936-63
World light heavyweight
champion 1952-62
Ring record: 234 fights, 199
wins, 26 losses (7 stoppages);
145 inside-the-distance wins, 8
draws; 1 no contest*

Archie Moore was not just an outstanding ring general but also a great showman, whose methods of self-projecting publicity were picked up and perfected by the young Cassius Clay. Long before Clay was declaring himself 'The Greatest', Archie used to get up to all sorts of tricks to keep himself in the headlines. He orchestrated a crack at Rocky Marciano's world heavyweight title by writing personal letters and sending telegrams to the sports editors of every major newspaper in the United States, and he also had 'Wanted' posters printed showing himself as sheriff and Rocky as the 'wanted' man.

These sort of gimmicks are all very well provided you can fight, and Archie could handle himself in the ring as well as any fighter in the history of boxing. He was an outstanding welterweight as an amateur and then turned professional as a middleweight at the age of 16 – or, more probably, 19. Moore went through his career insisting that he was born in 1916, but his mother innocently revealed after he had become world light heavyweight champion in 1952 that he had in fact been born three years earlier. 'I guess she should know 'cos she was there at the time', said Archie with a shrug of his wide shoulders and a sly old chuckle.

Moore was a professional for 26 years during which he scored a record 145 inside-the-distance victories. He was not a devastating one-punch finisher, but used to soften up his opponents with a steady stream of blows that were at their most effective when delivered as two-fisted hooking counters. Archie was too good for his own good and was avoided by a procession of champions, but he finally got his chance of a shot at the world light heavyweight title after agreeing to have the influential Jack Kearns as the eighth manager of his career on terms hardly favourable to the boxer. In about his 156th fight (his early record is incomplete), after 17 years as a professional and aged either 36 or 39 he at last became champion of the world when he outpointed Joey Maxim in St Louis on 17 December 1952.

Archie was forced to make his first two defences against Maxim, winning both contests on points. He reigned as champion over the next ten years, making occasional forays into the heavyweight division and then dropping back to see off his latest challenger. Nicknamed the 'Mongoose' and 'Ageless Archie', he used to shed more than a stone in no time at all to make his defences. He loved to be a man of mystery, and used to claim that he had a secret diet that had been passed on to him by an Aborigine during a fighting tour of Australia in 1940.

In June 1956 old Archie came to London to defend his title against British-based West Indian Yolande Pompey. It developed into a dull affair as Moore seemed to be interested in doing only just enough to sneak each round. Referee Jack Hart warned both boxers in the ninth round that they should snap into action or risk disqualification. Archie responded with a thundering attack in the tenth round that left Pompey a wreck. His championship reign seemed certain to end in Montreal in December 1958 when Yvon Durelle decked him three times in the opening round, but the 45-year-old maestro battled back to stop the French-Canadian in the 11th.

Moore came out top in nine title defences before being stripped of the title when well into his 40s and fighting mainly as a heavyweight. He made two challenges for the heavyweight crown, dropping Rocky Marciano for a short count before being knocked out in the ninth round and then going down in five rounds to Floyd Patterson in a fight for the vacant title following Rocky's retirement.

'Ageless Archie' became a fourth-round victim of young Cassius Clay in 1962, the master given a lesson by the pupil. Four months later he had his final fight, knocking out Mike DiBiase in three rounds, before retiring to concentrate on a career as an actor and occasional boxing coach. There have been few to touch him either as a ring master or as a larger-than-life personality.

Archie Moore (right) on the attack against Yolande Pompey in London in 1956. Archie won in the tenth round.

JOSE NAPOLES

Jose Napoles
Born Oriente, Cuba, 13.4.1940
Career span: 1958-75
World welterweight champion
1969-75
Ring record: 84 fights, 77 wins,
7 losses (4 stoppages); 55
inside-the-distance wins

Jose Napoles ducked out of Cuba shortly after the rise to power of Fidel Castro, who banned professional boxing. He based himself in Mexico and on the foundation of a long amateur career and 18 paid fights in Havana he built one of the most impressive of all modern ring records. Nicknamed 'Mantequilla' (smooth as butter), he reigned as world welterweight champion for more than six years apart from one temporary setback, and he made 15 successful defences before losing his crown to Britain's John H. Stracey in what was to prove his last fight.

Napoles had three uncles who organised boxing promotions in Santiago, and he reckoned that by the time he was 15 he had taken part in more than 300 contests at ten cents a fight. His official amateur record showed 145 bouts of which he lost only one. He made his professional debut at the age of 18 as a lightweight, and lost once in 18 outings before making his home in Mexico in 1962.

After winning 55 of his 59 contests, he challenged Curtis Cokes for the world welterweight title in California in 1969 and stopped the highly rated Texan in 13 rounds. Cokes was convinced it was a freak performance and he travelled to Mexico City confident that he was going to regain the championship. This time Napoles stopped him in ten rounds to emphasise the fact that he was exceptionally talented. He had a vast repertoire of punches, and was a master of pacing a fight and increasing his power just as his opponents sensed they were getting the better of him.

Emile Griffith and Ernie Lopez were both seen off by Napoles before he suffered a shock defeat against 9-1 underdog Billy Backus in Syracuse, the referee stopping the title fight in the fourth round because the Cuban had sustained a cut eye. Six months later, on 4 June 1971, Napoles regained his crown by stopping Backus in eight rounds.

He came to London in 1970 to defend the title against British champion Ralph Charles, and just as ringside spectators were beginning to think he was overrated he knocked out Charles in the seventh round with a blistering volley of punches that were thrown so quickly that his gloves were a blur.

Napoles mowed down all the leading challengers, but then reached too high when making a bid for the world middleweight championship against Carlos Monzon in Paris in 1974. The Argentinian was too big and strong for him and pounded his way to a seventh-round victory.

Rumours gathered strength that Napoles was taking boxing less seriously after his hammering by Monzon. He was said to be enjoying the high life and putting little effort into training. John Stracey, a competent and determined fighter from London's East End, chose just the right moment to tackle him in Mexico City on 6 December 1975. He survived the shock of a first-round knock-down to fight back and wear down the old champion. The referee stopped the bout in the seventh round with Napoles helpless on the ropes as Stracey battered away at him with both hands.

It was a magnificent performance by Stracey, but the Napoles he beat was nothing like the force he had been during the several years when he looked the greatest welterweight champion since Sugar Ray Robinson's days in the 10 stone 7 pounds division.

Opposite: Jose Napoles knocks Roger Menetrey back with a thundering left hook during his defence of the world welterweight title in Grenoble in 1973. The Cuban scored a comfortable 15-round points victory.

AZUMAH NELSON

Azumah Nelson
Born Accra, Ghana, 19.7.1958
Career span: 1979-
World featherweight champion
1984-88; world super
featherweight champion 1988-
Ring record: 32 fights, 31 wins,
1 loss (1 stoppage); 22 inside-
the-distance wins

Azumah Nelson launches a
long-range missile of a right —
the style of power punching
that has taken the African to
the top.

Azumah Nelson rivals Dick Tiger as the greatest fighter ever to come out of Africa. Like Tiger, he became a double world champion, winning championships at featherweight and super featherweight, and when he started to eye the lightweight title held by Pernell Whitaker a lot of experts rated his chances of completing a championship hat-trick.

Nelson's story is not the traditional one of a rags-to-riches fighter — he was the son of a wealthy merchant in his native Ghana and money was never his motivation for taking up boxing. He did not have his first contest until the comparatively late age of 17, but he quickly took the eye with his natural boxing skills and devastating punching power.

Within three years of his first bout he won a gold medal at featherweight in the 1978 Commonwealth Games, at which the bantamweight champion was Irishman Barry McGuigan. The following year, while doing his national service in the army, he collected another gold medal in the fiercely competitive World Military Games. Beaten only twice in 50 amateur contests, he turned professional in 1979 and went immediately into the ten-round class.

After winning his debut on points over ten rounds in Accra, he won the Ghanaian featherweight championship in his second fight and within another

18 months he had captured the vacant Commonwealth 9 stone title by knocking out Australian Brian Roberts in five rounds.

Nelson got too ambitious when he challenged outstanding world featherweight champion Salvador Sanchez for his title in New York on 21 July 1982. He came in as a last-minute substitute in only his 14th professional fight and put up a brave challenge before being stopped in the 15th and final round. Sanchez would, no doubt, have featured in my top 100 but for his tragic death in a car crash just a few weeks after his winning defence against the African.

In December 1984 Nelson, never afraid to go into his opponent's territory, travelled to San Juan to challenge two-time world champion Wilfredo Gomez for his WBC featherweight title and powered his way to victory in 11 rounds. Nelson defended his championship six times, including a one-round demolition of Britain's Pat Cowdell whom he took out with as good a left uppercut as I have ever seen delivered.

Cocky to the point of arrogance, Nelson did not go out of his way to win popularity with some of his taunting comments about opponents, but there was no questioning his ability. He was finding the 9 stone poundage difficult to make, and he relinquished his crown to go in search of the super featherweight championship. He fought Mexican Mario Martinez for the vacant title in Los Angeles on 29 February 1988 and gave a magnificent all-round boxing display on the way to a 12-round points victory. In a return match he knocked Martinez senseless with a vicious barrage of punches in the final round.

Nelson had set his sights on a big-money showdown with Barry McGuigan, but Jim McDonnell got the doubtful privilege of sharing the ring with him after he forced the Irish idol into retirement. The Londoner put up a brave show but was outgunned, and after knocking him out in the 12th round for a fifth successful defence of his super featherweight title Nelson reached for a bridge too far against Pernell Whitaker. He battled bravely but was clearly outpointed over 12 rounds in a bold but abortive move into the lightweight division.

MICHAEL NUNN

Michael Nunn
Born Davenport, Iowa,
14.4.1963
Career span: 1984-
World middleweight champion
1988-
Ring record: 35 fights, 35 wins;
23 inside-the-distance wins

Michael Nunn, like so many youngsters, was drawn to boxing through watching Muhammad Ali in action on television while he was a kid growing up in Davenport, Iowa. He picked up a lot of Ali's flashy tricks, and early in his professional career he was dismissed by the critics as too much of a showboating exhibitionist who slapped rather than punched properly with the knuckle part of the glove. But Nunn silenced the sneerers when he stopped 1984 Olympic gold medallist Frank Tate in nine rounds to win the IBF middleweight title in 1988.

His victory over Tate in his 31st professional contest earned him new respect from opponents and ringside reporters alike. Until this showdown in Las Vegas on 28 July 1988 it was 'Golden Boy' Tate who had been considered the better prospect, but Nunn dictated the fight from the first bell and demoralised his opponent with a magnificent display of boxing. Tate was rated the stronger puncher, but it was Nunn who went closest to

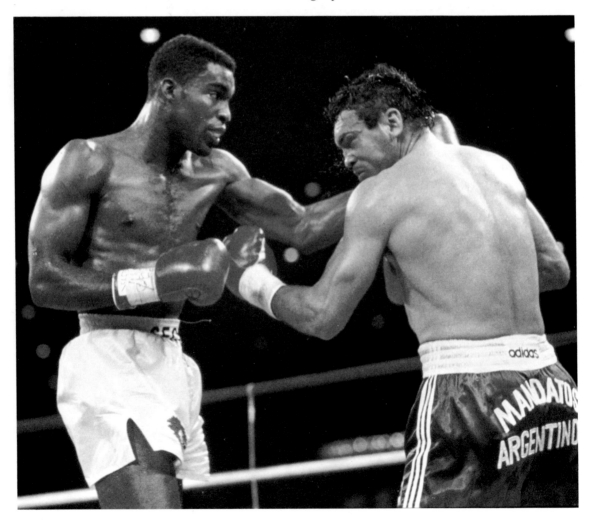

170

scoring a knock-out when he dropped Tate with a thumping left to the body near the end of the eighth round. Immediately the ninth round started Nunn drove Tate back to the ropes and was hitting him at will when the referee quite rightly stepped in. It was a win that did wonders for the confidence of Nunn, and he began to add jolting power to his fancy dan boxing skills. He stopped the alleged 'iron man' of the ring, Juan Roldan, in eight rounds, and then poleaxed his rival, WBA champion Sumbu Kalambay, in just 88 seconds.

Standing 6 feet 2 inches, he had learned how to make best use of the reach and height advantage that he enjoyed in most fights, and from being a safety-first boxer who was often jeered he developed into a great crowd-pleaser. Promoter Bob Arum went so far as to describe Nunn as 'the best boxer since the days of Muhammad Ali'. I think Sugar Ray Leonard might have wanted to dispute that, and Arum seemed to change his tune after Nunn slipped back into his old boring ways when he struggled to steal a majority points victory over tough Iran Barkley in a title defence in August 1989. 'Nunn must realise that he has a duty to entertain the public', said Arum after Michael's pedestrian points victory had been booed by the spectators.

Nunn then started to undo all his good self-promotion work by getting involved in a couple of out-of-the-ring altercations, and he had a bust-up with the management team that had guided him to world title status after an amateur career during which he won a Golden Gloves title.

But Nunn continued to do all the right things inside the ring, and a points victory over world welterweight champion Marlon Starling in Las Vegas on his 27th birthday on 14 April 1990 increased his stock. He started looking forward to big-money fights against the likes of Don Curry, Thomas Hearns and — the one he wanted most of all — Sugar Ray Leonard.

Opposite: Michael Nunn connects with a left on his way to an eighth-round knock-out victory over Juan Domingo Roldan in their world middleweight title fight in Las Vegas in 1988.

LASZLO PAPP

Laszlo Papp
Born Hungary, 25.3.1926
Career span: 1957-65
European middleweight
champion 1962-65
Ring record: 29 fights, 26 wins;
15 inside-the-distance wins, 3
draws

Laszlo Papp knocks out
Frenchman Francois Anewy in
the third round of his fifth
professional fight in Paris in
1958.

Laszlo Papp is a legendary figure in boxing because of his feat of becoming the first man to win three successive Olympic titles. He then became the first 'Iron Curtain' boxer to be allowed officially to turn professional, and was undefeated and ready to challenge for the world middleweight title when the Hungarian Government suddenly barred him on the grounds that his newly-won wealth was not compatible with his country's socialist principles. How Laszlo must wish that glasnost had come 25 years earlier!

Papp, a stocky, compact southpaw with a lethal left hook, started boxing as an amateur in Budapest in the last year of the Second World War and was coached by national team trainer Zsiga Adler – 'Uncle' Zsiga, Laszlo used to call him. He came to London in 1948 to capture his first Olympic Games gold medal at middleweight, outpointing Britain's Johnny Wright in the final. I took part in the 1952 Olympics in Helsinki and saw Papp boxing beautifully to win the light middleweight title. This was a newly-introduced division. If he had defended his middleweight championship he would have come up against a young American called Floyd Patterson.

What impressed me most about Papp was the accuracy of his punches. He was happiest when counter punching but could also be the aggressor when it suited him, and he rarely wasted a single punch.

Dissatisfied with his token job as a librarian, Laszlo already had the taste to become a professional, and when he approached the Hungarian authorities he was told they would consider his request only if he won a third gold medal in the 1956 Olympics in Melbourne. Papp duly did his duty, outpointing future world light heavyweight champion Jose Torres for his record hat-trick.

The Hungarian authorities, picking up the pieces after the 1956 uprising, dragged their heels when Laszlo pressed for his right to become a professional. They finally gave in on the understanding that his wife, Erszebet, and 11-year-old son remained in Budapest while he based himself in Vienna, starting a paid career at the age of 31.

For many years Papp had suffered from brittle bones in his hands, but this did not stop him punching his weight and in eight years as a professional he stopped 15 of his 29 opponents. He won the European championship in 1962 by stopping Dane Chris Christensen in seven rounds, and over the next three years only British champion Mick Leahy managed to stay the course with him.

Papp, a handsome man with a distinctive moustache and crinkly black hair, was being lined up for a shot at the world title held by Brooklyn's Joey Giardello when the Hungarian Government suddenly lowered the iron curtain on him. They played on his national pride, and pointed out that it was bad for the morale of his countrymen to see him flaunting his riches while they were working conscientiously for the good of Hungary.

Knowing that he could not get his wife and son out of Budapest, Papp reluctantly retired at the age of 38 and became the national team coach. He had never been beaten as a professional and lost just 12 of 230 amateur contests. In another time and another place, I am convinced he would have become an outstanding world professional champion.

FLOYD PATTERSON

Floyd Patterson
Born Waco, North Carolina,
4.1.1935
Career span: 1952-72
World heavyweight champion
1956-62
Ring record: 64 fights, 55 wins,
8 losses (4 stoppages); 40
inside-the-distance wins, 1
draw

Floyd Patterson had the fastest fists in the west, and I can vouch for that statement. We fought at Wembley in 1966, and I obtained first-hand evidence of the speed of his punches. I had been giving at least as good as Floyd had been dishing out in the first three rounds, but was suddenly overwhelmed early in the fourth by a lightning combination of left and right hooks. I went down for a count of nine with blood streaming from my old hooter. 'Blimey,' I thought to myself, 'I'd better do something about this.' So I went looking for him with my faithful left hook, but he found me instead with a corker of a straight right and it was goodnight nurse. I'd been hit harder in my life but never with quicker punches.

Guided by Cus D'Amato – the man who later discovered Mike Tyson – Floyd followed Rocky Marciano as world heavyweight champion when he knocked out 'Ageless' Archie Moore in five rounds in a fight for the vacant title on 30 November 1956. At 21 years and 11 months he was then the youngest heavyweight champion of all time, a record he has since lost to Tyson. Just like Tyson, he was discovered while boxing at a corrective school to which he had been sent after getting into trouble on the mean streets of Brooklyn.

Boxing brought order and discipline to his life, and he turned professional after winning the gold medal in the middleweight division at the 1952 Helsinki Olympics. He developed a distinctive style, launching sudden two-handed attacks from behind a high guard that became known as his 'peek-a-boo' method.

Floyd did not have the best of physiques for what was to become the era of the super heavyweights and he adopted risky attacking tactics in a bid to make up for his lack of weight and reach. He would lunge forward with both feet off the ground in an effort to get maximum power into his punches, but it meant he often left himself open to counter blows and in seven of his 13 title bouts he was knocked down 16 times. The cautious D'Amato rarely allowed Patterson into the ring with legitimate contenders and he steered Floyd through successful defences against Tommy Jackson, Pete Rademacher (the 1956 Olympic champion making his professional debut), Roy Harris and Britain's Brian London, who hardly made an aggressive move before being knocked out in the 11th round. Then Floyd's world was turned upside down when he underestimated Ingemar Johansson and was stopped in three rounds after walking into the right hand punch that became known as 'Ingo's Bingo'. Patterson created history by becoming the first heavyweight champion to regain the title but his 'bogeyman' was waiting around the corner for him in the menacing shape of Sonny Liston. When they first met in Chicago in 1962 Liston bludgeoned him to defeat in two minutes six seconds. Floyd was so ashamed of his performance that he left the stadium by a back exit wearing a false moustache and glasses so that nobody would recognise him and perhaps ridicule him. No wonder some people called this complex character Freud Patterson. Ten months later Liston gave an action replay of the first fight, this time stopping the powerless Patterson in two minutes ten seconds.

Archie Moore bows to the supremacy of Floyd Patterson, who became world heavyweight champion at the age of 21 in 1956.

He did not don a disguise when leaving the dressing-room after his second humiliation. He knew he had to learn to live with himself, and he regained his self-respect with two brave shows against Muhammad Ali. He made unsuccessful bids to regain the title for a second time against first Ali and then Jimmy Ellis.

Floyd had been a top-quality fighter, but never an outstanding champion because he simply wasn't big enough and had a suspect chin. He will always be haunted by the memory of Liston, who I felt sure could have beaten Floyd 100 times out of 100. But 'Freudian Floyd' ironed out his psychological problems after retiring and gave a lot back to the game he served with such distinction as a New York boxing commissioner.

WILLIE PEP

Willie Pep must have danced, skipped and run more miles during his 26-year career than any other boxer in history. Willie was not a devastating puncher and relied on his skill and speed of foot to outpace and out-manoeuvre opponents. He was so elusive that he was nicknamed 'Will o' the Wisp', and he won no fewer than 165 contests on points. Willie boxed his way through a remarkable total of 1,964 rounds, not including dozens of exhibition bouts. Just to put that in context, Pep boxed more rounds than Rocky Marciano, Joe Louis, Muhammad Ali, Larry Holmes and Sonny Liston put together. I boxed 381 rounds over a period of 17 years and thought I was overworked, but full-of-pep Pep made me seem almost like a part-time professional.

There are even more remarkable statistics to come about the man born Guglielmo Papaleo, the son of a Sicilian immigrant. Willie won the Connecticut State amateur titles at flyweight and bantamweight and then turned professional at the age of 18. He put together 62 contests without a single defeat in his first three years as a professional before dropping a narrow points decision to future world lightweight champion Sammy Angott. Willie then went another five years without a defeat. No modern boxer has come close to his astonishing record of just one loss and one draw in his first 137 fights. He set another record in 1942 when, aged 20, he became the youngest world featherweight champion in history. Willie

Willie Pep
(originally Guglielmo Papaleo)
Born Middletown,
Connecticut, 19.9.1922
Career span: 1940-66
World featherweight champion
1942-50
Ring record: 242 fights, 230
wins, 11 losses (6 stoppages);
65 inside-the-distance wins, 1
draw

Willie Pep scores with a right hook on his way to a revenge victory over Sandy Saddler in the second of their world title wars in New York in 1949. Pep won on points over 15 rounds.

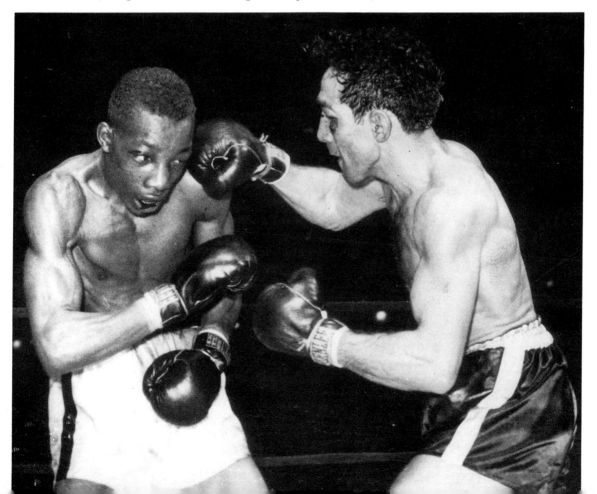

ruled the featherweight roost for six years before he got involved in a violent four-fight series with Sandy Saddler. The rule book was tossed aside as the two bitter rivals launched themselves into all-out wars in which no holds were barred. Saddler came out top with three victories to one by Pep and each time the world 9 stone title was at stake.

Willie won 11 championship fights and should have been a wealthy man, but gambling and business losses combined with the alimony needed for three ex-wives meant he had to box on far longer than was good for him. He got himself back into championship contention by winning 60 of 64 contests after losing his crown to Saddler, and was rewarded with a non-title fight against new world champion Hogan 'Kid' Bassey. The tough Nigerian stopped Pep in nine rounds, and that should have been his swansong. But pressing financial problems forced him into a comeback after a four-year retirement, and he won nine contests in 1965 before an ordinary fighter called Calvin Woodland outpointed the 43-year-old veteran on 16 March 1966 to convince him that it was time to quit the ring for good. He became a referee, moving around the ring at a rate of knots that reminded ringside spectators of his golden days as the fleet-footed Fred Astaire of boxing.

PASCUAL PEREZ

Pascual Perez was like a sawn-off Rocky Marciano, standing just 4 feet 11 inches tall but packing a wallop in both fists that could lift opponents off their feet. Known to his fans at home in Argentina as Pascualito, he dominated the world of little fighting men for six years after winning the Olympic gold medal at flyweight in London in 1948.

It was a real rags-to-riches rise to fame for Perez, the second youngest of nine children born to poor parents. The temptation was to turn professional as soon as he won the Olympic title, but he was befriended by Argentinian dictator Juan Peron, who presented his family with a large house and persuaded Pascual — then working as a caretaker — to continue to box as an amateur for the honour of his country.

He finally turned professional with Peron's blessing in 1952 at the age of 26, and proceeded to pound his way to the top of the ranking lists. Perez was unbeaten in his first 50 fights and took the world 8 stone championship from Japan's Yoshio Shirai in his 24th contest. He made 14 successful title defences, and included among his victims was British champion Dai Dower. The skilful Welshman was taken out with a single punch in the first round of a world title challenge in Buenos Aires in 1957.

Pascual Perez
Born Mendoza, Argentina,
4.3.1926
Career span: 1952-64
World flyweight champion
1955-60
Ring record: 91 fights, 83 wins,
7 losses (3 stoppages); 56
inside-the-distance wins, 1
draw

Pascual Perez retains his world
flyweight championship in
Tokyo in 1955 with a fifth
round knock-out victory over
challenger Yoshio Shirai.

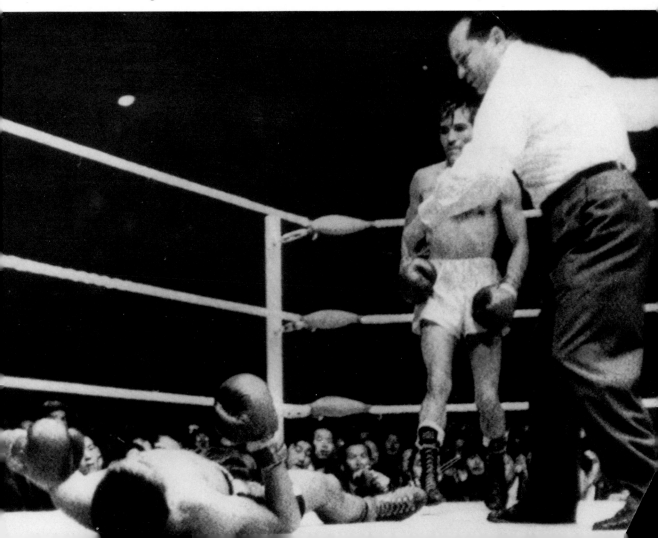

Pascual got himself involved in politics when he was criticised for making several visits to Peron after his exile, and then he too went into temporary exile after being involved in a car crash in which a motorcyclist died. It was ruled an accident, but Perez did not hang around for the court hearing. Throughout 1959 he fought only in Japan, dropping a points decision to Sadao Yaoita in a non-title fight and then stopping him in 13 rounds in the return with the championship at stake.

His title was snatched from him in Bangkok on 16 April 1960 when he was outpointed by Pone Kingpetch, who had a six-inch height advantage and was supported from the ringside by the King of Thailand. The years were beginning to tell on the 34-year-old Argentinian, and in a return match with Kingpetch five months later he was beaten in eight rounds, the first time he had been stopped in 57 professional contests.

Much of the fire had gone out of Perez, but he continued to fight for another four years, and 27 successive victories convinced him that he was still a force on the world stage. But then four defeats in six fights, including two stoppages against opponents he would have destroyed in his peak years, made him realise that, at 38, he had come to the end of the road.

Life did not treat him kindly after he had lost the world championship. His wife, who had also been his business manager, divorced him and he was left virtually penniless, continuing to fight purely to keep food on the table. In 1977 he slipped into a coma and died at the age of 50 from liver failure. But his name will always live on in boxing – along with that of Carlos Monzon – as the greatest fighters ever to come out of Argentina.

SUGAR RAY ROBINSON

Sugar Ray Robinson – the *original* Sugar Ray – is second only to Muhammad Ali in my book as the greatest boxer of all time. I shall just quickly summarise his career to explain why he was considered by many to be, pound for pound, the most formidable fighter ever to climb into the ring: he was world welterweight champion for four years before abdicating when he won the world middleweight crown, a title he captured a record five times; he was on the brink of winning the world light heavyweight championship until overcome by heat exhaustion when in sight of victory against Joey Maxim; in a span of 25 years he contested 25 world title fights; he fought 19 world champions, never took the ten-second count in 202 fights and was beaten only 19 times.

When he was a kid known by his real name of Walker Smith, he used to tap dance on the sidewalks of Harlem to earn money for his divorced mother who had brought him and his sisters from Detroit to New York City. He was hooked on the fight game from an early age and often carried the bag of his idol Joe Louis when the 'Brown Bomber' was going to and from the gymnasium. In an exceptional amateur career he won all of his 85 contests, 69 of them inside the distance and 40 in the first round.

He turned professional in 1940 after winning Golden Gloves titles at featherweight and lightweight, and – according to legend – he acquired the name Ray Robinson when substituting for another boxer of that name. His manager, George Gainford, claimed to have given him his nickname. A reporter said, 'That boy of yours is a real sweet mover'. 'Yes,' said George, 'as sweet as sugar.'

Sugar Ray's most distinctive characteristic apart from his flashing fists was his rhythm and balance. He used to appear in a nightclub act as a dancer, and you could have set him to music when he was performing in the ring with a grace and a style that was almost balletic ... until he let fly with his ferocious combinations that owed more to ballistics than the ballet. His physique was just about perfect: loosely muscled and with powerful shoulders tapering to a narrow waist all set on long, slim and strong legs on which he could have run marathons.

A charismatic character outside as well as inside the ring, Robinson won 40 successive fights before dropping his first decision to the 'Bronx Bull' Jake La Motta. It was their second of five meetings and the only one in which Ray came off second best. He went unbeaten for the next eight years and 91 fights, and on 20 December 1946 he won the vacant world welterweight title by outpointing Tommy Bell over 15 rounds in New York City.

Sugar Ray made five successful defences before very reluctantly relinquishing the title, having ripped away the world middleweight championship from his old rival La Motta with a savage 13th-round victory in Chicago on St Valentine's Day 1951. Travelling with an entourage that included his personal hairdresser, a French tutor, a trumpeter and a dwarf, this born entertainer took things too easily on a tour of Europe. He completely underestimated British champion Randolph Turpin, who

Ray Robinson
(originally Walker Smith)
Born Detroit, Michigan,
3.5.1921
Career span: 1940-65
World welterweight champion
1946-51; world middleweight
champion 1951-60
Ring record: 202 fights, 175
wins, 19 losses (1 stoppage);
110 inside-the-distance wins, 6
draws; 2 no contests

Ray Robinson – the original 'Sugar Ray'.

relieved him of his title with a brilliantly earned points victory at Earls Court on 10 July 1951.

Robinson whipped himself into magnificent shape for the return at the Polo Grounds, New York just 64 days later, but was struggling with a badly cut right eye as the evenly balanced fight reached the last moments of the tenth round. Then, like a true champion, he produced a winning punch just when it was needed. A thundering right cross dropped Turpin for nine, and he was under heavy attack on the ropes when referee Ruby Goldstein stopped the fight with eight seconds of the round left. An indication of Robinson's magnetic pulling power is that there was a crowd of 61,370 at the Polo Grounds, a record attendance outside the heavyweight division.

Following winning defences against Carl 'Bobo' Olson and Rocky Graziano, Sugar Ray challenged Joey Maxim for the world light heavyweight championship. The ringside temperature was well over 100 degrees – too hot for referee Goldstein, who collapsed at the end of the tenth round and had to be replaced. Robinson was way ahead on points, but he was so exhausted and dehydrated that he was unable to come out of his corner for the 14th round. It was the only time he was ever stopped, and it is fair to say that he was conquered by the conditions rather than his opponent.

He announced his retirement from boxing and was inactive for two years before making a comeback in January 1955. In his seventh fight of the year, on 9 December 1955, he recaptured the world middleweight title for a second time by knocking out 'Bobo' Olson in two rounds. Then, on 2 January 1957, he lost the championship to fighting Mormon Gene Fullmer when he was outpointed over 15 rounds. Their return title fight four months later ended with Fullmer counted out in the fifth round and Robinson back on the middleweight throne.

Sugar Ray was an ex-champion before the year was out, dropping a points decision to Carmen Basilio after 15 ruthlessly hard rounds. That would have been enough for most men, but the extraordinary Robinson won the title for a fifth time on 25 March 1958 when he outpointed Basilio in another slam-bang of a fight.

Time was beginning to weigh on Sugar Ray's shoulders and everybody would have been happy to see him retire as champion, but he needed a vast income to support his flamboyant lifestyle. He lost his title to Boston fireman Paul Pender and, for once, was also outpointed in the return. At the age of 40 he held Gene Fullmer to a draw in an NBA middleweight championship contest, and boxed on for another four years before at last conceding that his magic had deserted him. His death at the age of 68 in 1989 from Alzheimer's disease extinguished one of boxing's brightest ever lights. The legend of Sugar Ray will live on forever.

ERNIE RODERICK

Ernie Roderick
Born Liverpool, 25.1.1914
Career span: 1931-50
British welterweight champion
1939-48; British middle-
weight champion 1945-46
Ring record: 138 fights, 110
wins, 24 losses; 44 inside-the-
distance wins, 4 draws

Ernie Roderick was one of those unfortunate boxers whose peak years were lost to the Second World War, but either side of the war years he provided enough evidence to prove that he was one of the most gifted technicians ever produced by Britain. He was a great admirer of his fellow-Merseysider Nel Tarleton, and admitted that he based his style of boxing on that of the featherweight friend who eventually became his brother-in-law when he married Nel's younger sister.

Ernie, who boxed regularly from the age of eight, had been a professional for nine years before he got the chance to challenge for the British welterweight championship at Liverpool Stadium on 23 March 1939. He was matched with a Scotsman called Harry Owens, who fought under the ring name of old-time bare-knuckle fighter Jake Kilrain. Roderick was a solid rather than spectacular puncher, but he hit too hard for Kilrain, who was counted out in the eighth round.

The victory earned Ernie a crack at the world welterweight championship at the new Harringay Arena, a contest arranged by famous Liverpool matchmaker Johnny Best and promoted by the Greyhound Racing Association. It was just Roderick's luck that the title was in the keeping of one of the all-time greats, Henry Armstrong. 'Homicide Hank' went into such a deep sleep in the dressing-room before the fight that he had to be slapped awake by his manager Eddie Mead. There was nothing sleepy about Armstrong in the ring, however, and he chased and harried Roderick for 15 rounds on his way to a clear points victory. Only Ernie's great defensive skills coupled with his courage saved him from a knock-out defeat against an opponent who was conceding nearly 11 pounds.

There was no disputing Roderick's domination of the domestic scene, and he held the British 10 stone 7 pounds title for nine years. He won a Lonsdale Belt outright by beating Norman Snow and Arthur Danahar, and then immediately after the war he captured the British middleweight crown by outpointing Hampshire's Vince Hawkins. He then went hunting the European welterweight championship relinquished by Marcel Cerdan, and outpointed French Algerian Omar Kouidri to win the vacant title.

Ernie chose to concentrate on his 'natural' welterweight division after losing the British middleweight title back to Hawkins, and travelled to Paris in 1947 to defend the European championship against Frenchman Robert Villemain, who forced him to retire after nine rounds.

He returned to domestic matters, and successfully defended his British welterweight crown against Gwyn Williams and Eric Boon before being judged to have lost on points to Henry Hall in 1948, a decision described to me by that fine reporter Peter Wilson as the worst he had ever seen in a British championship contest.

Roderick retired two years later at the age of 36 and after a 19-year career in which he was always a credit to British boxing. He might have achieved much more on the world stage but for the war cutting into his career.

Opposite: Ernie Roderick stuns Henry Armstrong with a right uppercut, but 'Homicide Hank' quickly recovered to pound his way to a points victory.

BARNEY ROSS

Barney Ross
(originally Barnet David
Rosofsky)
Born New York City,
23.12.1909
Career span: 1929-38
World lightweight, junior
lightweight and welterweight
champion 1933-38
Ring record: 81 fights, 74 wins,
4 losses; 22 inside-the-distance
wins, 3 draws

Barney Ross was a ring hero, then a war hero, and a hero for all seasons of the Jewish fraternity, for whom he represented the last of the truly great Jewish fighters who illuminated the 1920s and 1930s with their memorable boxing exploits. If a film was ever made of his life and times it would rival anything in the *Rocky* series.

When Barnet Rosofsky was born in Manhattan, doctors feared for his life because at birth he was found to be suffering from arthritis and a weakness of the lungs. So Barney was a battler from life's first bell. He moved with his family to gangster-controlled Chicago in the roaring '20s, and was coached as an amateur by former world lightweight title contender Packey McFarland at, of all places, the Young Catholic Youth Centre. He won two Golden Gloves titles as a featherweight, and quickly became known as the 'Pride of the Ghetto' to his army of fans on Chicago's tough West Side. Ross had no option but to turn professional in 1929 after gunmen shot and murdered his father in his grocery store. 'I had to become the breadwinner for the family', he said.

He perfected an aggressive style of fighting, forcing opponents back behind a whirlwind of punches that used to overwhelm them. Barney was beaten only twice in his first 60 contests and in 1933 won the world lightweight and junior welterweight titles by outpointing Tony Canzoneri over ten rounds. They were re-matched over 15 rounds and Ross again won on points, using his bewildering speed of both hands and feet to unsettle his tough and talented opponent.

Barney, who punched too quickly to pack a really devastating blow, had to relinquish his lightweight title because of increasing weight. In 1934 he set his sights on the welterweight championship and was involved in an unforgettable three-fight series with Irish-born ring master Jimmy 'Baby Face' McLarnin. All three classic contests went the full 15 rounds, Ross winning the first and third bouts to confirm his standing as the world's number one welterweight.

Blessed with a granite chin and a big heart, Barney was never stopped throughout his career and managed to last the distance against a peak-power Henry Armstrong in a 15-round thriller staged at Long Island City Bowl on 31 May 1938. Armstrong won on points to add the world welterweight crown to his collection, and Barney decided to retire at the age of 29 after what was only his second defeat in 15 world championship contests, all of which went the distance.

He joined the US Marines immediately after the Japanese attack on Pearl Harbor, and declined a soft desk job. He qualified as a sergeant and was decorated for bravery after being wounded in action during a jungle battle at Guadalcanal. Barney fought his greatest battle to beat a drug addiction caused by an overdose of morphine while he was being treated for his war wounds. After earning the admiration of his many fans by getting himself straightened out he was finally beaten by cancer, and died following a long illness at the age of 58. Barney remains a hero for all seasons.

Opposite: Barney Ross staggers Tony Canzoneri with a right uppercut on the way to retaining his world lightweight title with a 15-round points victory in New York in 1933.

SANDY SADDLER

Sandy Saddler
Born Boston, Massachusetts,
23.6.1926
Career span: 1944-56
World junior lightweight
champion 1949-50; world
featherweight champion
1948-56
Ring record: 162 fights, 144
wins, 16 losses (1 stoppage);
103 inside-the-distance wins, 2
draws

Sandy Saddler was the first world champion forced to give up his title because of an accident *outside* the ring. He was involved in a car crash while travelling as a passenger in a New York taxicab in 1956 and suffered injuries that threatened his eyesight. Reluctantly, at the age of 30, he retired from the ring and as the featherweight champion of the world.

Saddler was never really a popular champion because he tore the title away from the idolised Willie Pep, winning a vicious, 'anything-goes' four-fight series 3-1. After taking Pep's crown for a second time in 1950 Saddler was considered too choosy about which challengers he met, but he had

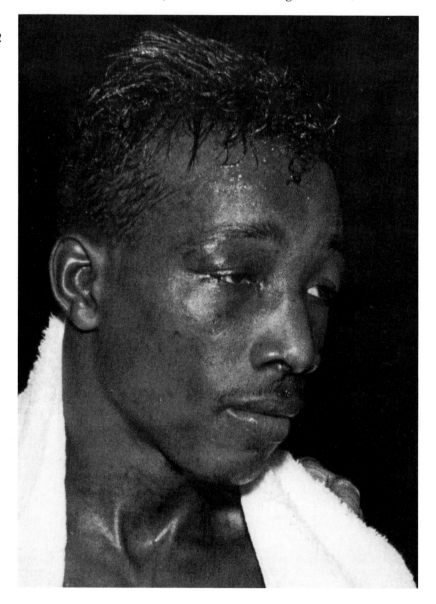

Sandy Saddler, who really made the feathers fly.

come up the hard way and was in no mood to let his championship go easily. He was quite understandably bitter that he had had to pay Pep a reported $25,000 for the privilege of fighting him for the title the first time around.

The son of a West Indian immigrant, Sandy grew up in the tough New York district of Harlem and was a professional by the age of 17. He had to battle through 93 contests before finally getting a shot at Pep in New York on 29 October 1948, winning by a dramatic fourth-round knock-out to become the new 9 stone champion of the world. There has rarely been a taller featherweight title-holder. He stood just over 5 feet 8 inches and had long, spidery arms and legs. Making full use of his enormous reach, he would keep opponents on the end of a snaking left jab and then knock the heart out of them with destructive hooks and uppercuts thrown in sudden clusters. Evidence of his punching ferocity is that he won more than 100 fights inside the distance.

Pep regained the title with a points victory at the end of a savage brawl in New York four months after Saddler's first victory. Willie had to have 11 stitches in facial wounds, while Sandy was fit to fight again the following month. Before the year was out he had beaten Orlando Zulueta for the vacant world junior lightweight title, but the only thing that interested him was the chance of a third fight with Pep. The 'Will o' the Wisp' wilted in their showdown in New York on 8 September 1950, Saddler winning in the eighth round. He confirmed his superiority over Pep the following year with a ninth-round victory in a fight regarded by onlookers as one of the roughest ring battles ever witnessed in modern boxing.

The featherweight championship was then put in cold storage while Saddler served Uncle Sam for two years as a US Army private based for much of his time in West Germany. He kept in trim by training with the Army boxing division and on his discharge resumed as champion, clearly outpointing interim title-claimant Teddy Davis over 15 rounds in New York on 25 February 1955.

Sandy made one more defence – a 13th-round stoppage of Flash Elorde in San Francisco on 18 January 1956 – before the crash that ended his career when he was past his peak but still the unquestioned number one featherweight in the world.

VICENTE SALDIVAR

*Vicente Saldivar
(originally Vicente Samuel
Saldivar Garcia)
Born Mexico City, 3.5.1943
Career span: 1961-73
World featherweight champion
1964-70
Ring record: 41 fights, 38 wins,
3 losses (1 disqualification, 2
stoppages); 27 inside-the-
distance wins*

Vicente Saldivar was one of the finest fighters to come out of Mexico, and to say that is just about the highest possible praise because the Mexicans have produced an army of exceptional champions. I choose Saldivar to represent Mexico in this hit parade because in Britain his name is revered almost as much as in his own country.

He will be remembered for all time by British fight fans in general and Welsh supporters in particular for his epic three-fight serial against 'Merthyr Marvel' Howard Winstone, one of the most gifted of all post-war British champions. They met in London in 1965, in Cardiff in the summer of 1967, and finally in Mexico City in October 1967. Saldivar won the first two contests by the narrowest of points margins, and then came from behind to stop Winstone in round 12 of their last battle. It says a lot for the great sport of boxing that after they had knocked hell out of each other Vicente and Howard became close mates, and the Welshman was Vicente's personal guest at his home during the 1968 Olympics in Mexico City.

Saldivar's story is the classic poverty-to-prosperity tale that can be traced in the background of so many fighters. He was one of a family of nine brought up on the shanty side of town in Mexico City, and became a fighter because it was the natural thing to do. Vicente won a Mexican Golden Gloves title as a bantamweight, which spoke volumes for his ability because in Mexico bantamweight boxers almost grow on trees.

Standing only 5 feet 3 inches tall, Saldivar had a short body that was packed with power and his square, southpaw stance made him an awkward handful for orthodox opponents. He became Mexican featherweight champion in 1964 in his 24th contest and this set him up for a crack at the world title held by skilful Cuban champion Sugar Ramos. Most experts expected Ramos to retain the championship, but Saldivar would not be denied and crash-bashed his way to an 11th-round victory. He was a fighting champion and successfully defended the title eight times in just over three years before announcing his retirement after his third victory over Winstone.

Saldivar got itchy feet and fists after 18 months out of action and made a comeback in July 1969 when he outpointed Jose Legra, one of the fighters who had briefly held the world title following his retirement. He then travelled to Rome to challenge Frenchman Johnny Famechon for his old crown on 9 May 1970, and a hard-earned 15-round points win restored him as champion.

On paper he was favourite to retain the title against Japan's Kuniaki Shibata in Tijuana in 1970, but after being badly cut his famous stamina suddenly deserted him and, in the 13th round, he was stopped for the first time in his career. His only previous defeat had been a disqualification in his 17th fight against Emiro Durgel, which he quickly avenged.

Vicente tried another comeback in 1973 after a two-year lay-off, but failed in a bid to win the featherweight title for a third time when Brazilian Eder Jofre knocked him out in four rounds. The boxing world was rocked 12 years later by the news that Vicente had died of a heart attack at the age of 42.

*Opposite: Vicente Saldivar
(left) meets Howard Winstone
head-on in Cardiff in 1967.
This was the second of their
three classic contests. The
Mexican master won the first
two on points, and the third
when he forced a 12th-round
retirement.*

DAVE SANDS

*Dave Sands
(originally David Ritchie)
Born Burnt Ridge, New South
Wales, 4.2.1926
Career span: 1943-52
Australian and
Commonwealth middleweight
champion 1946-52; Australian
light heavy and heavyweight
champion 1948-52
Ring record: 104 fights, 93
wins, 8 losses (1 stoppage); 62
inside-the-distance wins, 1
draw; 2 no contests*

Dave Sands put Australia on the boxing map with his ring exploits in the immediate post-war years, and was poised to become even more famous when he was killed in tragic circumstances. He had signed to fight British champion Randolph Turpin in London for the vacant world middleweight title when the truck he was driving to a lumber camp in Dundog, Australia, overturned. Sands was trapped underneath and died shortly after being rushed to hospital. He was 26 and in his prime.

The son of an Aborigine mother and a Puerto Rican father, Sands started to box with makeshift gloves against his three brothers in the outback of northern New South Wales. When he was 16 he hitchhiked 300 miles south to Newcastle to join his eldest brother, who had started a professional career. He was given a job cleaning the gymnasium, and when gym owner Tom Maguire watched him sparring he realised that this was one of the greatest natural fighters he had ever seen. Instead of cleaning gyms Dave started to clean up the opposition after making his professional debut at the age of 17.

He won his first 18 contests inside the distance, showing little polish but punching with such strength with either fist that it cancelled out the advantage his opponents had in skill and experience. Dave gradually learned orthodox techniques to harness his raw power, and in 1946 – his fourth year as a professional – he annexed the Australian middleweight and light heavyweight titles. Stories filtered back to England that the Aussies had discovered their greatest fighter since Les Darcy knocked over the world's finest middleweights in the first quarter of the century. We realised the rumours were not exaggerated when Sands twice outpointed useful Watford boxer Alex Buxton, who toured Down Under before becoming British light heavyweight champion.

Sands came to London in 1949 and, overawed in his debut, was outpointed by Philadelphian Tommy Yarosz. But he won his next six fights in England, including a one-round destruction of Dick Turpin for the Commonwealth middleweight championship. When he returned home in 1950 he outpointed future world middleweight champion Carl 'Bobo' Olson and completed a hat-trick of Australian titles by winning the heavyweight crown. The first moves were made to match Sands with Randolph Turpin, who had sworn revenge for his brother's defeat, but the fight was put on ice while Randy got involved with Sugar Ray Robinson for the world championship. Sands went instead to the United States where he again outpointed Olson and then stopped Henry Brimm in ten rounds to earn the world number one contender's position.

He stopped off in London after his successful trip to the United States and, handicapped by a gashed left eye, suffered a shock seventh-round defeat against hard-hitting Trinidadian Yolande Pompey. It was Dave's first stoppage in what was his 100th fight. Within a year one of Australia's greatest ever boxing heroes was dead.

Opposite: American Mel Brown ducks under a right from Dave Sands. The Australian won this chief supporting contest to the first Turpin-Robinson world title fight in 1951 on points over ten rounds.

MAX SCHMELING

*Max Schmeling
(originally Klein Luckaw)
Born Brandenburg, Germany,
29.9.1905
Career span: 1924-48
World heavyweight champion
1930-32
Ring record: 70 fights, 56 wins,
10 losses (5 stoppages); 38
inside-the-distance wins, 4
draws*

Max Schmeling became the only champion to win the world heavyweight title while on the canvas. He was put there by a low punch from Jack Sharkey in the fourth round of a 1930 championship contest to find a successor to the throne vacated by Gene Tunney. Within seconds Schmeling's voluble manager Joe Jacobs was up on the ring apron demanding that the referee disqualify Sharkey. Eventually the referee, Jim Crowley, reluctantly agreed to the demands of Jacobs after consulting the two ringside judges – much to the disgust and anger of the near-80,000 crowd at the Yankee Stadium in New York. This did not make Schmeling the most popular of champions, particularly as he became the first fighter to take the heavyweight crown away from North America (Bob Fitzsimmons adopted American citizenship).

Schmeling, a competent boxer with a paralysing right hand punch, was a seasoned professional by the time he lifted the world title. In six years he

had lost only four of 49 fights and was the European and German light heavyweight champion before stepping up into the heavyweight division. He launched his career in the United States in 1928 with five successive victories. A year after winning the championship in such unsatisfactory circumstances, Schmeling proved his ability to the doubting American fight fans by stopping vastly experienced Young Stribling – the 'Pride of Georgia' – in the last seconds of a 15-round title defence. The champion was then pressed into giving Sharkey a return at Long Island on 21 June 1932, and he lost a narrow points verdict and the title.

The beetle-browed German's most famous victory was to come. Promoter Mike Jacobs fed Schmeling to the up-and-coming Joe Louis, who had been a winner of all his 27 fights. Schmeling was not given a hope of victory, and was thought to be there purely as cannon fodder for the devastating Louis. But Schmeling, by then a cagey veteran of 31, wrecked the script and million-dollar world title plans when he grounded the 'Brown Bomber' with his favourite straight right in the fourth round and finally knocked him out in the 12th. This shock victory by Max was later avenged by Louis with a devastating first-round knock-out in a title fight in which racial hatred poisoned the atmosphere because of Hitler's doctrine. Schmeling returned to Germany where, 11 months after his humiliating defeat by Louis, he won the European heavyweight championship by knocking out Adolf Heuser in one round in Stuttgart.

During the war, Schmeling served as a paratrooper and was wounded at the Battle of Crete. He made a brief comeback in 1947 and then retired to run a mink farm, and he also had the lucrative franchise to distribute Coca-Cola in Germany. As far as German fight fans were concerned, Max had always been the real thing!

Opposite: Max Schmeling is flattened by Joe Louis in the first round of their world heavyweight title fight in New York in 1938. Louis savagely avenged a 12th-round knock-out defeat inflicted by Schmeling in 1936.

MICHAEL SPINKS

Michael Spinks
Born St Louis, Missouri,
13.7.1956
Career span: 1977-88
World light heavyweight
champion 1981-85; IBF world
heavyweight champion 1985-88
Ring record: 32 fights, 31 wins,
1 loss; 20 inside-the-distance
wins

Michael Spinks owes his place in my top 100 to his achievements in the light heavyweight division. I never really took him seriously as a heavyweight, and Mike Tyson obviously shared my opinion, judging by the contemptuous way he knocked him out in just 91 seconds of a farce of a fight in 1988.

One of seven children raised in a St Louis ghetto, he and his older brother Leon created ring history when they became the first brothers to win gold medals at the same Olympics in the 1976 Montreal Games. Michael won at middleweight and Leon at light heavyweight.

Both turned professional the following year, and Leon was rushed to the top with indecent haste. He outpointed a fading Muhammad Ali to win the world heavyweight title in only his eighth contest and immediately lost it in a return match, and from then on it was downhill all the way for a young man who proved unable to handle his sudden exposure to fame. Michael, though younger, was a considerably more mature and controlled person. He picked his way carefully to title status, challenging Mustafa Muhammad for the WBA light heavyweight championship in his 17th fight and in his fifth year as a professional. He boxed intelligently to win on points.

Over the next four years Michael made ten winning defences, impressing with his ring strategy and punching power. Only two of his challengers managed to last the distance. A fraction over 6 feet 2 inches tall, Spinks operated behind an authoritative left jab and his follow-through right was a bombing punch that could disrupt the defences of the strongest opponents. He could sometimes be aggravating with his negative tactics, which included going walkabout during contests, but his avowed intent was not to take a single unnecessary punch and nobody should criticise him for that common sense approach.

Like so many light heavyweight champions before him, Michael was drawn by the glory and the gold promised in the heavyweight division. He challenged Larry Holmes for the IBF version of the world heavyweight crown in Las Vegas on 22 September 1985, and after 15 rounds was adjudged to have won on points. My sympathy was with Holmes, who claimed he had been the victim of boxing politics. When they met in a return seven months later Holmes seemed to have done enough to have regained his title, but again the judges awarded the points decision to Spinks. He stopped an ordinary Norwegian called Steffen Tangstad in four rounds and then the lack-lustre Gerry Cooney tamely surrendered in five rounds, a victory that set Spinks up for a challenge against Mike Tyson.

Spinks bulked himself up to weigh close to 15 stone but still looked to me to be just a blown-up light heavyweight. He froze on the night and was knocked cold in just 91 seconds in a 'fight' that did nothing to show world heavyweight championship boxing in a good light. It was the one and only defeat of Michael's career and he retired with a few million dollars nicely tucked away in the bank. He will be remembered as a magnificent light heavyweight champion who took the heavyweight division for a profitable ride.

Opposite: Michael Spinks
attacks to the body on his way
to relieving Larry Holmes of his
world heavyweight title.

JOHN L. SULLIVAN

*John Lawrence Sullivan
Born Roxbury, Massachusetts,
15.10.1858
Career span: 1878-1905
World heavyweight champion
1882-92
Ring record: 42 fights, 38 wins,
1 loss (1 stoppage); 33 inside-
the-distance wins, 3 draws*

John L. Sullivan was the last of the bare-knuckle champions, a larger-than-life character who earned his 'Boston Strong Boy' nickname by astonishing feats of strength. When he was just 16 he lifted a streetcar back on its rails, and he could hoist a full barrel of beer above his head like a weight-lifter. Mind you, he usually preferred to drink the barrel dry first. Modesty never became him and he used to swagger into bar-rooms and shout: 'I'll fight any man in the house!' There were rarely any takers. He had an enormous capacity for drink until later years, when he travelled the United States as an evangelist preaching against the evils of alcohol.

Sullivan won the bare-knuckle version of the world heavyweight title in 1882 when he battered Tipperary's Paddy Ryan into submission in nine rounds in Mississippi City. When they met in a return wearing gloves in New York City three years later police clambered into the ring and stopped the fight in the first round to save Ryan from annihilation.

The son of Irish parents, Sullivan was crowned Queensberry world heavyweight champion when he beat Dominick McCaffrey over six rounds in Cincinnati on 29 August 1885. In 1887 a group of wealthy sportsmen in Boston clubbed together and presented their hero with a beautiful belt that was studded with 397 diamonds setting out his name as undisputed champion of the world. This was their gesture to try to end disputes about Sullivan's right to the title. Six months later he travelled to Europe for his only fight outside the United States. He was ahead on points against game Englishman Charlie Mitchell in a return fight at Chantilly, France, when appalling weather forced an abandonment of the contest as a draw after 39 rounds. They had met in New York five years earlier when Birmingham-born Mitchell, conceding 33 pounds, became the only fighter to knock Sullivan off his feet before being pounded to a third-round defeat.

John L. used to rely on sheer brute strength to win his contests, knocking the spirit out of opponents by shrugging off their best punches and then pounding them with wild but effective roundhouse right swings. His most famous victory came when he knocked out Irishman Jake Kilrain in the 75th round of a brutal battle to retain his bare-knuckle title in 1889. It was the last fight staged under London Prize Ring rules.

There has rarely been a greater hero in American sport than John L., and grown men cried when a pot-bellied, out-of-condition Sullivan was knocked out by James J. Corbett in the 21st round in New Orleans on 7 September 1892. Both men wore five-ounce boxing gloves. It was Sullivan's only defeat in 42 fights. He retired after a couple of exhibition bouts, toured as an actor and remained an idol until his death at the age of 59. Remembering that he reigned before there were such things as television sets or even radios and that 'media hype' was an unknown phrase, Sullivan must go down as one of the most phenomenal figures in the history of boxing. He more than anybody revealed why the world heavyweight title is known as 'the greatest prize in sport'. It brought him fame that has already lasted a century beyond his peak fighting days.

Opposite: John L. Sullivan, the last of the bare-knuckle champions.

NEL TARLETON

Nel Tarleton
(originally Nelson Tarleton)
Born Liverpool, 14.1.1906
Career span: 1926-45
British featherweight champion
1930-45
Ring record: 144 fights, 116
wins, 20 losses; 40 inside-the-
distance wins, 8 draws

Nel Tarleton won the British featherweight championship three times during a career in which he defied medical experts by continuing to box despite having only one sound lung. He was desperately ill with pleurisy and pneumonia in 1937, his seventh year as a professional. When one of his lungs collapsed, doctors feared for his life, let alone his boxing career. He not only conquered the illness but also boxed on for another eight years, during which his name became a byword for boxing skill. To Nel, boxing truly was the Noble Art.

The eldest of eight children born and brought up in his beloved Liverpool, Nel was christened Nelson, but when he launched his pro career as a bantamweight in 1926 (with a defeat!) the promoter could not get his full name on to the poster and so it was cut to Nel. To all Merseyside fans he became known and idolised as 'Nella'.

Nel Tarleton in typical hit-and-hop-it action. He was a master at piling up the points with his left jab.

Tarleton was a shade over 5 feet 9 inches tall and he used a long reach to full advantage. He was a perfectionist at punch placing, and could be devastating when on the attack. But connoisseurs considered him at his most impressive when boxing on the retreat, slipping and sliding out of range of his opponent's punches and landing beautifully controlled counters. One of the first rules of boxing is that you should stay off the ropes, but Nel became a master at using them to his advantage. He would roll on them, avoiding punches by a whisker, and then bounce off them and launch attacks that caught his confused opponents completely off balance.

A Northern Area 9 stone title-winner in 1928 and then British champion from 1930, he went on to make two challenges for the world featherweight title, both of them staged in the open air on that great football stage of Anfield and both of them against bulldozing American southpaw Freddie Miller. Each time – on 21 September 1934 and 12 June 1935 – he was pipped on points.

Nel won six of eight contests in the United States and also tried his luck in Australia, but it was in England that he was the hero of all boxing fans who liked to see skill and technique in the ring. He revealed his undoubted world class when he held highly rated world bantamweight champion Al 'Panama' Brown to a draw over 15 rounds at Liverpool in 1932.

In all Tarleton fought ten times for the British featherweight title, losing twice and creating history by becoming the first man to regain the championship on two occasions. Each title fight went the distance.

After serving in the RAF during the war Nel got himself into peak condition for one more defence against rising London star Al Phillips, whose aggressive style of fighting had earned him the nickname the 'Aldgate Tiger'. They battled in Manchester and 39-year-old Nella, 14 years older than his challenger, came from behind to snatch a points victory against Phillips, who was handicapped by cramp in his leg. For Nel it was the end of a glorious career and he had won a second Lonsdale Belt outright – 'one each for my twins, Brian and Sandra', he said.

Nel, the man who was never once stopped in the ring, died after a long illness two days before his 50th birthday in 1956. His funeral brought Liverpool to a halt, and he is lovingly remembered on Merseyside as a gem of a boxer and as a gentleman both in and out of the ring.

DICK TIGER

Dick Tiger
(originally Richard Ihetu)
Born Amaigo, Nigeria,
14.8.1929
Career span: 1952-70
World middleweight champion
1962-65; world light
heavyweight champion
1966-68
Ring record: 81 fights, 61 wins,
17 losses (2 stoppages); 26
inside-the-distance wins, 3
draws

Dick Tiger had more ups and downs in his boxing life than you will find in a mountain range, but the fact that he won both the world middleweight and light heavyweight championships in the second half of his chequered career is proof enough that he deserves his place in my personal hall of fame.

Born Richard Ihetu and brought up in tribal traditions in the Orlu region of Nigeria, he started his professional career in Lagos in 1952. Dick adopted his nickname 'Tiger' as his surname when coming to Britain in the wake of his countryman Hogan 'Kid' Bassey, who won the world featherweight title in 1957.

He was beaten once in his 16 contests in his homeland, avenging his defeat when taking the Nigerian middleweight title from Tommy West in 1954. A year later he set sail for Liverpool and based himself on Merseyside under the management of the vastly experienced Tony Vairo. Nobody could have believed they were watching a future double world champion when he lost his first four contests in England on points. His future looked so bleak that his manager arranged for him to work for his daily bread in a Liverpool paint factory.

Tiger's fortunes changed dramatically in May 1957 when he was matched with exciting Paddington prospect Terry Downes at Shoreditch Town Hall. Terry's connections studied a Tiger record that was studded with six defeats and convinced themselves that he would not trouble crashing, bashing Downes. But the Nigerian pounded Downes into a sixth-round surrender, and from then on he was suddenly considered championship material rather than a stepping-stone for prospects.

He gained nine more wins in the next nine months, and also drew over ten rounds with British champion Pat McAteer, who he then knocked out in nine rounds, relieving him of his Commonwealth championship.

Tiger's switchback career then suffered more setbacks when he dropped points decisions to Americans Randy Sandy, Spider Webb and Rory Calhoun. He based himself full-time in the United States from the summer of 1959 and after he had lost and regained his Commonwealth championship against Canadian Wilf Greaves he set up a crack at the world title held by fighting Mormon Gene Fullmer. On 23 October 1962 he outpointed Fullmer, drew with him in a return and then stopped him in seven rounds in his native Nigeria on 10 August 1963 to become universally recognised as world champion.

A stocky 5 feet 8 inches, Tiger was a workmanlike rather than stylish boxer. He had enormous reserves of stamina and wore opponents down with heavy two-fisted attacks which were at their most effective when delivered from close range. After losing his middleweight crown on points to American Joey Giardello on 7 December 1963 he had to wait nearly two years before getting a chance for revenge. He literally took it with both hands, clearly outpointing Giardello in the return.

Four months later Tiger dropped a disputed points decision and his title to Emile Griffith. At 37 he was finding it hard to keep down to 11 stone 6

pounds, and elected to campaign as a light heavyweight. On 16 December 1966 he stunned Jose Torres when he became the first boxer this century to move up from middleweight champion to win the world light heavyweight crown. He scored a unanimous points decision over the skilful American-based Puerto Rican, and beat him on a split points decision in the return five months later.

Tiger's brief reign as light heavyweight king was ended when Bob Foster knocked him out for the only time in his career in four rounds in 1968. He was 41 when he finally decided to end his eventful career following a ten-round points defeat by Emile Griffith in 1970. Much of his money had gone to his tribespeople to help them in their civil war struggle in Nigeria and he returned home a hero, but he became a victim of cancer and was, tragically, dead within a year of settling down in his homeland.

Dick Tiger drops Rubin 'Hurricane' Carter in the fourth round of their non-title fight in New York in 1965. Tiger won on points over ten rounds against the highly-rated American.

GENE TUNNEY

Gene Tunney
Born New York City,
25.5.1897
Career span: 1915-28
World heavyweight champion
1926-28
Ring record: 83 fights, 77 wins,
1 loss; 45 inside-the-distance
wins, 3 draws; 1 no decision, 1
no contest

Gene Tunney was the most calculating of all the heavyweight champions. Everybody was convinced that Jack Dempsey was unbeatable, but Tunney knew he could be mastered with the right tactics. He considered boxing an art form, perfecting and polishing his skills in the gymnasium, and he always made a close study of his opponents. It was in the US Marines during the First World War that he first came to prominence as an outstanding ring technician while boxing as a light heavyweight. Tunney out-thought all his opponents, and after reversing his one and only defeat by Harry 'Smash and Grab' Greb, he campaigned to challenge for Dempsey's crown.

Tunney was not the run-of-the-mill hungry fighter from a poor background. He was brought up in Greenwich Village by comfortably-off

parents, and it was against their wishes that he turned professional at 18 rather than following a literary career. He was unbeaten in his first 14 contests before joining the US Marines, winning the US Expeditionary Forces light heavyweight title in France.

A stylist with a rapier-like left jab and a solid right cross, he took the American light heavyweight crown from Battling Levinsky in 1922. Four months later Harry Greb gave him a terrible hiding that put him on his back in bed for a week, but in four subsequent contests he got the better of Greb. He then started to campaign for the heavyweight title by eliminating each of the leading contenders until Dempsey, who had managed to duck outstanding black challenger Harry Wills, could not ignore him any longer. They finally met in a rainstorm in Philadelphia on 23 September 1926, and Tunney cleverly boxed on the retreat to win an undisputed points victory over ten rounds, the maximum allowed under Philadelphian law.

Tunney gave Dempsey a revenge chance a year later in Chicago and came perilously close to losing the title in the famous 'battle of the long count'. Dempsey dropped Tunney in the seventh round and hovered over the dazed champion, ignoring the referee's instructions to go to a neutral corner. By the time Tunney was back on his unsteady feet, 14 seconds had ticked away. Tunney danced away from further trouble and repeated his ten-round points victory. Gene always maintained that he could have got up before the ten-second count if it had been necessary, and the referee said that Dempsey had only himself to blame for not immediately abiding by the new rules and going to a neutral corner.

Following his two victories over Dempsey, Tunney successfully defended the title once more against New Zealander Tom Heeney at the Yankee Stadium in New York City on 26 July 1928. The fight did not capture the public imagination and promoter Tex Rickard lost $150,000. After stopping Heeney in 11 rounds, Tunney married a wealthy heiress, Polly Lauder, and retired from the ring. He turned the brain power that had brought him so much success in the ring to business pursuits and became an executive director of several major companies. Gene had the satisfaction of seeing his son win a seat in Congress, and continued to be a highly respected and popular character right up until his death in 1978 at the age of 81. He has gone down in boxing folklore as the thinking man's champion.

Opposite: Jack Dempsey slips to the canvas during his second contest with Gene Tunney.

RANDOLPH TURPIN

Randolph Turpin
Born Leamington,
Warwickshire, 7.6.1928
Career span: 1946-64
World middleweight champion
1951
Ring record: 75 fights, 66 wins,
8 losses (5 stoppages); 45
inside-the-distance wins, 1
draw

Randolph Turpin had an extra-special talent that, for my money, made him pound-for-pound the greatest of all Britain's post-war champions. His life became twisted by tragedy, but while he was at his peak he was a magnificent fighter whose ring exploits inspired an army of youngsters to reach higher standards. I was one of them, and I will always cherish memories of Turpin when he was the king of the ring.

Born in Leamington in the heart of England, he followed two older brothers into professional boxing. His eldest brother, Dick, created history by becoming the first black boxer to fight for and win a British championship. Jackie was a good class featherweight. But it was Randolph who grew up to become world class.

Randy, as he was popularly known, started to establish himself as an outstanding boxer while serving as a cook in the Royal Navy. He won an

Randolph Turpin shakes hands with Albert Finch at the weigh-in for their British middleweight title fight in 1950. Randy won by a knock-out in the fifth round to avenge the defeat of his brother, Dick.

ABA welterweight title at the age of 17 in 1945 and captured the middle-weight championship the following year before starting his professional career. It was obvious that he was the most gifted of the Turpin brothers, but his strong-willed mother insisted that brother Dick should have the first chance of winning a British title.

Breaking through the disgraceful colour bar in 1948, Dick took the British middleweight crown from Vince Hawkins. When he lost it to Albert Finch, Randolph quickly restored family pride by stopping Finch in five rounds to become the new champion on 17 October 1950. Four months later he won the European title by knocking out Dutchman Luc van Dam in just 48 seconds.

Turpin had a superb physique that gave him the appearance of a Greek god in the ring. He was a master of orthodox boxing skills, had a textbook left jab that came straight from the shoulder and he was blessed with knock-out punching power in both hands. Sugar Ray Robinson completely underestimated him during a tour of Europe in 1951 and was out-thought

Randolph Turpin knocks Sugar Ray Robinson off balance with a left jab, his winning weapon in their first world title fight in London in 1951.

and out-fought over 15 rounds at Earls Court as Turpin won the world middleweight title on a wildly memorable night.

Just 64 days later, on 12 September 1951, Turpin seemed on the way to successfully defending the title in a return with Robinson in New York when the mighty Sugar man flattened him with a thundering right hand punch in the tenth round. Turpin somehow managed to get to his feet, but was under pressure on the ropes when referee Ruby Goldstein pulled Robinson off and raised his hand with just eight seconds to go to the bell. Sugar Ray had such a bad cut eye that it was doubtful whether he could have come out for another round.

There were still some exceptional performances to come from 23-year-old Turpin, but he was never quite the same formidable force after that defeat by Robinson. In 1952 he outpointed weight-weakened Don Cockell to win the British and Commonwealth light heavyweight titles, and beat South African George Angelo for the vacant Commonwealth middleweight championship. The following year he beat Frenchman Charles Humez on points in defence of the European middleweight title.

This victory earned him a contest with Carl 'Bobo' Olson for the vacant world middleweight championship, but – weighed down by domestic worries – he gave a below-par performance and was outpointed over 15 rounds in New York. Worse was to follow in 1954 when he was knocked out in 65 seconds when defending his European title against Tiberio Mitri in Rome.

Turpin won British light heavyweight title fights against Alex Buxton and Arthur Howard, but his skill was disappearing as fast as the fortune he had earned in the ring. After a disastrous two-round defeat by Yolande Pompey in 1958 he got involved in wrestling and pirate boxing shows. On 17 May 1966 the greatest British boxer of my lifetime, depressed by financial and domestic troubles, shot himself a month before his 38th birthday.

MIKE TYSON

Mike Tyson was touted as unbeatable until the unfancied James 'Buster' Douglas came along and handed him a mummy and a daddy of a hiding. Douglas exploded the myth of Tyson's invincibility by knocking him out in ten rounds in Tokyo on 11 February 1990 in what was expected to be just a routine defence for the man who, a little over three years earlier at the age of 20, had become the youngest world heavyweight champion of all time.

I never got completely carried away with the 'Tyson is unstoppable' hysteria because too many of his opponents had been of little more than average ability or way past their peak. There was no doubting that he had sledgehammer power in his punches, but I wanted to see how he would react once somebody was brave enough, strong enough and skilful enough to hand him some of his own medicine.

Frank Bruno showed that Tyson could be hit and hurt by staggering him in the first round of their world title fight, and that should have sounded alarm bells. Too many of his opponents had frozen with fear because of the hype that surrounded 'Iron' Mike, but Douglas realised that he was only human and thoroughly deserved his unexpected victory.

I was disgusted when the dollar-chasing boxing politicians tried to take the glory away from Douglas because of a slow count by the referee after Tyson had dropped him in the eighth round. Douglas was clearly listening to the count, and it was not his fault that the referee was tolling three seconds behind the official timekeeper.

Boxing had saved Tyson – a street mugger when he was just a kid growing up in Brooklyn – from a life behind bars, but I was never happy with the way he conducted himself as world champion. He adopted an arrogant, bully-boy attitude hardly becoming the heavyweight king, and his often undisciplined behaviour in his domestic life did not set a good example to youngsters looking up to him as an idol.

Tyson seemed to lose his way when the two mentors who guided him away from a criminal existence, Cus D'Amato and Jim Jacobs, both died. It was D'Amato, Floyd Patterson's former manager, who had taken Tyson out of a reform school and adopted him, teaching him about life as well as about boxing. He listened and learned, and after failing to make it into the United States team for the 1984 Olympics in Los Angeles he made a sensational start to his professional career by winning his first ten fights in a total of only 16 rounds.

In his 28th fight and at the age of just 20 years, four months and two days, he knocked out Trevor Berbick in two rounds to take over from Floyd Patterson as the youngest world heavyweight champion in history. In eight title fights he beat 'Bonecrusher' Smith (pts 12), Pinklon Thomas (rsf 6), Tony Tucker (pts 12), Tyrell Biggs (rsf 7), Larry Holmes (ko 4), Tony Tubbs (rsf 2), Michael Spinks (ko 1) and Frank Bruno (rsf 5). But his life outside the ring was in such turmoil that it was a wonder he could concentrate on his boxing career. His stormy marriage to actress Robin Givens lasted just six months, he wrote off a car in what was reported to be a suicide attempt

Mike Tyson
Born Brooklyn, New York City, 30.6.1966
Career span: 1985-
World heavyweight champion 1986-90
Ring record: 37 fights, 36 wins, 1 loss (1 stoppage); 32 inside-the-distance wins

Mike Tyson is about to deliver the knock-out punch against former world champion Larry Holmes in the fourth round of their title fight.

and he parted with trainer Kevin Rooney and teamed up with boxing 'overlord' Don King rather than his official manager, Bill Cayton.

He appeared to be cracking under all the pressure, and so we should not really have been that surprised when 'Buster' Douglas exposed his limitations. It will be fascinating to see how Tyson reacts to the humiliating defeat by Douglas. He was, without question, an outstanding champion but, in my opinion, he fell short of the qualities of the true greats like Joe Louis and Muhammad Ali.

JERSEY JOE WALCOTT

Jersey Joe Walcott became, at 37 years 6 months, the oldest man to win the world heavyweight championship when he knocked out Ezzard Charles with a cracking left hook in the seventh round of their title fight on 18 July 1951. It had been a long, hard haul to the top of the mountain for Walcott, who had started out in life as Arnold Cream. He borrowed his ring name from a famous welterweight boxer who had been world champion at the turn of the century.

Jersey Joe, a God-fearing man who always carried a Bible with him outside the ring, had been a hungry fighter in the truest sense. He had a wife and six children to feed and continually had to answer the call of the ring to make ends meet. Walcott had lied about his age so that he could launch his professional career at barely 15, and he had been swindled so many times by unscrupulous managers and promoters that he kept giving up boxing in disgust. His ring record shows 69 contests, but there were many early fights that went unrecorded.

His hungriest years were between 1938 and 1945 when he had just seven fights and he went on the dole to pay the food bills. One freezing cold evening in the winter of 1945 Walcott was visited by a boxing manager called Felix Bocchicchio, who wanted Joe to sign with him. Walcott pointed to an empty coalbin in the corner of his living-room and said: 'Mister, if you can keep that bin full for me I will fight for you'. Over the next eight years under Bocchicchio's shrewd management Walcott earned enough to buy a coalmine. In their first two years together Jersey Joe fought 21 times, losing just three matches and avenging each defeat. His victims included top class fighters of the calibre of Joe Baksi, Lee Oma and Joey Maxim.

Walcott took part in eight world title fights including two with Joe Louis and four with Ezzard Charles. He was a crafty and shifty counter-punching box-fighter who could bewilder opponents with clever footwork and feints, and he had the punching power to finish fights with one well-executed blow. He was particularly successful with his potent left hook, the punch with which he knocked out his old rival Ezzard Charles in seven rounds to win the world championship at the fifth time of asking in 1951 after campaigning for 20 years as a professional.

His brief reign as world champion ended when he came up against a human destroyer by the name of Rocky Marciano. He was outboxing and outfoxing Rocky and on the way to a points victory when in the 13th round the 'Brockton Blockbuster' caught up with him and dropped him for the full ten-second count with a devastating right cross to the jaw. In the return Joe – understandably – did not seem to have his heart in the job and caved in under the first telling punch that he took.

Jersey Joe became a respected boxing official after his retirement, and refereed the second Liston-Ali fight, getting in a right old mix-up when Sonny went down and out to what seemed a tame punch. As a member of the 'left hookers club' I will always remember him for the way he finally won the title at the age of 37. The punch that knocked out his old adversary Ezzard Charles was one of the most deliberate and beautifully executed left

Jersey Joe Walcott (originally Arnold Raymond Cream)
Born Merchantville, New Jersey, 31.1.1914
Career span: 1930-53
World heavyweight champion 1951-52
Ring record: 69 fights, 50 wins, 18 losses (6 stoppages); 30 inside-the-distance wins, 1 draw

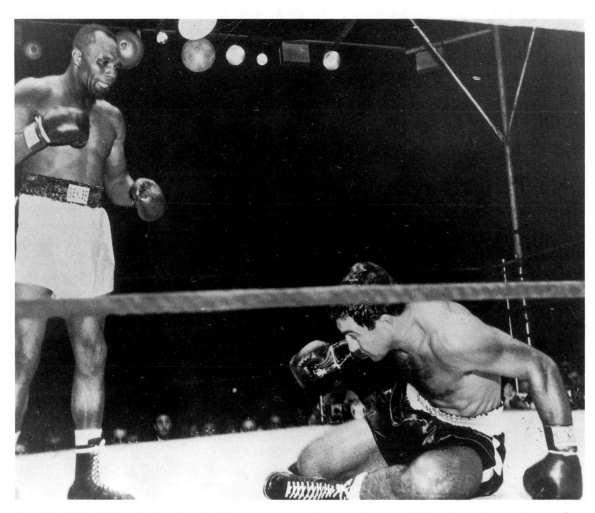

Jersey Joe Walcott drops Rocky Marciano in the first round of their world title fight in 1952. The 'Rock' recovered to win in the 13th round.

hooks I have ever seen thrown. If you get the chance to see it on video, you will understand exactly what I mean. He had clearly decided to throw the punch at least five seconds before its delivery and performed an almost rhythmic dance to make sure he got maximum leverage. It was the punch of a master craftsman who described his left hook as 'the best tool in my bag'.

MICKEY WALKER

Mickey Walker is considered to have been one of the most ferocious fighters ever to have climbed through the ropes. He was nicknamed the 'Toy Bulldog' because of his grim determination not to let go once he had an opponent on the hook. His punches came in avalanches and because they were thrown so quickly he was not the hardest of hitters, but their sheer quantity used to reduce his rivals to wrecks.

Mickey, raised in the Irish district of Elizabeth, New Jersey, started out as a professional welterweight at the age of 17 and before his 16-year career was over he was fighting — and beating — heavyweights, although standing only 5 feet 7 inches tall and rarely weighing more than 12 stone. He bridged two eras of boxing, taking the world welterweight title from old-timer Jack Britton in 1922 and boxing a draw with Jack Sharkey just 11 months before he became world heavyweight champion in 1931.

While giving the impression of being just a slugger in the ring, he was a much shrewder technician than most spectators realised. He had powerful forearms on which he used to block many punches, and he was adept at rolling, bobbing and weaving to avoid being hit as he pressed constantly forward behind whirlwind fists.

He could be a wild man both inside and outside the ring, and the stories are legion of how he used to leave the bed of a latest girlfriend to fight and then go on an all-night drinking spree. One story passed down through the generations is that he and the equally boisterous Harry Greb brawled on the corner of Times Square in the small hours of the morning in the summer of 1925, continuing where they had left off in a world middleweight title fight won on points by Greb just the previous evening. Another tale is that he climbed into the ring the worse for wear with drink when defending his welterweight title for an eighth time against Pete Latzo in Scranton on 20 May 1926. He had just about sobered up when he was announced as a points loser and ex-champion.

Walker won the middleweight crown later the same year when out-pointing the talented Tiger Flowers. His first defence was against British champion Tommy Milligan in London, where he tried to persuade promoter C.B. Cochran to book the Prince of Wales as referee because he was so keen on an honest decision. The reason for his concern became apparent when it was discovered that he and manager 'Doc' Kearns had bet his entire £20,000 purse that he would win. Milligan, a good class fighter from Wishaw in Scotland, was counted out in the tenth round.

After two successful defences against Ace Hudkins, Walker relinquished the middleweight crown in 1931 to chase bigger prizes. He made two challenges for the world light heavyweight title, losing on points to Tommy Loughran in 1929 and then suffering the same fate against Maxie Rosenbloom in 1933. The following year he beat 'Slapsie' Maxie on points in a non-title fight.

Despite his lack of inches he made big inroads into the heavyweight division and beat rated fighters of the time like Johnny Risko, Paulino Uzcudun and King Levinsky. His draw with Sharkey lifted him into a

Mickey Walker
(originally Edward Patrick Walker)
Born Elizabeth, New Jersey, 13.7.1901
Career span: 1919-35
World welterweight champion 1922-26; world middleweight champion 1926-31
Ring record: 163 fights, 115 wins, 21 losses (5 stoppages); 61 inside-the-distance wins, 4 draws; 22 no decisions, 1 no contest

contender's position, but his dreams of capturing the heavyweight title disappeared when he was pounded to an eighth-round defeat by Max Schmeling on 26 September 1932.

Married seven times – three of them remarriages, or 'returns' as Mickey called them – he needed a lot of money to support his hectic lifestyle. He had gone through a vast fortune by the time he retired in 1935, but found a new and contrasting way of making a living. Mickey became an artist of some repute and had several exhibitions of his oil paintings. He left his signature on two different types of canvas.

Mickey Walker, the 'Toy Bulldog'.

FREDDIE WELSH

Freddie Welsh had an extraordinary career that started and ended in his adopted country of America and during which he commuted to his homeland of Wales to prove himself the best lightweight on either side of the Atlantic. He was a master of defensive boxing, and in a 163-fight career was only ever stopped once – and that by the brilliant Benny Leonard when Welsh's best days were far behind him.

Freddie Welsh
(originally Frederick Hall
Thomas)
Born Pontypridd, Wales,
5.3.1886
Career span: 1905-22
World lightweight champion
1914-17
Ring record: 163 fights, 120
wins, 27 losses (1 stoppage); 30
inside-the-distance wins, 16
draws

Freddie Welsh, a master of the
defensive arts.

215

There are two stories as to how he got the name of Freddie Welsh. One is that when he emigrated to Philadelphia as a youngster he did not want his mother to know he was punching for pay. The other, and you can take your pick as to which is the true version, is that he adopted his name after the ring announcer had mixed up his name with the fact that he was Welsh and introduced him for his debut as Freddie Welsh.

One certain fact is that he was an exceptionally gifted boxer who perfected the art of blocking punches with his gloves and elbows, slipping inside leads and then working away with both hands from close range. He was not an upright, British-style boxer but fought out of a crouch with his arms held in a criss-cross guard. A measure of his ability is that among the opponents he beat were legends of the ring like Abe Attell, Johnny Summers, 'Peerless' Jim Driscoll, Willie Ritchie, Matt Wells, Ad Wolgast, Battling Nelson and Charley White.

He outpointed Summers on 8 November 1909 to win the first NSC Lonsdale Belt, and the following year beat his great Welsh rival Jim Driscoll in a showdown in Cardiff. An intelligent but sometimes arrogant man, Welsh taunted Driscoll throughout the fight until the usually impeccably behaved Cardiff man lost his temper and was disqualified for butting in the tenth round.

Welsh added the European and Commonwealth championships to his collection and then took the world lightweight title from Willie Ritchie on a C.B. Cochran promotion in London on 7 July 1914, fighting for expenses only and squeezing to a points victory by just a quarter of a point. Freddie cashed in on his championship over the next three years in the United States, beating Ad Wolgast three times – once with the title at stake – and then outpointing Charlie Wright over 20 rounds in another title defence.

He was 31 and past his prime when he went against the wishes of his trainer and agreed to a third fight with 21-year-old Benny Leonard after meeting him in two no-decision bouts. In no-decision contests there could be no official winner and the verdicts were left to the ringside reporters, but any stoppage was recognised and Leonard took over as world champion when he forced the referee's intervention in the ninth round. It was not Welsh's night. His manager ran out on him after Freddie had discovered that he had bet his entire $5,000 purse on him to beat Leonard. He had fought for nothing.

Welsh served as a captain in the US Army based in Washington in the last two years of the first World War, and then continued his career for six more fights before retiring to run a health farm that hit financial problems. He died penniless in New York in 1927 at the age of 41.

PERNELL WHITAKER

Pernell Whitaker was, for me, the outstanding champion in the 1984 Olympics in Los Angeles, and it was obvious that he would make an impact as a professional. He is a stylish southpaw who moves around the ring with the dazzling footwork of a skilled disco dancer, and there are few boxers around to match his ability to make opponents miss with clever feints and subtle shifts of direction. Although he is not a devastating puncher, he hits hard enough to earn respect and the cumulative power of his combinations has brought him a good percentage of inside-the-distance victories.

Pernell is nicknamed 'Sweet Pea' and he is a 'now-you-see-me-now-you-don't' operator who pounds his opponents with solid counter punches after tricking them into unguarded situations. An indication of his standing in the fight game is that he was voted the Ring Fighter of the Year for 1989, an accolade earned ahead of a procession of exceptional boxers.

He was brought up in the shadow of the Scope, a sports arena in Norfolk,

Pernell Whitaker
Born Norfolk, Virginia,
2.1.1964
Career span: 1984-
World lightweight champion
1989-
Ring record: 21 fights, 20 wins,
1 loss; 11 inside-the-distance
wins

Virginia. The main entrance was just a dozen steps across the road from his house, and as a youngster growing up with four sisters and two brothers in a tough ghetto area he used to dream of one day topping the bill there. Whitaker would have made an even quicker rise to the top as a professional but for a succession of hand injuries and a broken ankle that prevented him boxing on a Virginia Beach bill featuring all America's 1984 Olympic champions. He still managed to steal the show by climbing into the ring for a marriage ceremony with his bride Rovonda.

In March 1987 Whitaker's manager Lou Duva decided to gamble on a short-cut to championship class by agreeing for Whitaker to fight experienced Roger Mayweather after only 12 professional contests. He revealed a maturity gained in more than 200 amateur bouts by surviving an early knock-down to win on points against the future world champion.

This victory brought Whitaker into world title contention and he challenged Mexican Jose Luis Ramirez for the WBC lightweight championship in Paris on 12 March 1988. To most ringsiders Whitaker appeared to have coasted to an easy points victory, but a split decision went against him and he collapsed to the canvas in sheer disbelief when the verdict was announced. To add to his misery he also collected another broken hand. Within a year he became IBF lightweight champion by outpointing Greg Haughen in Virginia on 18 February 1989, and six months later he got his revenge on Ramirez, outboxing him over 12 one-sided rounds to add the WBC title to his collection. Whitaker underlined his exceptional quality when he gained a unanimous 12-round points victory over dangerous world super featherweight champion Azumah Nelson in Las Vegas on 19 May 1990.

Previous page: Pernell Whitaker (right) is short with a jab against Mexican Jose Luis Ramirez in Paris in 1988. Whitaker dropped a hotly disputed points decision, but gained revenge in a return match.

JIMMY WILDE

Jimmy Wilde was called the 'Ghost With a Hammer in his Hand'. It is one of the most fitting nicknames ever hung on a sportsman. Jimmy was a physical freak. On tip-toe he was only a shade over 5 feet 2 inches tall and the most he ever weighed in the ring was 7 stone 10 pounds. His legs were spindly, and he had pipestem arms strengthened by digging at the coalface in the mine where he worked for six years from the age of 12. But he stands like a giant in boxing history because of the way he terrorised the world's flyweights in the hungry days when the 8 stone division was heavily populated and fiercely competitive.

Wilde started boxing for pennies in the miners' clubs and Welsh boxing booths when he was a schoolboy. He officially turned professional at the age of 18 and went unbeaten in his first 98 contests, 67 of them ending inside the distance. There was nothing orthodox about his style. He held his hands low at the hip like a gunfighter and used to weave in towards his opponents on light feet, rocking them with punches thrown from a crouch. His shoulders turned like a golfer taking a swing and every punch landed with maximum impact. He had the power to lift lightweights off their feet.

When he arrived at the famous Ring in Blackfriars in 1912 to make his London debut – after 28 victories that had largely gone unreported – the wife of promoter Dick Burge said to her husband on seeing Jimmy: 'You can't let that poor little mite get in the ring. Give him a good meal and send him home'. 'But I'm a married man with two children, mum', said an indignant Wilde. 'Let me fight and you'll have a different opinion of me.'

Jimmy duly knocked out the highly rated son of Walworth lightweight hero Matt Wells in the first round, and within a year he had captured his first title – the British 7 stone championship – that he took from Billy Padden with an 18th-round stoppage in Glasgow on New Year's Day 1913. He often fought two and three times a week, and his first defeat came in 1915 when he ran out of steam and was stopped in the 17th round of his challenge for Tancy Lee's British and European flyweight titles.

His greatest boxing triumphs came while he was serving as an Army physical training instructor during the First World War. He became British flyweight champion by stopping Joe Symonds in 12 rounds on 14 February 1916, and then two months later laid claim to the world crown when he stopped Johnny Rosner in 11 rounds.

He avenged his one defeat by Tancy Lee when he stopped the Scot in 11 rounds to add the British and European titles to his world crown on 26 June 1916, and then in December of the same year he knocked out Young Zulu Kid in the 11th round of a world title defence in London.

Having seen off all the leading flyweights, Jimmy started to knock over such notable bantamweights as Joe Lynch and Pal Moore and in an end-of-wartime charity contest halted outstanding featherweight Joe Conn in 12 rounds while conceding two stone. Wilde was not permitted to receive a fee for the fight, but the promoters showed their gratitude by presenting his wife with a bag of diamonds worth £3,000.

Jimmy Wilde
Born Tylorstown, Glamorgan,
15.5.1892
Career span: 1910-23
World flyweight champion
1916-23
Ring record: 145 fights, 141
wins, 3 losses (3 stoppages); 99
inside-the-distance wins, 1
draw

Jimmy Wilde, the 'Ghost With a Hammer in his Hand'.

In 1920 the 'Mighty Atom' toured the United States where he won 12 out of 12 fights. He was now 29 and his fire was beginning to go out, and it was poor judgement to agree to fight world bantamweight champion Pete Herman in London in 1921 when he gave away over a stone. Jimmy battled with all his heart but was rescued by the referee in the 17th round. Two years later he made an even worse decision when, against the wishes of his wife and after two years' retirement, he travelled to New York to meet Filippino Pancho Villa and was counted out flat on his face in round seven. It was a sad end to one of the most amazing of all boxing careers.

HOWARD WINSTONE

Howard Winstone can be bracketed with his countryman 'Peerless' Jim Driscoll and Merseyside master Nel Tarleton as the most skilful feather-weights to have been bred in Britain. He did not have the power of Barry McGuigan, but he was a superb ring technician who during a smashing career won two Lonsdale Belts outright, reigned as European champion and was, briefly, a world title-holder.

These were remarkable achievements by Winstone considering that an accident while working in a factory during his amateur days threatened to end his career. He was operating a machine when he got his right hand trapped. Howard lost the tops of three fingers, and though he continued boxing there was an undoubted reduction in his punching power. In 1958 he won the ABA bantamweight title followed by the Commonwealth Games gold medal in his homeland of Wales.

Howard Winstone
Born Merthyr Tydfil,
15.4.1939
Career span: 1959-68
World featherweight champion
1968
Ring record: 67 fights, 61 wins,
6 losses (3 stoppages); 27
inside-the-distance wins

Howard Winstone, the
'Merthyr Marvel', receives his
trophy from old adversary
Vicente Saldivar after beating
Mitsunori Seki in 1968.

He turned professional under the guidance of former British welterweight champion Eddie Thomas, who concentrated on improving Howard's already excellent technique. His main weapon was a stabbing left jab that landed with uncanny accuracy, and his combination punches were delivered with lightning speed. I thought Terry Spinks was fast, but Howard outdazzled him at Wembley in 1961 when overpowering him to take away his British 9 stone title with a tenth-round stoppage.

Winstone took part in 17 title contests during his career, successfully defending the British championship six times and winning eight European title fights. He lost neither of these titles in the ring. He was unfortunate that there was an outstanding featherweight champion on the world throne in the shape of Mexican Vicente Saldivar, who was forced to reach down into his boots to win three thrilling fights against the Welsh idol.

When his old rival and close pal Saldivar retired Howard won the WBC version of the world featherweight title by stopping Japanese Mitsunori Seki in nine rounds at the Royal Albert Hall on 23 January 1968. That was the good news for Howard. The bad news was that he had got to the top of the mountain just as his reserves of stamina were beginning to run out. The wars with Saldivar had drained him and he was starting to struggle to make the 9 stone weight limit.

It was not the old, sparkling Winstone who defended his world championship against Cuban Jose Legra at Porthcawl on 24 July 1968, and he was stopped in five rounds — a defeat that triggered his retirement from boxing as undefeated British and European featherweight champion.

The last time I saw Howard at a boxing promotion he appeared to weigh nearly as much as me. But he seemed content with life and had a wide, easy smile lighting his face. When he climbed into the ring to be introduced to the crowd he got the sort of warm reception that made it clear that he remains an undefeated champion in the minds and hearts of the fans.

TONY ZALE

Tony Zale used to work in the steel mills in his hometown of Gary, Indiana, and was such a rough, tough handful in the ring that he was known as the 'Man of Steel'. There have been many more skilful middleweights than Zale, but rarely any as strong and aggressive.

The son of Polish immigrants, Zale had a long and impressive amateur career during which he started to build his reputation for hardness. He lost only eight of 95 amateur contests, and won 50 of them inside the distance. He had steel fists to go with his steel chin.

Zale turned professional in 1934 at the age of 21 after winning a Golden Gloves title at lightweight and reaching the finals as a welterweight. He became disheartened by a sequence of nine defeats during his first two years in the paid ranks and returned to the steel mills while he considered his future in boxing.

He returned full-time to the ring in 1937 and gatecrashed the world ratings by outpointing NBA world champion Al Hostak over ten rounds. This earned him a return with the title at stake, and on 19 July 1940 he took over as the new champion when he knocked out Hostak in 13 rounds. Zale again knocked out Hostak in two rounds in a third meeting, and then

Tony Zale
(originally Anthony Florian Zaleski)
Born Gary, Indiana, 29.5.1913
Career span: 1934-48
World middleweight champion 1940-48
Ring record: 87 fights, 67 wins, 18 losses (5 stoppages); 45 inside-the-distance wins, 2 draws

Tony Zale on his way to a third-round knock-out victory over old rival Rocky Graziano in their dramatic world middleweight title fight in Newark in 1948.

223

gained universal recognition as champion in 1942 when he outpointed George Abrams over 15 rounds.

Tony lost four years of his career to the war, serving in the US Navy before resuming as middleweight champion in 1946. Rocky Graziano had emerged as his number one contender, and Zale had six warm-up contests that he won in rapid time before giving Graziano his first crack at the title in New York on 27 September 1946.

Zale had to get off the canvas to win a vicious battle in the sixth round. Ten months later it was Graziano's turn to climb off the floor to stop the 'Man of Steel' in six rounds and become the new champion. On 10 June 1948 Zale won the rubber in convincing fashion, knocking Graziano out in the third round to regain the championship. It was a dramatic climax to a thrilling serial that captured the imagination and interest of thousands of American fight fans who followed it as closely as the baseball world series.

When he was a kid, Zale had dreamed of being a baseball pitcher and spent hours practising his throws. This had left him with 'pitcher's' elbow, which handicapped him in the second half of his career, and he needed surgery after losing his title to Frenchman Marcel Cerdan, who stopped him in 11 rounds on 21 September 1948. The defeat convinced him that it was time to duck out of the sport to which he had given his all.

He had an interest in a car showroom in Chicago in partnership with a local baseball star, and kept close contact with boxing as a referee and youth coach. Last word on Zale goes to Rocky Graziano, who said of his old rival: 'When we fought each other our attitude was kill or be killed. Years later I still woke up in a sweat thinking I was back in the ring with Zale. Believe me, he *was* a man of steel'.